T0086406

NO PROOF AT ALL

NO PROOF AT ALL

A CURE FOR CHRISTIANITY

C. BOYD PFEIFFER

Algora Publishing
New York

© 2015 by Algora Publishing.
All Rights Reserved
www.algora.com

No portion of this book (beyond what is permitted by
Sections 107 or 108 of the United States Copyright Act of 1976)
may be reproduced by any process, stored in a retrieval system,
or transmitted in any form, or by any means, without the
express written permission of the publisher.

Library of Congress Cataloging-in-Publication Data —

Pfeiffer, C. Boyd.
   No proof at all: A cure for Christianity / C. Boyd Pfeiffer.
       pages cm
   Includes bibliographical references.
    ISBN 978-1-62894-171-5 (soft cover: alk. paper) — ISBN 978-1-62894-172-2 (hard
cover: alk. paper) — ISBN 978-1-62894-173-9 (eBook) 1. Christianity and atheism. 2. Faith
and reason. 3. Religion and science. I. Title.
   BR128.A8P44 2015
   230—dc23
                                    2015027676

Printed in the United States

To those groups, individuals, devout Religionists, Sunday school teachers, TV evangelists, fundamentalists, evangelicals, ministers, rabbis and priests whose hypocrisy, bias and ignorance of religion has caused me to carefully re-read the Bible and to critically re-think Christianity.

Table of Contents

INTRODUCTION	1
CHAPTER 1. THE BASICS OF CHRISTIAN BELIEF	9
CHAPTER 2. BACKGROUND OF BIBLICAL TEXTS	19
CHAPTER 3. GOD AND GODS: MONOTHEISM AND POLYTHEISM	29
CHAPTER 4. MAN-MADE ASPECTS OF RELIGION	41
CHAPTER 5. WHY PEOPLE BELIEVE WHAT THEY BELIEVE	49
CHAPTER 6. MIRACLES	57
CHAPTER 7. BIBLICAL PHYSICAL IMPOSSIBILITIES	65
CHAPTER 8. BIBLICAL IMMORALITIES	75
CHAPTER 9. BIBLICAL CONTRADICTIONS AND ERRORS	81
CHAPTER 10. PRAYER	91
CHAPTER 11. PRAYER PROBLEMS AND PRAYER THOUGHTS	99
CHAPTER 12. THE TEN COMMANDMENTS — FOUR UNIMPORTANT ONES	109
CHAPTER 13. THE TEN COMMANDMENTS — FOUR IMPORTANT ONES AND THOSE LEFT OUT	121
CHAPTER 14. ETERNITY AND HEAVEN/HELL	129

CHAPTER 15. PROPHECY   137

CHAPTER 16. SCIENCE AND THE SCIENTIFIC METHOD   145

CHAPTER 17. MORE SCIENCE, MEDICAL ADVANCES AND STUDIES   151

CHAPTER 18. RELIGIOUS HEALING AND FAITH HEALING   161

CHAPTER 19. SHOW ME THE MONEY!   171

CHAPTER 20. THE DISCONNECT OF FAITH FROM REALITY   179

CHAPTER 21. A CURE FOR CHRISTIANITY — CONCLUSION   189

AUTHOR'S BACKGROUND   205

BIBLIOGRAPHY   223

Introduction

No one book can provide exhaustive coverage of the broad subject of religion and faith in an advanced, literate civilization that enjoys the benefits of scientific knowledge. Instead, I will attempt to cover — or at least introduce — the subject from the standpoint of common sense, logic, understanding of reading, and various interpretations of Biblical and religious meanings and content. You don't have to be a scholar to read this book. You do have to examine each chapter and subject critically, which is what you want to do anyway.

If you are a devoutly religious person who accidentally picked up this book, congratulations. You are about to embark on a voyage of curiosity and discovery, one of hopefully many voyages into the foibles of religion. Some of these voyages will come from chapters here. Many more will come from books written by qualified Biblical authors.

If you are a Christian who accidentally picked up this book, be careful. Of course, you can easily put it back on the library or book store shelf. After all, one of the easy cop-outs for religionists is the simple statement, "God can do anything He wants. God can do everything."

That assertion, however, doesn't give us any reason to accept an explanation that ignores the laws of physics, chemistry, mathematics or other sciences. It usually ends the conversation, forestalling the difficult process of actually taking the trouble to think things through.

The highly religious are often stuck with past ignorance, myths and superstition. Religion seems to stifle verbal intercourse and thoughtful reflection and discussion.

In an Internet column (Religious Skepticism Examiner on Examiner.com), I ran a piece on 1 Kings 7:23, where the Bible is wrong in calculating *pi*. This section, on casting (molding) a circular reservoir (called a "sea"), notes that the diameter was ten cubits and the circumference was 30 cubits. That can't be. With a ten-cubit diameter, the circumference would be 31.14159 cubits. Convert all this to feet (a cubit is 18 inches, the length of a forearm, or 1.5 feet) and the diameter would be 15 feet, with the circumference at 47.124 feet — not 45 feet.

One commenter noted: "If the Bible is wrong, then God is also wrong and that just isn't possible.... I am no math expert. I just thought you might want to have your facts correct when writing an article criticizing God."

The problem is that *Pi* is a mathematical constant, and the constant is 3.14159. It doesn't matter what measurement system is used, but you can't change systems in mid-calculation and you can't bend the facts using different measurement systems throughout. And whoever wrote I Kings should have known this. 1 Kings was written in about 900 BCE. The Babylonians of 1900–1680 BCE had already calculated *pi* to about 3.124. The early Egyptians figured *pi* to 3.1605. Both were closer to reality than the Bible. Also, God is supposed to be omniscient — he would have (should have) known true *pi* to dictate it for the Bible.

You can have your own opinions, but you can't have your own facts. However, faith and belief seem to trump hard evidence and facts with many religionists. Christians have Jesus walking on water, feeding thousands with a little bit of bread and fish, raising the dead, healing anyone of anything, returning to life after death by crucifixion, talking to God, talking to Satan, flying around in the sky, adjusting the catch of fishermen based on the side of the boat from which they are netting, and having a parthenogenesis birth. The religious have "faith" which means that they have nothing. Faith is a term only used when there is no evidence to back up the "belief."

Go back into the Old Testament and you have the sun standing still, a man comfortably living in a fish (Leviathan) for three days, a flood (Noah) rising 30 feet 3 inches per hour for 40 days (by comparison, wet parts of Madagascar record 15 feet of rain annually), miraculous writing of commandments on stone tablets, a stick that turns into a snake, a snake that turns into a stick, fingers writing on a wall, floating iron axe heads, partings of river waters, plagues, a woman made from a rib, a person turned into a pillar of salt, a talking donkey, whales that eat tiny krill but which can also swallow a person, bushes that burn without burning up, people in a fire without being harmed, people in close company with lions without becoming lunch, a magical fruit, and a talking lizard that becomes a snake.

The irony of all this is the preposterousness of all of Judaic/Christian belief, in fact all or any religious belief, in that believers accept things that nowhere else in life would be accepted or even considered as anything but a fairy tale.

As to examples of morals, and basic rules for living, we would all be better off reading and following Aesop's Fables. Aesop (620–560 BCE), a slave, wrote tales with great morals. Apollonius of Tyana, a 1st century philosopher, wrote of Aesop that "he made use of humble incidents to teach great truths and after serving up a story, he added to it the advice to do a thing or to not do it." We would have learned as much, and quicker, from Aesop as we think that we do from the Bible without the uncertainty of the scriptures and the evil of God.

This does not mean that you have to have personal knowledge of, or experiments in, all knowledge for you to know the truth. I have no knowledge of how speak Farsi, Swahili, or Welsh, but I trust that many can and that they can translate back and forth between those languages and English. I also trust that there are those who to the best of their knowledge study and know — and can read and write — ancient Hebrew, Aramaic and Greek and know the nuances or major differences between those languages of several thousand years ago and modern translations and language use of today.

I use the same facts, analyses, truths, science, logic and understanding to determine that miracles can't happen. The word "miracle" is used all the time, but what is defined as a miracle today comes nowhere near the divine, contrary-to-common-sense-and-facts supernatural result that we would have to have for a true miracle. We have remarkable coincidences but no miracles.

We also have to look at prayer and wonder why the Christians, Jews and Muslims do not insist — flat out insist — on tests to prove the validity of this most important aspect of their religions. The bottom line is that careful repeatable, double blind tests on true prayer show that prayer does not work, and that there is no proof of anything at all ever being accomplished through prayer and prayer alone. The proof of prayer not working is there.

You can find immoralities in the Bible through God ordering mass killings of innocent peoples. You find other immoralities of God ordering/asking Abraham to kill and sacrifice his son Isaac. The fact that God rescinded this demand just in the nick of time and before Abraham nicked Isaac's neck with the killing knife does not change anything.

Just the idea of killing someone to "prove" that you love God is disgusting and abhorrent. Let's put this in a modern, though maybe slightly less gruesome scenario.

"Hey Junior," Dad calls out to his son, "do you love me?"

"Yes, Dad, of course!"

"Junior — do you *really* love me?" continues Dad.

"You know that I love you Dad, I'd do anything for you. I'd do anything you want me to. I love you!"

"OK, then, prove it. You know where I keep my 12 gauge 870 Remington shotgun? You know where I keep the shells? Go get it and load it. Use number 2 shot. Then take Duke, your German shepherd, outside. Shoot him. Shoot him in the head, point blank range. If you really want to prove that you love me, prove it. Kill Duke. That will prove your love for me by following my instructions."

Even assuming that Dad stops this horror just before Junior yanks the trigger on old Duke and blasts Duke's head into gray brain chowder, the palpable disgust and horror of all this is obvious. That anyone — particularly a parent — would ask a child or anyone to "prove" anything such as love, loyalty, faithfulness, obedience, fidelity, devotion, and care by killing a loved and cherished pet or anyone or anything is abhorrent. Then substitute a loving (?) God, asking this of one of his own subjects, one of "his chosen people?" Disgusting! There is no other word for it.

Were such a demand to be made in a modern world, I am sure that Child Protective Services would be on that father and home life like Duke on a dog biscuit to remove that child from the horrors of that household and the evil intent and sickening suggestion — demand — of that abusive father.

Since the gospels (Matthew, Mark, Luke and John) wrote about Jesus's life of 33 years, this would include information that would predate his death by 30 plus years. And these gospels were written 30 to 70 years after the death of Jesus. Thus, it would be as if I, in 2015, were writing about the Korean War (1950–1953) at the earliest, or World War I (1914–1918), in the case of John's later writing. And remember that this earliest Christian period was a time when there were no books, newspapers, TV, DVDs, Internet, libraries or copying machines. It was all written or transcribed from oral tradition, just as I would have to do from personal oral accounts — and nothing else — of World War I or Korea, were I writing today about these events and using the same basis of information. I am not sure that you would — nor should you — trust the accuracy of my accounts of 50 to 90 years ago.

Today we have, from some religions, mistakes and foot-dragging in stem cell research, birth control methods, alleviation of pain, euthanasia, human genome advances, biomedical and biomechanical studies and further evolutionary advances which are the foundation of all biology today.

The one big question is: why does religion — specifically Christianity — exist at all today with the advances of knowledge that we have had since the first century? It is talked about as a religion of a monotheistic God, when it is obviously a religion of a henotheistic or polytheistic god with three parts — a God, his son Jesus and an outside spirit (Holy Ghost), the last of some ill-defined purpose. The role of this religion in society is also strange, given the cultural inculcation of religion into society and the role it plays — without any evidence of its evidentiary existence — in daily life.

The Ten Commandments continue this charade, despite the fact that two of these commandments (do not covet; respect your parents) are minor players in any culture. If the Ten Commandments were written by a god as claimed, then the first four commandments are the rantings of an anxious, nervous god with severe insecurity and low self-esteem issues. The four commandments that remain were a part of societal rules long before the thoughts of any tribe of Israelites, rantings of Old Testament prophets or the highly disturbed writings of the Old and New Testaments.

Religious healing was common in the Old and New Testaments. But there is no proof other than the myth of the Bible that any of this was true. There are no more proofs of this Godly or religious (or Christian) healing than there is of the existence of Roman and Greek gods such as Zeus, Jupiter, Hercules, Venus, Apollo, Aphrodite, Diana or other gods such as Thor of the Vikings or Ra of the Egyptians.

Sadly for all, the standard or traditional churches and ministers do nothing — NOTHING — to condemn this trickery in which people are duped into discarding proven medical remedies and to giving money to the charlatans who practice this fakery and financial conning. There is no insistence by "legitimate pastors" (or is that an oxymoron?) that those who perform "healing" on stage or on TV prove their success.

Those practicing this chicanery ought to be made to prove results, just as results are tested and proven in pharmaceuticals with the FDA and medical procedures. If they cannot prove their faith healing and demonstrate that "Jesus heals," then they should be arrested, jailed and tried for practicing medicine without a license. In addition, traditional clergy of standard denominations and churches should be ashamed of themselves for not condemning the practices and the thievery of the fakes in the so-called religious community. We as a society should also condemn the medical community and politicians for not going after these thieves.

We should condemn those in the justice system on both state and federal levels for not seeking out those preachers who steal this way and trick people into believing the nonsense that they are selling. In addition, laws should be enacted on a federal and/or state level that would prohibit this anywhere, anytime, by anyone. In addition, it should be a felony for anyone — including parents, family and church members — to allow such faith healing of minors who legally have no recourse and no right to control their lives or their choices in life or medical services. Even now, there are some states that would give me a pass if I were a parent "laying hands" on my diabetic child, or using "anointing oil" to cure a brain tumor in my baby, or mounting a "prayer chain" in my church to cure my teenage child of cancer.

In addition, we will look at the man-made aspects of religion, and there are many. Today, Jesus would be wearing clothing from Wal-Mart or Target, appropriate to the occasion, dining on simple food with others, and meeting casually with others to press his message. He would not be a Baptist, Presbyterian, Methodist, Lutheran, Catholic, Jehovah's Witness, Mormon, Seventh Day Adventist, Episcopalian or Pentecostal.

He would not be competing with the flashy ministers of this world with their tailored TV clothing, rings, expensive cars, several mansions, boats, Swiss bank accounts, private (leased or owned) planes for travel, and expensive vacations.

Following the stories and tales in the New Testament, services with Jesus would most likely be quiet discussions. The man-made aspects of most church services with the singing, tithe collection, more singing, reading of Biblical verses, sermons, church news, benediction, announcements of new and continuing church events to keep everyone in line, etc, would not be followed. The money for huge cathedrals and churches that are used only once each Sunday could be spent on buildings and services to truly help others, to truly extend help to fellow mankind. Money could be spent on hospitals, clinics, homeless shelters, schools (secular, please), soup kitchens, dormitories or apartments for the poor and struggling, shelters for abused women and their children, clothing for the very poor, food, jobs, job training, guidance, counseling, rehab services and counseling. This could all be done without the punishment of having to listen to a Jesus-sermon before receiving the benefit of the meal, clothing, or other help. Without the money spent on churches and the like — all exempt from property tax which costs the rest of us USA citizens $71–$100 billion annually — the world would be a much better place and far advanced intellectually, scientifically, and culturally from the religious conscripts to society that we endure today.

One of the particularly egregious annoyances of Christianity and perhaps other religions is the current TV trend of "prosperity gospel" or "prosperity religion" in which TV hucksters preach that you have to "plant your seed." What they mean, of course, is that you have to send them money under the pretence that this is giving money to God or Jesus or the Holy Ghost, or some such deity, all for a godly purpose. Under this "prosperity preaching" scam, these hucksters preach that God will reward you ten-fold or a hundred-fold or some similar nonsense. It is all along the lines of preaching that you are a Christian, therefore better than others who are non-Christian, that you deserve the money and wealth that comes with believing, that all you have to do is to give big to get big. It is greed and avarice under the cloak and guise of Christianity, Jesus, God, religion and the larcenous preachers trying to filch money from those who can least afford it. It is sad that the wealthy ministers all get the money and their "salaries" by extorting it from the poor, the deluded, the helpless, the hapless and the hopeless who are perhaps giving with their last bit of money in the bank or from their most recent Social Security check.

For some, believing, especially the parts about the pleasures of heaven and the agonies of hell, is nothing more than buying (or believing in) fire insurance. Drop enough money in the plate each week to make sure that your fire insurance stays in effect. For others, it is buying into the circular argument that the Bible is true. God wrote the Bible. Buy into the Bible because the Bible was written by God. What does the Bible say? It says to believe in God and everything in the Bible. — But this is a circular argument.

Many believe because others believe, or to make Mom happy, to advance a career, because the Bible stories are nice moral stories (no, they are not!), because there are no negatives to believing (yes, there are!), to wanting a life after the life on this earth (there isn't one!), to be with family and friends after this life is over (see above!), to provide answers to the big "WHY?" as to our life here on earth: what are we for, what does the future hold for us?

Unfortunately, there is a disconnect between God, religion, faith and hope on one side and the reality of life as we enjoy it and live it today on the other. The disconnect involves the value of prayer (it does not work), the lack of information about heaven and hell, the false belief in the resurrection (can't happen) and other magical Biblical events.

The cure for Christianity can only come by starting — or re-starting — to examine the Bible, starting not with faith but with a blank slate. To start with a blank book and examine religion under that premise, as you would do in any real experiment, or test of anything in life, may lead you to some surprising conclusions. It might lead you to a new open way of thinking and to a careful view of what we know — really know — vs. what we only make up or want to invent about religion. Hopefully such a process will help you become a critical thinker and careful analyzer of the various beliefs of different religions. Wanting to believe something does not make it true. As the TV science and cosmological documentaries narrated by Morgan Freeman say, "Question everything."

This does not mean that you have to give up your religion to study the basics of Christianity and religion. It only means that you have to suspend your belief for a short time as you test the waters with a new way of thinking and examining your beliefs — this time using only facts, science, truth, logic, knowledge and a basis of the scientific method as a way to measure facts and truth against your assumptions about religion and Christianity. Let's start.

Chapter 1. The Basics of Christian Belief

For most, the basis of Christianity is found in John 3:16. It says as a direct quote from Jesus: "For God so loved the world that he gave his one and only Son, that whoever believes in him shall not perish but have everlasting life." (Note that some Biblical scholars do not consider this a quote from Jesus, while they still consider it a basis of Christianity.)

That this is the basis of Christian belief is also reinforced by additional writing in John 3:17–21, again considered by many as a quote from Jesus: "For God did not send his Son into the world to condemn the world, but to save the world through him. Whoever believes in him is not condemned, but whoever does not believe stands condemned already because he has not believed in the name of God's one and only Son. This is the verdict: Light has come into the world, but men loved darkness instead of light because their deeds were evil. Everyone who does evil hates the light, and will not come into the light for fear that his deeds will be exposed. But whoever lives by the truth comes into the light, so that it may be seen plainly that what he has done has been done through God."

While the Old Testament is part of the total Bible that includes the New Testament, it is the 27 books of the New Testament with the basis of Christ-belief that make it Christian. It is the 39 books of the Old Testament (Protestant) in combination with the 27 books of the New Testament that make up the 66 books of the total Bible. And virtually all Christian religions consider the entire Bible — including the Old Testament — as important.

In addition, Christians ignore or waffle around the passage of Matthew 5:17 which seems to tie the Old and the New Testaments together. It says in this passage, as a direct quote from Jesus, "Do not think that I have come to abolish the Law or the Prophets; I have not come to abolish them, but to fulfill them. I tell you the truth, until heaven and earth disappear, not the smallest letter, not the least stroke of a pen (the "jot" and "title" of other translations), will by any means disappear from the Law until everything is accomplished." That surely ties together the New Testament of Jesus and the Old Testament of the Israelites.

Many (maybe most) Christian religions consider that the Bible is the basis and the ONLY basis for any belief, any study, any substance of early religious life. The New International Version for example lists this in the Preface after describing the mission and aim of the translators involved. "In working toward these goals, the translators were united in their commitment to the authority and infallibility of the Bible as God's Word in written form. They believe that it contains the divine answer to the deepest needs of humanity, that it sheds unique light on our path in a dark world, and that it sets forth the way to our eternal well-being."

What this means of course is that this NIV edition is perfect or the word of God is perfect, and that the Bible contains no mistakes, errors, evil, contradictions and falseness. But if God did not pick perfect people for this task, would not God be ultimately responsible?

Another strange thing about religion is the extremes to which believers go in their choice of denominations and sects, beliefs and practices. You can find this in from the Shiite and Sunni versions of Islam to the extremes of Hinduism and Buddhism, and in the reformed and orthodox examples of Judaism (the parent of Christianity), as well as in the various Christian denominations.

A rational thinking person would assume that all Christian religions would subscribe to the same basic beliefs. That is not the case. Particularly with the Protestant religions there are different views and time schedules as to the anticipated return of Christ, the Rapture, premillennialism, tribulation, pretribulational return of Christ, postmillennialism, amillennialism, dispensational millennialism, resurrection, and progressive dispensationalism.

One of the problems of describing Christianity is that there are few basics on which all agree, other than the John 3:16 verse mentioned above. Most participants would agree broadly that the ultra formalized Catholicism includes specific Pope-controlled views which include a prohibition of the use of contraception or any sort of birth control, fasting or avoidance of certain foods during Lent, required church attendance each and every week, belief in the Eucharist rite that the wafer and wine when blessed by a priest is the true, real, biological body and blood of Christ, that there is a heaven and hell and purgatory, that confession of sins regularly to a priest is a must of the faith, that infant baptism is definitely preferred to prevent a baby from going to hell. There are also the highly stylized rituals of the various venerations of

Mary and established saints, various approved practices relating to sexuality, a condemnation of homosexuality, and a condemnation of masturbation.

And the extremes are extreme. The Catholic Church is often condemned for its apparently weak stance on pedophilia committed by priests, particularly involving altar boys. Other churches are often at fault in similar or even worse crimes. (Jehovah's Witnesses were recently found guilty and fined $12 million for similar pedophilia crimes and sexual abuse of children.)

The Catholic Church has also spent millions to silence those have been abused from suing the Church for past assaults. Major newspapers have reported of payments of $20,000 to priest pedophiles to encourage them to retire. This was not payment to the victims of such abuse, but payment or a "bribe" to the perpetrators (Catholic priests) to encourage them to get out of the altar boy–pedophilia business. According to the NY Times, this was done in the Milwaukee Archdiocese when governed by Archbishop Timothy Dolan before he became a prominent spokesperson for the Catholic Church (frequently on TV) and Archbishop of the New York Archdiocese. Nothing was said about the victims and no reports were made to the police, nor were charges filed against the accused priests.

At the other extreme are the basic fundamentalist protestant religions who believe in faith healing and use of prayer, anointing with oil, written prayer requests, church or other prayer chains, and laying on of hands (not medication) to heal parishioners including minors such as their own children. (What adults do or do not do is up to them, but to withhold proven medical aid to children is unconscionable. Unfortunately, some states allow this by parents, with no penalty, even if — as often happens — the child dies from the lack of good medical help.)

In addition, there are the fundamentalists — primarily in the South and the Ozark and Appalachian areas — who practice snake handling and drinking of poison as a rigid adherence to Mark 16:9–20. This section has been discounted by true Biblical scholars as something that is false that was added to Mark after the original writing.

Adherents do handle poisonous snakes as a result of their belief, and do drink very dilute poisons, usually strychnine. The results are that few die of the diluted strychnine, but some believers die each year from being bitten by snakes.

There is more idiocy. Many Christians, mostly of the fundamentalist ilk, believe that God controls the weather (God controls everything!) and thus controls who will live or die in a tornado, hurricane, tsunami, monsoon, earthquake, volcano, or anything else in nature. They also believe that God controls life and death in an airplane crash, and that God and Jesus control sporting events, at least American sporting events.

In a survey by publicreligion.org, 53% of those polled believed that God rewards those athletes who have a religious faith with good health and success. Forty percent of minority Christians and 38% of white evangelical Protestants agree that God does play a role in the outcome of sporting events.

Just look at the 2013 Super Bowl game. The Baltimore Ravens won the Super Bowl in an orgiastic bouillabaisse of black-outs, early Baltimore touchdowns, San Francisco comebacks during the second half, stuff-strutting Beyoncé.

What is lost in all this is the question how the Ravens won. What was the governing force in their win? According to the TV reports of Baltimore City prior to the game, it seemed to be in part at least a result of the positive attitude of the Sisters of Mercy, a Catholic order of nuns associated with Mercy Hospital. Photographed and questioned for the news media prior to the game, they were ebullient in their positive attitude for the forthcoming ultimate football game. Why would they not be ebullient? After all, they had Jesus on their side. Jesus can't lose can he?

Then again, you had the Ravens kicker, Justin Tucker, a devout Catholic. He is always shown making the sign of the cross on his chest before every kick. With that going for you, you can't fail, can you?

Of course, this also poses other questions. Suppose that God liked the Ravens and Jesus liked the 49ers? What then? Suppose the Holy Ghost did not like either of them and had wanted the Patriots to win over the Ravens in their matchup prior to the Super Bowl? Suppose that the nuns of Mercy Hospital had no strong allegiance to any team? Suppose Justin Tucker had forgotten to make the sign of the cross in an earlier game that caused a loss for the Ravens?

The insanity continues. The original Mormons did not mind taking multiple wives (in fact, encouraged it) but did not (and do not) drink caffeine such as coffee and caffeinated soft drinks. They also have religious underwear, which many non-Mormons refer to as "magical underwear." This is seemingly identical to what most would refer to as "long Johns" but which has been more recently (1840s) shortened and abbreviated so as to end at the knees and elbows instead of the ankles and wrists as originally mandated. Since then it has been further shortened with the tops resembling a halter top for women and a Tee shirt for men. The bottoms are still like long swim trucks.

Most Baptists eschew dancing and drinking alcohol but do not mind subjecting their wives to second class citizenship and life identical in philosophy (if not technology) to the feudal and nomadic primitive peoples right out of the stone age and from which modern Judaism and Christianity arose some three thousand (two thousand with Christianity) years ago.

Martin Luther, with his beliefs, set the stage for the Nazi treatment of Jews, suggesting in the 1500s the killing of them, burning synagogues, destroying religious books and literature, taking over their homes, and banning them from German cities. So much for early Protestant Christian tolerance.

Jehovah's Witnesses do not allow blood transfusions. Amish are sure that if you leave their faith, you have a one-way, non-refundable ticket to hell. The Christian Scientists believe that you do not need modern medicine to heal diseases. You just need belief, not unlike the other primitive fundamentalist religions. Scientologists (if you want to count as a religion a belief system made up by a science fiction writer L. Ron Hubbard) shun former members who have left the "religion" as do Amish, and for the same reasons.

The simple declaration of John 3:16 was not enough for those in and of the church to control the faithful of the early church. Thus the necessity of creeds. These were written by supposedly learned bishops and priests of the time, and they still serve as documents of belief. Prior to some of these, there was even less uniformity of belief or understanding. In fact, early on, Christianity was just a modification of Judaism and Judaic belief. Jesus was a Jew, and if you are a believer of the Bible, perhaps a very good Jew. The new faith of Christianity had this new guy, and his followers after his death, taking the ball and running with it for a while, just as Moses, Joshua, Abraham, David and others had done.

Some of the more well known of these creeds include the Nicene Creed (325 CE), the Apostles' Creed (390 CE), and the Westminster Confession (1646 CE). Of these many creeds, the Nicene Creed codified the concept of the Trinity while the Second Council of Orange (529 CE) addressed the concept of original sin.

Early on there was no uniformity as to which books should be incorporated into the so-called New Testament, and only through committees and other gatherings of priests were decisions made as to what was to be included. There is also an expanding bibliography of gospels or books such as The Gospel of Mary, The Gospel of Judas, The Gospel of Thomas and others that were not and are not included in the New Testament.

The final approval according to the Catholic Church (the only church at the time) was that the 39 books of the Old Testament and the 27 books of the New Testament (for a total of 66 books) were codified in 393 CE at the Council of Hippo and in 397 CE at the Council of Carthage. And these decisions were made by men just like you and me. Naturally women, being second class citizens at the time, were not allowed in these meetings. Only men were allowed — just ordinary men.

The idea of a Christian Trinity including God, Jesus and the Holy Ghost was not decided until perhaps 325 with the Council of Nicea when the

Nicene Creed was created. There was an earlier mention of "trinity" in 170, but it was a different concept than we use today. This concept was developed by Theophilus of Antioch with a later mention in the early 3rd century by the church writer Tertullian. A more recent codification of this occurred in the Fourth Lateran Council of April 19, 1213, under Pope Innocent III, which solidified this concept of a Trinity.

A continuation of that Fourth Lateran Council (1215) also spelled out the rules by which Jews were to pay a "Jew tax," wear special Jew-identifying clothing, be barred from public office, and keep out of public view and off the streets on Christian holidays. So much for Catholic discrimination against Jews which set the stage for Luther and his book *"On the Jews and Their Lies"* and future discrimination against Jews.

Thus, these early books of the Christian Church, the creeds the church leaders want you to believe and follow, and the concepts of basics such as the Trinity were not developed until long after the death of Jesus and long after the writings of the basic books of the New Testament — Mark, Matthew, Luke and John.

To these bare bones basics, more and more has been added and more and more division has occurred among religions. The sharpest division took place on October 31, 1517, when Martin Luther posted his 95 Theses or objections to indulgences; this was posted on the door of the Catholic Church in Wittenberg, Germany. The Pope objected, as he had done with an earlier cleric, Andreas Boderheim von Karlstadt (1480–1541) who had written about a wider range of Catholic Church corruptions than the sale of indulgences which Luther addressed.

Other rites and beliefs bounced all over the place and have for centuries. Some churches use wine and a wafer to symbolize the blood and body of Christ in their communion. Some use a crumb of bread and grape juice. The Catholics believe that the wafer and wine, when raised up and blessed by the priest, becomes the REAL body and blood of Christ, never mind the ridiculousness of this or the symbolic cannibalism of this belief. (Also, never mind the possibility that, were this true, we could probably work our way along to determining the DNA of said Christ.) Some churches have communion with every service, others once a week (usually Sunday), still others monthly.

The idea of a Christian church service differs entirely from that presumably called for by the New Testament. In this, you find in Matthew 6:5 Jesus in a direct quote, a calling for the use of prayer only privately, only in your room or closet and with the door shut, and never in a synagogue, temple (Jesus was Jewish, after all) or church, never outdoors as Billy Graham used to do in sports stadiums, never on street corners as Jimmy Swaggart used to do in the South, never out loud and before thousands as is practiced by Joel Osteen, John Hagee and others.

This section reads, "And when you pray, do not be like the hypocrites, for they love to pray standing in synagogues and standing on the street corners to be seen by men. I tell you the truth, they have received their reward in full. But when you pray, go into your room, close the door and pray to your Father, who is unseen. Then your Father, who sees what you have done in secret, will reward you. And when you pray, do not keep on babbling like pagans, for they think they will be heard because of their many words."

Christian worship, as defined by the Bible, implies only private praying as per the above, along with worship involving a gathering of a few friends and similar Christian believers. This you can find in the Bible, in which it is stated that when two or three believers are gathered together "in my name" (i.e., to worship Jesus and God) this seemingly constitutes a "church service."

One irony is that Christianity requires belief that Jesus rose from the dead after being crucified, and that three days later he physically rose to heaven. This, of course, must be accepted as absolute verified belief, the truth, the same way that you accept all "facts." Muslims believe a similar set of "facts" about their prophet Muhammad. In 632 CE Muhammad took a spirited trip from Syria to Mecca or Jerusalem (it is unclear as to the proposed history here) on the back of his winged white horse Buraq. From here he rode Buraq into the heavens to see Allah. So, you see, we have one prophet riding a white horse to the heavens, while another prophet (according to many non-Christian religions), Jesus, with no such horse as Buraq, also goes to heaven. We are required to recognize as truth the assertion that the prophet not riding a horse (or horse-like carrier) to God is true, while Muhammad's trip is totally fiction. Of course, there is no explanation for any of this.

Certainly, the Bible and the principles of all religions include some basic moral guidelines that are useful. Admonitions to not lie, to not steal, to not kill, to love thy neighbor, to be giving and good are the way that mankind should live — regardless of religion. But these thoughts long precede religion and Christianity and are part of tribal beliefs and societies since the development of civilization. Mankind — as we know mankind today — goes back about 195,000 years to the central Rift Valley of Africa and before that from evolving primates for millions of years. The skill of writing only arose in the last 10,000 years; goodness and morality certainly were evolving with mankind long before that, and references to such were included in early writings long before mankind's creation of gods and religions.

And against the "love" promoted in the Bible, you have to consider the sheer evil of most religions of the past and present. In the Old Testament you find Moses killing 3,000 of his men because they did not accept the Ten

Commandments. God, through David, killed 70,000 Israelites because David conducted a flawed census. Perhaps hundreds of thousands or more of first-born Egyptians were killed as a result of Passover, all on God's orders. Joshua, on God's orders, killed tens of thousands or more Canaanites in 30 plus cities as a result of an unwarranted Israelite attack of Canaan. This included killing babies, pregnant women, old men, crippled old women, children and families. All this of course is in the Bible (Joshua 6:20) which is claimed as the unvarnished, unaltered, absolute, literal "word of God."

Christians, as a result of their teachings and beliefs, are big on mission work. Of course, "missionary" can mean many things. In the case of Christians, it almost always means proselytizing to the world about Christianity. The question is — Why? If God were truly omnipotent, could he not, with a snap of his fingers, cure the ill and infirm, eliminate true evil, help with crops for food, and supply clean potable water? Why does it take people — the religionists or others — to do this with God claiming the credit?

Certainly it is laudable to help others with medical help, education, building, educating and similar improvement goals, but these things are secular in nature. When it comes to a religion, most parts of the world have their own religion or religions. Why mess up these people by trying to teach them something else and converting them to a different, equally delusional belief? It is certainly good to improve the lot of others with clean water, better agriculture, improved housing, education and basic sanitation, but groups that are not religious do this all the time. The atheist Richard Dawkins (author of *The God Delusion*), through his foundation, helps underdeveloped peoples. That's great. Some non-religious charities work in specific areas, such as building improved housing, educating and building schools, improving sanitation, creating clean water wells, creating medical clinics, providing medical help and operations, agricultural help, industrial training and aid. Christians do these secular tasks, yet want to be credited as doing it in the name of God or Jesus.

This is certainly better than killing those with other beliefs (or no beliefs) as the Catholic Church did by burning with so-called witches, heretics, infidels and heathens during the Inquisition in Europe, roughly from 1212 to 1765. Those "witches" in America were hanged – not burned as was often the case in Europe. Galileo was not killed, burned at the stake or tortured (although many thousands of others were) — but he was friends with one of the Popes. After he proved, in the early 1600s, that the solar system and our earth are heliocentric (the earth goes around the sun) and not geocentric (the sun goes around the earth), he was told that he was wrong, and he was confined to house arrest for the rest of his life. It took the Catholic Church

362 years to apologize to him (in 1992) and to indicate that Galileo is/was right and that the Pope was wrong.

Another aspect of Christianity is the constant hop-scotching of material to make the point that religion wants to make. You can and will find all sorts of things mentioned in sermons and listed in religious books to "prove" the points desired by those of faith. An example is God stopping Abraham from killing Isaac in the famous (or infamous) Old Testament story. The horror of God insisting on this killing by Abraham and then stopping it at the last minute is looked upon as an example of God's love rather than the horror involved.

An example of God's "love" is that of Joshua under God's order, killing all in the cities of Ai, Jericho, and some 30 other cities listed in the book of Joshua. There are three main things wrong with the story as viewed by Christians. The story of the Israelites taking over Canaan notes the following:

- God gave or promised the land to the Israelites.

- God helped the Israelites to take the cities and the land through warfare inflicted by the Israelites on the Canaanites, this warfare being helped by God.

- God ordered Joshua to take the cities and to kill everyone in each city, right down to babies, pregnant women, old people and even domestic stock. (Joshua 6:20)

There are five problems with this narrative featured in a book that is considered a moral guide:

1. The land was not empty nor God's to give away. The Canaanites were there and doing quite well in their cities and on their land where they had settled long ago.

2. The Canaanites were not warring with the Israelites.

3. God — if you believe the Bible — aided Joshua and the Israelites to take the cities through a ritualistic marching around the walls of the city (at least Jericho), on the seventh day of which the walls of the city would fall down and allow the Israelites to enter the city and kill everyone. If you believe all this, God was being discriminatory.

4. Killing everyone including babies, pregnant women, old people, mothers, and even domestic stock makes God a contract killer, not a benevolent deity, in ordering this killing by Joshua.

5. Recent and voluminous archeological studies have shown that there is and was no existent city at the spot of Jericho and those diggings in that area and resulting artifacts only show a people

living there and dying out or moving on 300 years prior to Joshua as described in the Bible. It just didn't happen.

Then there is Christianity's belief in the impossible. One main example which all seem to ignore is the idea that prayer can do something — anything. Check Chapters 10 and 11 for more on this. There is also the idea of inanimate, often inorganic objects being responsible for some Christian good or "blessing." On a TV show entitled *The Real Housewives of New Jersey*, the crew of wives and husbands were on an RV trip along the West Coast when they encountered a narrow road. Looking for help, one of the housewives noted, "It's a good thing that I brought my rosary on this trip. We're not in a sports car." Yeah, lots of luck with that one and a hunk of metal in the shape of a religious medal keeping an RV from going of the road and over a cliff.

The ridiculous point was, obviously, that just the mere presence of a thing — the Catholic rosary — on the trip would keep them all safe. The same level of hocus pocus is available in the idea of a figurine (idol?) of Mary on the dashboard of a car, in a boat, or hanging on a wall in a house. Sure, that little hunk of metal, plastic or wood is going to protect you from all evil!

You find the same concept with the blessing of religious figures insuring protection and happiness for a new born baby and insuring that God, Jesus, the Holy Spirit or an angel would be looking over the baby and protecting it. The Catholic idea of the cracker (host) and wine becoming with the priests blessing the true, real body (flesh) and blood of Christ only speaks of some form of cannibalism instead of a religious rite designed to protect the user or to honor Christ.

This is also found with Protestants, particularly the TV charlatans who, for a phone call and your credit card, will send you a prayer shawl, a small vial of anointing oil, holy water, prayer beads or a blessed bookmark for your Bible.

Chapter 2. Background of Biblical Texts

A basis of journalism is that you always go back to the original source of information for the truth. For example, you might read or hear that TV evangelist Pat Robertson said that Hurricane Katrina was God's retribution for Ellen DeGeneres living (or performing — stories vary) in New Orleans. Her lesbian lifestyle was the reason for God unleashing the violent forces of nature on the city, forces which ultimately killed 1800 people. This statement was not made by Pat Robertson. (According to reports, there was a satirical article on this in Dateline Hollywood.)

This story evolved from some of the other crazy and ridiculous things that Robertson has said over the years, but this is not one of them. Nor, to the best of my knowledge, did any other fundamentalist, evangelical preacher say this, although John Hagee came close.

According to reports, John Hagee did comment on New Orleans and Katrina as follows: "All hurricanes are acts of God because God controls the heavens. I believe that New Orleans had a level of sin that was offensive to God and they were recipients of the judgment of God for that."

A reference to Pat Robertson and gay rights or homosexuality did tie in to Orlando, FL. After an Orlando, FL, gay rights parade, Pat Robertson did say that he was not sure that he would want to be around that area, presumably due to the possible retribution from God by some means, including hurricanes or maybe lightning.

As much as I am revolted by Pat Robertson and his "let's pretend" religion and his general lack of reason and logical thinking, we have to give him this one. Pat Robertson has said some disgusting and crazy things about not wanting to be in Dover, PA, because of the legal stand and court decision on preventing magical creationist teaching in concert with evolution in a science class. But he has not said anything about Ellen DeGeneres in connection with Katrina in New Orleans. And if he or others had said such, you would have to wonder about a God or god who would trade the lives of 1800 people and the discomfort/dislocation — to say the least — of hundreds of thousands of others just to get to one lesbian performer and to teach her a lesson!

You certainly have to wonder about John Hagee and his statements. A more recent statement made by Hagee is that all atheists should be thrown out of the country — forced to leave their American homes where they were born and raised. Instead of atheists, substitute the word blacks, Jews, Democrats, Mormons, bakers, bankers, UPS drivers or others, and you might have a different perspective on this. After all, we cherish the idea that it is a free country, and all of the above, including (with freedom of religion) atheists, are allowed to live here and to worship — or not.

Small nuances and variations as to history are only of interest to historians and scholars. In the case of religion in general, it can involve the whole world. For example, Christianity involves 2.2 billion people. Christianity wants to bend and blend any "Christian" story or "fact" to fit the puzzle where the devotees want the pieces to fit.

You also have to be careful with various translations from earlier periods. Time has a way of changing the meaning of words and phrases. Take the word "gay." The word "gay" currently means — most of the time — homosexual, and has supplanted the words "queer," "fag" (mostly English — and also meaning cigarette). At one time, even "queer" did not mean homosexual — it only meant different, unusual, odd, singular. It had nothing to do with sex or sexual preference.

Originally, "gay" meant happy, spirited, and joyful. It had nothing to do with sex. The movie "The Gay Divorcee" (1934) with Fred Astaire and Ginger Rogers had nothing to do with homosexuality or lesbianism, with a plot that only referred to a woman trying to get a divorce. The "gay" in the title referred to her spirited and joyful take on the world.

The Stephen Foster (1826–1864) song "My Old Kentucky Home" has as its first two lines: "The sun shines bright on my old Kentucky home; 'Tis summer, the darkies are gay. . ." When the song was written, probably in 1852, the word "gay" was meant to mean joyful and happy. Similarly the word "darkies" to identify blacks (then slaves) would not be used at all today, or at least not used without explanation.

The Bible has similar problems in translations and usage from the original writings. In the Bible, the original passage described Mary, the mother of Jesus, as a "young girl." This was in a time when there were lots of young girls, and during this reportedly promiscuous era, not all of them would be virgins or inexperienced in sexual activities. The original writing prophesying this mother of the coming Messiah was in Isaiah and was written in Hebrew. However, with the translation of the story into Greek and its inclusion in Luke, the term was changed to "virgin."

The word "almah" (or alma) as used in Hebrew in Isaiah meant "young girl." If the writer of Isaiah had wanted to use "virgin" as a specific word, he would not have used alma/almah, but would have used "bethulah" (or betulah) which specifically means "virgin" in ancient Hebrew. When this prophecy from Isaiah was translated into Greek for the book of Luke, the Hebrew word almah (young girl) was translated as the Greek word "parthenos" or "parthenogenesis," meaning virgin birth, or birth without the presence of a father or sperm to fertilize the egg.

(Note that parthenogenesis is a standard term used in biology to describe a virgin birth, so far proved only in some plants, some insects, a few fish, a few lizards such as the American blue-tailed skink, a shark or two, along with few other rare examples. It is biologically impossible among humans.)

This switch to parthenogenesis from Isaiah to Luke was by intent, but whether this was with the intent of deceit, just a mix-up to fulfill a prophecy to make Jesus appear to be more than he really was is lost to antiquity. The fact remains that the vague "young girl" of Isaiah became the definitive, precise "virgin" of Luke. Obviously, a "young girl" most likely would be a "virgin" unless she were married, in which case the term "young girl" would not have been used. A "virgin" might or might not be a young girl, since many a single lady has gone through her life without having had sexual intercourse.

Most likely through the error of "almah" becoming "parthenos," this Hebrew/Greek translation "mistake" became a basic tenet of the Catholic Church with the Immaculate Conception and, subsequently, the virgin birth of Christ. It is also an aspect of the Protestant denominations.

Do you really want to accept as your religion one which has in a fundamental document of belief a translated word with a definitive and exact meaning other than the original word that has and had only a vague or questionable meaning in Biblical reference?

There is also the problem of the origin and safekeeping of all the original books of the Bible and specifically New Testament. Some proselytizing missionaries were once asked about the location of all the originals of the gospels — Matthew, Mark, Luke and John. "Oh, they are in various libraries, churches, monasteries and research institutions throughout the world," was the quick and casual reply. The lady of the team was quite sure of herself — happy to answer this seemingly simple question.

Nope, not right — not even close. The fact is that there are NO originals — as in NONE, ZIP, NOTHING — remaining. All we have are copies of copies of copies of copies of copies, along with scraps from the Dead Sea Scrolls, the Nag Hammadi Library and some other sources that suggest a similarity to a little bit of the gospels or which in part echo the same thought. We do have the fourth century documents Sinaiticus and Vaticanus, which are the oldest extent copies of the almost complete Bible. That's not much to go on and definitely not enough to use for basing a strong belief in a "god" or on which to base so-called salvation and where or how you will spend eternity.

Recent reports indicate that we have found 6,000 copies of New Testament documents and that in these there are some 400,000 mistakes.

Before going further, it is good to look at when the original gospels were written, to the extent that we can know this. You get differing accounts of the writing of the four important canonical gospels — Matthew, Mark, Luke and John. This even varies between general overall sources by historians and those who are Christian theological sources. According to Matthew 2:1, Jesus was born during the time of Herod, who from historical references, died in 4 BCE. Thus, Jesus was born between 4 and 6 BCE. Luke 3:23 notes that "Jesus himself was about 30 years old when he began his ministry." Luke 2:1 notes that Joseph and Mary traveled to Bethlehem as required for a census called for by Quirinius, king of Syria. These two birth dates as per Matthew and Luke place the birth of Jesus about 9 years apart. There is evidence of this from Biblical historical references. The historical evidence of Jesus death at the age of 33 — after two to three years of preaching — places his death based on his birth between 27 BCE and 36 BCE.

Ironically, none of the gospels was written at the time when Jesus was alive and none of the writers knew Jesus. And the four gospels along with other books (27 in all) were not codified into the defined New Testament by the Church (Catholic Church) until 393 CE, following the Epistle Athanasius and occurring during the Council of Hippo and later (397 CE) during the Council of Carthage. It was not until 185 CE and the pronouncement of a Bishop Irenaeus that the four gospels of Matthew, Mark, Luke and John were even accepted by the Church as possibly authentic. Thus, the New Testament is not quite the definitive document that one might believe. And even today, there are arguments among scholars as to which if any other "books" (Gospel of Thomas, Gospel of Mary, Gospel of Judas and others) should be included into a complete and authoritatively accurate New Testament.

The best approximate dates of the four canonical gospels are as follows:
Matthew — from 50 CE to 70 CE
Mark — from 50 CE to the early 60s CE
Luke — from 59 CE to 63 CE.
John — from 85 CE to 100 CE.

Mark is considered to be the first of the gospels written. Matthew and Luke were both written around the same time, about 60 CE to 65 CE. John is always considered as the last written with that occurring around 90 CE to 100 CE.

So, the first of these four documents was written some 20 years after the death of Jesus. How much absolute detail and direct quotations do you remember accurately about some signal event in your life of 20 years ago?

Exactly when these were written would be nice to know, but the main point is that all were written long after Jesus had died. Realize also that the first century CE was not exactly the information age. Most people did not read and write. Most likely, Jesus and his disciples were illiterate. And plagiarism was not considered a bad thing. This was done to embellish, exaggerate, improve, hype up some facts or characters, and to make a tale better and more interesting than originally written.

There were no printing presses, phones, cameras, iPads, iPods, tablets, recording devices, no public or private libraries of any extent, no newspapers, writing paper, computers, TV, Internet, no History channel, no history courses in schools or the Lyceum where Aristotle taught. In short, there was nothing by which to learn and nothing by which to make exact written records of anything produced as a written document.

At the official level, the Roman Empire was a society that recorded anything and everything, from simple purchasing receipts to documentation and histories of wars and everything in between. There were no other reports of people — Jew or Roman — walking the streets. There are no extraneous (extra Biblical) reports of Jesus, miracles, his crucifixion, walking on water, or the dead (zombies?) walking around Jerusalem after Jesus died. (Matthew 27:52 says, "The tombs broke open and the bodies of many holy people who had died were raised to life. They came out of their tombs, and after Jesus' resurrection they went into the holy city and appeared to many people.")

If the dead walking around Jerusalem were not the equivalent of zombies, then what were they? If the walking dead were not worth recording by the Jews and the Romans, what would it take to be recorded in Roman records as newsworthy of the time? Some critics have referred to the Jewish historian Josephus as an argument against the above statement. But Josephus was born in 37 CE, three to ten years after the death of Jesus. Thus, assuming that Josephus was perhaps 20 or older before he would be recording Jewish history, he would have started in around 57 C.E., or some 25 years after the death of Jesus. Josephus as a historically accurate historian of all this is no more valid than the writings of Matthew, Mark, Luke and John.

Today, with instant reports of news from around the world, it is hard to imagine a time when we did not know instantly that a tsunami has devastated some part of the world, that guerillas are fighting to overthrow the government of a certain country, that minutes ago an airliner crashed.

Go back just 60–70 years to a time with little or no TV and you got weekly MovieTone reports during the short subjects of a movie. These reports, depending upon when you went to the movies and when they changed their MovieTone news, would give us news as recently as a week ago (the film had to be shipped and processed, then edited) on how the Marines were doing on Iwo Jima, the invasion of Normandy or the details of the Potsdam Conference.

Go back another 60–70 years and you have only newspapers able to report news, sometimes with woodcuts, or those new-fangled things called photographs, made off of glass plates. The idea of finding reliable, historically important works written in Biblical times with cuneiform, hieroglyphics, some clay tablets and a fair amount of papyrus, courtesy of Egypt, is difficult to comprehend. Mechanical copying methods were still 2,000 years away. In any case, this recording of events somehow excluded Jesus or any miracles, walking on water, feeding thousands with a few scraps of fish and bread, raising the dead, shifting demons from people to pigs, resurrection, and yes, zombies.

Copying by hand by scribes led to missed lines, duplicated words and lines (dittography), deliberate mistakes, deliberate modifications, accidental mistakes, accidental modifications, both accidental and deliberate misspellings, added lines or words and other accidental or deliberate errors from the original.

Copying was done in one of two ways. One, a monk or scribe could have a copy of the said document side-by-side with a blank tablet, scroll or sheet of papyrus and copy onto the blank sheet the words of the supplied document. Second, a reader could slowly and deliberately read out loud to a scribe or monk the words in the document — in short, dictation. Both methods led to mistakes small and large. In this latter case a mistake or change could occur with the reader or the copying scribe.

There would be only one original from which copies could be made. Once a copy had been made, that copy could be used as a document upon which other copies could be made. The original could be used to make another copy. Thus, in time you would only have copies of copies of copies of copies, sometimes almost ad infinitum, with each turn of copying leading to the possibility of more errors. An error in one copy would also lead to the same error of all subsequent copies made from that document, even if they were copied exactly as per the document used by the copying scribes.

Can you really totally accept without question a document with a possibly flawed background and history? Do you really want to believe that each word of this Bible, the inerrant word of God, is absolute, from God and exactly as God wrote it or had it written, when all we have are copies of copies? Do you really believe and accept that, even with the possible or probable errors inherent in a book like this, it is the word of God? Do you really accept an error-filled book of which we have no definitive facts as to the original meaning of words as the truth on which to base a life style, life meaning and life belief?

For Mark to write anything, approximately 20 years after the death of Jesus, would like me in 2015 writing about Bill Clinton entering office as President of the United State in 1993 and the 40 years of his life prior to this date. Would it be possible to get an accurate representation of a single person of that time, of his or her biography, of quotes and activities including daily life? It would be almost impossible to get any accurate rendering of such a time and such a person from 100 years ago.

Starting to get a little squeamish now about the accuracy and validity of the gospels and the life and death of Jesus? Good. Let's continue.

Think also of the many direct quotes of Jesus in the four canonical gospels. These are found in quote marks in many Bibles, printed in red in "red letter editions." Realize that under journalism rules, these quotes have to be the exact statement and exact wording of the person saying them — in this case Jesus.

How could anyone reasonably expect there to be accurate quotes from anyone over that period of time? Sure, I can remember from decades ago a quote, question or phrase of a friend or family member. Usually these are pithy or are statements that occurred during some seminal or major event so that such would be burned into my memory. But for the life of me I could not and would not pretend to remember lengthy passages or quotes from anyone, much less be able to repeat them verbatim and accurately.

For writing this section of this book, I did a count of the numbered quotes from Jesus as listed in these four gospels. In most cases, each numbered verse in the Bible is a complete sentence. In some cases, the quotes are part of a numbered sentence while in other cases you have two, perhaps three, sentences.

The numbers of verses per gospel, assuming that I did not miss one here or there, are as follows:

Matthew — 654 verses
Mark — 277 verses
Luke — 575 verses
John — 411 verses

Realize that these above are all direct quotes from Jesus, with no paraphrasing. It would take a memory expert to come close to anything like this, something just too far-fetched in the days of Jesus and among a nomadic people of almost illiterate tent makers and sheep herders. In some cases in Matthew, there are up to three and one-half pages of quotes or seven columns (most Bibles are in a two-column format) of text.

Realize that the earliest copies that we have are from the fourth century, somewhere in the period from 300 to 399 CE. These might be subtle changes or major changes, but they are changes. Realize also that while simple accidental mistakes could occur with hand copying from one document to create a second "identical" document, changes could also be deliberate. Particularly enthusiastic scribes and priests, to further push the faith, their messiah, and their version of religion, could have added, subtracted, changed or augmented things that change the meaning or add meanings that were not meant in the original document. And this could go on for a few centuries or more as Christianity changed and evolved and as scribes worked feverishly to encourage their particular dogma.

A prime example of all this can be found in Mark 16:9–20. My current version of the NIV translation states before this section, "The most reliable early manuscripts and other ancient witnesses do not have Mark 16:9–20." This is the section that also has direct quotes from Jesus, which can lead us back to previous pages about the accuracy of any quotes attributed to Jesus. If this quote from Jesus is questionable and this section possibly fabricated and false, can we really completely trust all the many other quotes from Jesus?

This highly dubious section is the basis on which Southern Appalachian churches and church members started handling rattlesnakes, drinking dilute strychnine, and speaking in gibberish (tongues) to supposedly "prove" their devout Christian faith. This was extremely popular as a primitive mountain expression of religious faith in the 1930s through the 1940s, but even continues today, although fortunately in reduced form and with fewer people and snakes. That also of course also means reduced numbers of deaths from poison and deaths or maimings from rattlesnakes.

It is also important to realize that all of these works in the gospels and elsewhere in the Bible were written without the language skills and notations that we use today. In the times when these were written, whether in ancient Hebrew, Aramaic or Greek, there were no definitive rules for upper and lower case to indicate proper nouns. Uppercase was not used to start a sentence and indeed there were no sentences as we think of them today. There were also no punctuation marks such as periods, commas and question marks. These came later in the evolution of writing. There was also no separate and specific capitalization, so that examples of writing of early Hebrew or Greek Biblical texts were often in capitals only, and often with no spaces between words. ThusyoucouldhaveasentencethatwouldlooklikethisormoretypicallybeincapitalsSOTHATITWOULDLOOKLIKETHIS. And spacing is important. The word "therapist" with the appropriate spacing becomes "the" "rapist." Or look at "tenants" such as a landlord would have, and note that the meaning is completely different with spacing, such as "ten" "ants." Even "landlord" has different meaning as two words — "land" and "lord." We also had early on obelism, in which manuscripts (all that was available then) were annotated or otherwise punctuated in the margins of the text to indicate the general location of various pauses, when reciting or speaking. Most of the population in ancient times was illiterate, so that lectures, speaking, and other oral displays of this written word were the only way that most would hear of the thoughts of others.

This lack of spacing and punctuation also led to confusion, or could even today lead to confusion. "God is nowhere" Does this simple three word sentence — or perhaps godisnowhere — mean that God is no where around and thus non-existent? Or does it mean that "God is now here", an omnipresent force, with us right now and at this present time? It could go either way.

All of this is possible with either original or accurately copied Biblical texts, since there was little in the way of punctuation in early times in alphabetic writings. Early punctuation marks consisted of only symbols for what today we call a period, comma and semicolon. Naturally all these varied greatly with different languages as they do today and also with different periods of history and civilization.

Then too, we have deliberate deceptions — lying about the Bible and faith — of the Biblical text from preachers when giving sermons or in Bible classes and Sunday School lessons. I was in a Sunday School class of a Presbyterian church when the subject was — or was supposed to be — on the origins of the gospels, their history and writing. In talking about Paul and Romans (not the four gospels of Matthew, Mark, Luke and John), the pastor noted the genealogy of Jesus, going back from Joseph to the Old Testament and David. I asked the obvious question as to why the genealogy would be traced back to and through Joseph, when Joseph obviously did not have anything to do biologically with the impregnation of Mary by God. The pastor mumbled something about Mary being involved with this, and then a learned church member in the audience piped up with the comment that the genealogy of Jesus as described in Luke can be traced from back from Mary to David. He was quite sure of this, as was the pastor. At the time, I did remember reading somewhere that there was a highly questionable theory about a possible indirect line from Mary to David. I pointed this out to the assembled audience, but was drowned out by another audience member espousing the same Mary–David connection.

It turns out that this mention of the indirect connection of Mary to David is questionably mentioned in some few extra-gospel documents. However, in the gospels you can find several sections that refer specifically to the lineage of Jesus being traced directly from Joseph back to David, as per Old Testament prophesy. Depending upon which way you are going, the line is always traced from father to son or from son to father. A daughter or mother is never mentioned.

Two of these occur in Luke, specifically Luke 2:4 and also more extensively in Luke 3:23–31 or 38. Luke 2:4 lists the following statement: "So Joseph went up from the town of Nazareth in Galilee to Judea, to Bethlehem the town of David, because he belonged to the house and line of David." That is a clear statement that Joseph was descended from David and that as the "father" of Jesus, that Jesus in turn was descended from David. Of course, he was not, as the literal Christians believe.

The second reference of Luke 3:23 to 31 or 38 lists the specific genealogy of Jesus from his "father" Joseph back to David. It begins: "Now Jesus himself was about thirty years old when he began his ministry. He was the son, so it was thought, of Joseph, the son of Heli, the son of Matthat, the son of Levi, the son of Melki, . . ." etc, with a series of commas down through "the son of David" and back further to "The son of Enosh, the son of Seth, the son of Adam, the son of God." Matthew 1:1–17 does the same thing in reverse, going from Abraham (and ultimately David) down to Joseph.

In short, there is no mention of Mary and her connection with the line of David in the Bible and there is only a reference of descent of sons — SONS — from David down to Joseph. Another interesting thing is that the genealogy of Jesus from David to Jesus or from Jesus to David varies in the two texts (Matthew and Luke) dealing with this and the birth of Christ. In Matthew, you have 27 ancestors of Jesus counting to David, while in Luke there are 42 ancestors listed. And there is no duplication of these ancestors between these two supposedly authoritative texts and basis for the New Testament.

What we have then is a complex listing and growing list of why these gospels — along with other Biblical texts — might not be as correct and accurate as Christians would like.

At the least, all this makes one wonder and perhaps question a lot about these texts in which many place so much faith. Much or all of that faith is obviously — very obviously — misplaced, flawed and totally without foundation.

CHAPTER 3. GOD AND GODS: MONOTHEISM AND POLYTHEISM

When I was little, I thought that I understood the concept of an all-powerful God and also understood his son Jesus. What I could never understand was the Holy Ghost or Holy Spirit as a third part of the Trinity. It was kind of like a ghost, floating around on the periphery of events but never doing anything and never of any real use. I could never understand the idea of the Trinity, either. The idea of Three-In-One might be fine for lubrication oil, but it is difficult to grasp as a triplet in one person.

And realize that early Christians, such as they were, did not get it either. It was not until the First Council of Nicea (in Anatolia, today part of Turkey, but then part of Greece), convened in 325 CE, that the Pooh-Bahs of the Christian religion decided that the Trinity concept was to be a part of the Christian religion. Until then, it was up in the air. It was studied, discussed, talked about, but still up in the air and only codified as something in which Christians HAD to believe in 325 CE.

Many others throughout history did not get the concept of the Trinity either. Michael Servetus, a Spanish theologian, did not get it at all and was quite vocal about it for the time period in which he lived (mid-1500s) both in his speech and writings, including books against the dogma of the Trinity. John Calvin of Presbyterian fame (b. 1509–d. 1564) was vehemently against the no-Trinity ideas of Servetus and thus in concert with the Inquisition, the Spanish courts and prevailing religion. The result was that Servetus was burned alive on a pyre of his own books written about the Trinity.

At the insistence of some — including Calvin — he was burned "slowly" so that his torture would last as long as humanly — or inhumanely — possible. Fortunately, burning at the stake and the Inquisition are not in vogue today (or at least are not legal) so I have no fear of stout fierce brigands and Christian bigots with smoky firebrands showing up at the front door to drag me and my manuscripts and books to the nearest bonfire.

In addition, many or most Christians have a problem with the Holy Spirit, Holy Ghost or whatever you want to call it. Many seem to understand the concept of a God and his son Jesus. God is the abstract entity, who according to Christians and their particular delusion may or may not have a form like a human. After all, the Bible says that humans were made in God's image. Thus, he must be like us or in correct chronology and sequence, we must be like him in appearance. He must have a face and eyes, and hands and fingers, and a body, in whatever forms that body takes. We know that fingers — ordered by God or really God's? — in Daniel 5:5 and Daniel 5:24 wrote on a wall to upset King Belshazzar; Daniel subsequently translated the writing. We know that God wrote the Ten Commandments on stone tablets. This was done several times — once with Moses breaking them after his time on Mount Sinai when he discovered golden calf worship going on upon his return down the mountain. The second time was to replace the broken tablets after destroying the golden calf (and along with the calf, we had the unwarranted killing of 3,000 members of the tribe who wanted to be left alone to worship their own way). Shame on God and Moses for not leaving people alone.

We know that, according to the Bible, Jesus was a person/God, the son of God, and the one crucified and in whom one must believe to gain heaven, avoid hell and accept the Savior. Presumably, since Jesus looked like any average man, and was made in God's image, then God looked like Jesus, or Jesus looked like God. We know that God and Jesus communicated, as per the pronouncements from God as to his pleasure with his son Jesus (Matthew 3:17 and elsewhere) and also Jesus' pleading to God when Jesus was on the cross being crucified.

What we know little or nothing about is the Holy Spirit. A spirit as defined by the dictionary is the basic life force of a person, the thinking, motivating, feeling part of a person as distinguished from the body or material physical part of a person. It can also be considered the life force, will, consciousness, soul and thought of a person, again separate from the skin and bones, organs and muscle of the body. But it is still part of that person and not a separate entity.

Of course, part of this might be the Holy Spirit or Holy Ghost entering us or being a part of us as per the soul of humans. The soul of course is that intangible part of us that is the true spirit of our bodies — ourselves — and that which leaves our dead body and goes to heaven upon our death. Of course for this, you also have to define death, since it comes to us in different forms. Final death, as we know it, comes to us with the death or destruction of our brain, since this is what makes me me and you you.

Ultimately, death ensues in all animals and plants. In higher animals such as mammals, this seems to result in a living animal often knowing or wondering about dead animals of the same species, usually a part of a group or family gathering. We have all seen on TV shows examples of lionesses, hyenas, or tigers touching, nudging, smelling and otherwise noticing and apparently wondering about — loving? — their dead.

We don't know, but this might even be a way of their conveying sorrow, loss, disappointment and the emotional pain of this loss. This seems to be especially poignant with the mothers of cubs or offspring which are caught and killed by a predator or lost in some natural accident.

This could well be the beginning of the concept of a soul, as a "life force" that is found in some people and things — living — and not in others — those dead. Thus, this realization of the differentiation of life and death might be the beginnings in early man of the realization that something it different and that the difference might be a concept that early man invented as a "soul."

While God, Jesus (New Testament) and the Holy Ghost/Holy Spirit are all mentioned in the Bible, they are not mentioned as the three-in-one deal. That only comes about as a man-made element later and long after the death of Jesus. In 260 CE Sebelius states that the "Father, Son and Holy Ghost are the names for the same God." The concept wobbles along for a while, but is finally codified and insisted upon by the man-made and man-invented Nicene Creed of 325 CE. The Council of Constantinople in 381 CE is also credited with the concept of the Trinity. In CE 388 an Emperor Theodosius insists that all people must worship the Trinity or else they will be punished. Thus, it was not really until the fourth century that the concept of the Trinity was made mandatory for belief as a result of a bunch of thugs sitting around a conference table for a while at some religious council or conference and making this up for everyone else to believe and accept — or else. Do you really want to believe that which is forced upon you by other earlier men with no more experience and less knowledge then you?

But if we want to strictly and literally believe in the words of the Bible, that divinity of Christ can also be subject to foolish mankind whim and questioning. For example if you read Isaiah, you find the following in Isaiah 7:15 "Therefore, the Lord himself will give you a sign; The virgin will be with child and will give birth to a son, and will call him Immanuel. He will eat curds and honey when he knows enough to reject the wrong and choose the right. But before the boy knows enough to reject the wrong and choose the right, the land of the two kings you dread will be laid waste."

Part of the premise of Christianity is that Jesus is divine, and always was divine and always will be divine until the end of his life at crucifixion. He is both a perfect human being and also perfectly divine. If you read the above, it might at first seem that Jesus, once born to Mary, is perfect, perfectly divine and when old enough will reject the wrong and choose the right. That's what the above quote says. Go ahead – read it again.

Thus, there was a time when Jesus was choosing things without knowing the right or wrong of them and thus choosing wrong things, making wrong choices. That makes Jesus wrong during part of his early life, thinking wrong thoughts, making wrong choices, choosing evil instead of good, perhaps without knowing it. But there is no doubt from this Isaiah quote that Jesus was wrong and bad part of the time as a child and thus not divine.

It also makes Jesus as a baby an atheist, just as we all are when we were babies or toddlers and before being brainwashed by our parents and others. To be bad and make wrong choices as Isaiah says, he would not have known God, or Godly ways, or his own divinity, if you want to follow this fanciful rabbit trail. If you are going to argue (as you will) that we all make bad choices and have bad thoughts when we are babies, then you are going to have to agree on the face of the above quote that Jesus did the same thing. He was wrong, thinking wrong things making wrong choices, and thus not divine. That sort of knocks out the whole Christian divinity fantasy.

But let's check this for a minute. Suppose that you were being asked to join, or did belong to, one of the many fraternal organizations that abound in this and some other countries. It could be the Rotary, Lions, Moose, Elks, Shriners, Masons, or Odd Fellows. For the sake of this hypothetical example, let's make up a fictional fraternal organization, the Meerkats. Then let's suppose that you learned that the Meerkats, with chapters and members all over the country and in general widely admired, have as a group the following characteristics. And note that you can check all this very easily on the Internet.

- That members have a very high percentage of their population — higher than the general population — buying porn on the Internet.

- That the incidence of domestic abuse among Meerkats is higher than for the general US population.

- That the incidence of Meerkat spousal abuse is higher than the average for the general population.

- That child abuse rates are also higher than for those not members of the Meerkats.

- That animal abuse, including dog fighting, is higher than for other non-Meerkat groups or the general population.

- That underage drinking is higher in Meerkat families than in the general population.

- That those who are Meerkats have in general less education than the overall population of non-Meerkats.

- That teenage pregnancy rates are higher in Meerkats than among non-Meerkats.

- That school drop-out rates are higher among Meerkat families than in the general population.

- That rape cases including date rape are higher in Meerkat families and among Meerkat youth than in non-Meerkat families

- That other crimes and disservices to society and crimes against humanity are also much higher with Meerkats than for the general US population.

- That women are disrespected, looked down upon, slighted, ignored and disparaged in general by Meerkats.

- That Meerkats have in general higher rates of alcoholism, drug use and more petty crime than non-Meerkats.

We could go on, but that is enough for now. Would you want to join an organization — this hypothetical Meerkat social organization — that had such a record, as proven by statistical figures, surveys, polls and studies? (Check the Internet.) What if these figures were from the United Nations reports, Center for Disease Control and Prevention, the Federal Bureau of Investigation, the National Institutes of Health, Federal Bureau of Prisons and from polling groups such as Harris, Pew and Gallop along with newspaper and media investigative reports?

But, by becoming religious, particularly Christian in this country, that is exactly — EXACTLY — what you are doing by joining a church, becoming religious and accepting Christianity. This does not mean that you are involved in any of these deplorable statistics or the activities which produce them. It does mean that you are joining a group to which these statistics apply. Substitute "Christians" for the "Meerkats" mentioned above and you have an accurate picture of Christianity and the Christian religion in society today.

Let's look at the following:

- A report by Benjamin Edelman of the Harvard Business School on anonymous receipts from major online adult entertainment providers finds that the residents of conservative and religious states (red states, in political parlance) consume the most porn, with less consumed by blue states or those with less religious attendance and fewer so-called conservative or religious values. Utah ranked the highest in porn consumption adjusted for population. Residents of Montana bought the least online porn.

Church goers did buy less porn on Sundays, but they made up for it during the rest of the week. There were 11 percent more porn subscribers in those states that banned gay marriages than in states that do not explicitly restrict gay marriage. Those states where the majority agreed with the statement "I have old-fashioned values about family and marriage" bought more porn subscriptions per thousand people than states where the majority disagreed.

More porn was also bought in states where the majority agreed with the statement that "AIDS might be God's punishment for immoral sexual behavior." Try telling that to an African child who innocently got AIDS from his mother or to an American wife who caught it innocently through her philandering husband.

- In a look at the religiosity of other countries, United Nations reports show that those countries that are less religious and more secular or secular-humanist have citizens with a higher incidence of education, health standards, women's rights, per-capita income, adult literacy, and similar societal standards. These top five nations with little or less interest about religion are Norway, Sweden, Australia, Canada and the Netherlands. High levels of religious belief and very low levels of atheism were found in the bottom of fifty nations of the world surveyed for this.

- In the United Nations report on the World Social Situation (2003), evidence was that of the forty poorest nations on earth, all but Vietnam were highly religious with very low or almost non-existent levels of atheism.

- In a study printed in the Journal of Law and Economics (2002), of thirty-eight non-African nations examined, the top ten with the highest rates of homicide were highly religious with very low or insignificant levels of atheism. Of the ten nations with the lowest homicide rates, all but Ireland were secular nations with high levels of atheism.

- According to a report from the United Nations on the World Social Situation (2003) the thirty-five nations with the highest levels of youth illiteracy rates were all highly religious, with very low or insignificant levels of atheism.

- Those countries that are the most religious on Earth — particularly those in Africa — have the highest rates of Aids and HIV infections. Much of this may be due to fundamentalist Christian or Catholic influence or intrusion into African lives with these western religions constantly and almost universally condemning sex education, birth control and the use of condoms.

- The use of a condom will not only markedly reduce births (with high birth rates also a severe problem for these poorest countries on earth), but also reduce or eliminate the passage of STDs including AIDS and HIV. Those countries such as Scandinavia which are generally irreligious or less caring about religion have more and better sex education and widely available birth control methods of all types. These countries experienced the lowest rates of AIDS and HIV infections.

- Information from the Federal Bureau of Prisons shows that approximately 80 percent of the inmates have some form of Christian belief.

This breaks down to the following, as per 1997 figures.

    Catholic — 39.164 percent
    Protestant — 35.0008 percent
    Church of Christ — 1.744 percent
    Pentecostal — 1.463 percent
    Jehovah Witness — 0.890 percent
    Adventist — 0.831 percent
    Mormon — 0.399 percent

The result for all of the above is 79.499 percent, roughly in line with the estimated nationwide population for the various versions of Christianity. For the general population, the figures are about 80 percent affirming a belief in Christianity; atheists and other non-believers number about 16 percent. It is hard to get an exact figure on them, due to the extreme unwarranted prejudice against atheists. Atheism makes many understandably want to hide their non-belief. But even with these figures, the number of atheists in prison numbers 0.209 percent.

Rather than matching the general population figure, as it does for Christians, this statistic shows that far fewer atheists are going to prison. That suggests that far more atheists are good people, people who stay out of trouble, people who do not violate laws (or people who do not get caught — take your pick). But the comparison of 79 percent prisoners in federal prisons vs. an 80 percent general population for Christians and a 0.209 percent prison population vs. an 8–19 percent general population for atheists suggests that atheists are far better citizens in their secular lives than are the so-called followers of Christ.

A look at statistics from polling and social studies agencies shows that most of the religious fervor in the US is in the South and Midwest. This is primarily of fundamentalist and evangelical faiths and churches. In the Northeast, as might be expected, there is a more secular view of life and less fundamentalist religious belief.

In the religious Southern and Midwestern states, you find far more of the less attractive segments of society. There is more domestic abuse, spousal abuse, child abuse, animal abuse, rape, petty crime, illiteracy, date rape, lower income, less education, out of wedlock pregnancy, drug use and alcoholism, all when compared to New England. This again seems to confirm that the more religious an area is, the less likely it is to achieve the better societal standards of a civilized nation or area.

The bottom line again, with all of this, is whether or not you would want to belong to a group that has such a dismal record in care and concern for family, friends, acquaintances, community, and society. If this were a report on the fictional and hypothetical Meerkats social and fraternal group, would you want to be a member? Would you want to go to activities — or bring your wife, husband or family and children to such activities, knowing that the group is comprised of less than sterling examples of humanity?

The idea of one god vs. a few gods or many gods is a one that has baffled and perplexed early man since those days before any religion was invented by early primitive man. For those at that time, the idea of many gods made sense and perhaps could even be argued that such ideas were the beginnings of science, our curiosity about the world and an attempt to explain it. Let's not place too much in this idea, since obviously early peoples and their many early gods were wrong. If nothing is known about the world or universe, it certainly seems to make sense that one god would pull the sun across the sky each day, that one would make thunder, another lightning, and still more would control the floods (think of the Nile), earthquakes, volcanoes (think of Hawaii or the South Pacific), tides, rain, (think of the monsoons of southeast Asia) and seasons. It could go on and on, but early peoples were concerned with the land and farming, hunting, food gathering and such, and sought answers for their daily or seasonal concerns. Only much later in these early civilizations did the concept of science as we understand it today develop the true reasons for the rains, tides, movement of the sun, the stars and earthquakes. Of course, much research, exploration and studies continue to go on today in these fields for further enlightening our discoveries of our world and universe.

But let's go back to the basics and simplistic aspects of religion and fables that we know are fables and fiction and not true. Let's look at the Santa Claus fable, myth, tale, or whatever you wish to call it. Of course, when we are young we are all enthralled with the idea of a big jolly giant, distributing presents throughout the world in one night and bringing us our wished-for gifts by sliding down the chimney. As we get older, we learn that this is just a nice little tale and that it is patently ridiculous. But why is it ridiculous? Let's look at the facts, or at least some of the facts.

1. Santa Claus has been around for hundreds of years and no one lives that long.

2. There is no way to live at the North Pole, Santa's year-long hang out.

3. Here is no such thing as an elf population to help Santa.

4. If there were elves, and since they would live at the North Pole with Santa, where would they get the electricity for lights and power tools, the necessary power machinery and materials necessary to make toys?

5. Since most toys today are made of plastic, how would elves get the ability to install and run injection molding machines?

6. Reindeer can't fly. Ever.

7. Neither Rudolph nor any other animal ever has or ever has had a red light bulb for a nose. Period.

8. The North Pole is too far north for reindeer or caribou, which are the same thing, but wild. Reindeer (domesticated) and caribou inhabit a band generally north of the 50th latitude around the earth of northern Canada, Finland and other Lapland countries in Europe and northern Siberia. They live not in perpetual ice and snow, but in tundra and taiga (boreal forest) regions.

9. To visit all homes in the world, Santa would have to visit 822 homes per second, according to scientists and demographers.

10. To visit all the homes in the world, Santa would have to travel at a speed of 650 miles per second. The space shuttle orbited the earth at approximately 18,000 per hour. That translates to about five miles per second, far short of the speed that Santa would have to achieve.

11. Santa cannot fit down most chimneys. Most would be tight for a small leprechaun, much less a large man.

12. If Santa could slide down a chimney, he would not and could not fit past the damper (a plate controlling the fire) set above the fireplace or firebox.

13. If the fireplace fire were burning when Santa arrived he would be killed by the flames when sliding down the chimney or end up in the nearest hospital burn unit.

14. There is no way for Santa to climb up the chimney if indeed he could fit in it and slide down.

15. Toys for all the boys and girls in the world would not and could not fit into one bag or fit onto one sleigh, Santa's favorite mode of transportation.

16. Santa could not physically eat all of the cookies and milk left out for him on the fireplace hearth by waiting boys and girls.

17. If Santa smoked a pipe as often portrayed, he probably would have died of lung cancer a long time ago.

18. Santa would not have time to show up at every shopping mall in every city.

19. There is no list of "good boys and girls" and "bad boys and girls."

20. The non-existent Santa does not have lumps of coal for the so-called "bad boys and girls."

We could go on, but you get the idea. Now, let's take a look at the "real things and events" of the Bible and of Christianity and see if they pass the logical, empirical evidence and fact tests.

1. The earth is older than 6,000 years as is often claimed by fundamentalist Christians.

2. People were not made from soil as is claimed by God for Adam, nor was a woman (Eve) made from Adam's rib.

3. Snakes do not talk.

4. Snakes do not eat dirt as is claimed for them by God in Genesis.

5. Donkeys do not talk (Balaam's donkey).

6. Axe heads do not float.

7. All the two million (conservatively) land animals on earth cannot fit in a 1,500,000 cubic foot boat (the Ark) as per Noah.

8. Animals could not migrate from their native habitat to the Mideast in time for the sailing date for Noah's Ark.

9. Enough of the right kind of food for each pair of two million animals could not be stored on the Ark.

10. Snakes cannot change into sticks as per Moses nor sticks back into snakes.

11. People (including Jesus) cannot walk on water or violate laws of physics.

12. People (including Jesus) cannot abstain from drinking water and eating food for 40 days. After three days without water, you die. Dead is dead.

13. People (including Jesus) cannot raise dead people back to life. Dead is dead.

14. People of the time (including Jesus) could not cure lepers. Leprosy is leprosy.

15. People (including the Israelites) cannot cause walls (Jericho) to fall down by blowing trumpets.

16. People (including Jesus) cannot go to heaven or visit God by flying in the air. People cannot fly — it is beyond our limits as we are subject to the laws of physics. Dead is dead.

17. People (including Jesus) cannot rise from the dead after being killed through crucifixion. Dead is dead.

18. The dead cannot rise from their graves (as per Matthew after Jesus' crucifixion) and wander through Jerusalem without being noticed. Dead is dead.

19. People cannot be turned into pillars of salt, as per Lot's wife.

20. People cannot "live" after death as per the concept of an afterlife or heaven and hell of the Christian religion. Dead is dead — really!

Similar ridiculous claims are made by other religions, including Islam, Hinduism, Buddhism, and Jainism. These are "known" by Christians to be completely false claims of a false religion. Why are outlandish claims of other religions obviously false while the equally outlandish claims of Christianity are true? What good, solid, factual, truthful, logical explanation is there for this phenomenon? The truth is that there is no basis for the "truth" of Christianity or its Judaic basis.

Chapter 4. Man-Made Aspects of Religion

Religion of all types is totally man-made. This includes the fanciful beliefs, the rites and rituals, the clothing, the special rules and restrictions on eating, dress and holy days. It includes the supposed but obviously made up Biblical miracles, current daily "miracles," religious violations of natural physical laws, and the supposed "real" transubstantiation of wine and cracker into the "real" biological body and blood of Christ as per the Eucharist of the Catholics. It is all as made up as are the stories of Winnie the Pooh, Alice in Wonderland, Dorothy in the Land of Oz, anthropomorphic tales of Aesop's Fables, or the science fiction of Jules Verne, Isaac Asimov, and Ray Bradbury.

Christian religious life and services would or should involve doing good and living well and morally and of course, following the precepts of Jesus. Instead, it seems to involve reciting religious literature, doing some few (often very few) good works, citing things that should be done to live a "Christian life" (words rather than action) or most often, condemning others for not doing certain things or living a certain way. Christianity, as with all things in life, should be about action and example rather than about words, "dos" "don'ts" and similar admonitions or restrictions. But that was not to be in Christianity and certainly is not the way it is today. As Friedrich Nietzsche said, "The Christian resolve to find the world evil and ugly, has made the world evil and ugly."

Take the Sunday service of most churches, be they backwoods Appalachian, tongue-speaking, snake-handling, strychnine-drinking fundamentalists or big city genuflecting Catholic adherents in their ornate cathedrals. The service is the same — stuck in a format that in Protestant churches generally includes an introduction, meeting of others in the church (shaking hands with those in neighboring pews), church announcements, perhaps a community report of some type.

There are names for each of these rites. There is also lot of sitting, standing and in some Protestant churches and especially in Catholic churches, a lot of kneeling or genuflecting. While this certainly helps with blood flow, I suspect that the real religious reason is that it involves and includes parishioners in the service and as a part of the involvement with the ministers and priests so as to be "included" in the religion and the worship of God. It is not just a show — it is a show-and-tell-and-participatory activity. That keeps the faithful devotees faithful and hopefully coming back for more. And tithing more consistently.

There is also a lot of singing and music, again to create the participation part of the service. There are hundreds, probably thousands, of religious songs used by the many Protestant and Catholic faiths and throughout their services. Depending upon the denomination and service, this might range from a stanza or two of two or three hymns, to all written and recorded stanzas of a dozen religious hymns.

There is no religious music. There are religious lyrics, just as there are often lyrics for lots of other types of music — religious, hip-hop, country, blues, bluegrass, marching, patriotic, swing, big band, symphony, chamber music, polka, honky tonk, and zydeco, as per a few examples. Christian music is only Christian music because of the lyrics. "Onward Christian Soldiers" and "Amazing Grace" have a completely different beat and pace than "Nearer My God to Thee" or "Silent Night, Holy Night." However, they are religious only in the sense of the lyrics added to the music involved.

Despite protestations to the contrary, it seems as if much in Christian rites and rituals was stolen from other earlier but similar religions such as Mithraism. Mithraism went back 1,000 years to roots in Zoroastrianism. And reports of Mithra existed long before those of Jesus. It just seems that Jesus and crew had a better PR department. They did overlap in time periods so that today it is sometimes difficult to determine who stole what from whom in the various rites and rituals. We do know that the Vatican is built on the ruins of an earlier Mithric church or meeting place. The history of Mithra is that he was born on December 25th, the winter solstice at the time. He — like Jesus — was also supposedly born of a virgin, had twelve followers or disciples, died, was buried, and later resurrected.

He also had a Eucharist communion rite. *The Jesus Mysteries — Was the "Original Jesus" a Pagan God?* By Timothy Freke and Peter Gandy lists this Mithric rite and statement as: "He who will not eat of my body and drink of my blood, so that he will be made one with me and I with him, the same shall not know salvation." That's from Mithra and Mithraism which through the early stages of Zoroastrianism predated Christianity by 1,000 years.

The Eucharist rite of Mithra is not unlike that from John 6:54–56 in a direct quote from Jesus. "Whoever eats my flesh and drinks my blood has eternal life and I will raise him up at the last day. For my flesh is real food and my blood is real drink. Whoever eats my flesh and drinks my blood remains in me, and I in him."

All this was in an effort to attract recruits to the religion, to dispel any negative aspects of their version of Christianity and to prove that their religion was the best. One of the larger groups which failed in their effort to become the big dog was the Gnostics. They were fairly liberal, tolerant of other views of Christianity and even other religions. They also had dozens of texts and gospels that did not meet the strident constructs of the literalist Christian religions. For this reason, many of these — perhaps most — were burned or destroyed.

The very fact that all Christian churches and denominations vary so widely is proof of several things. It is proof — or a strong suggestion — that the Bible is not true, or that the Bible was poorly written and filled with questionable statements, qualifications and wild inaccuracies. It is also proof that the Bible was written with the specific agenda of the writer/religion in mind, or that translations as to original meaning were poorly executed, or that there is no uniformity of thought, dogma, doctrine or philosophy in any of these claims of any religion as to being the one true religion. If there was a true meaning or outcome to all of this, there would only be one Christian religion instead of the many hundreds scattered around like cow pies in a pasture.

Regardless of the outcome of any of the above, or a conclusion of the possible inconsistencies, it remains that there can be no true Christian religion. If there were provable truth in any of this, it would logically eliminate various religious doctrines and dogmas. It would have a concurrent, uniform thought among all Christian theologians of all otherwise different religions that exist today.

Thus, the writing, reading, understanding, and universal conclusions of all would have to be the same. The fact that they are not proves that the man-made fallacies of each aspect of "understanding" "truth" and "validity" of the so-called Biblical truths were cobbled together by individuals who were and are in total conflict with the thinking of other individuals or religions. Most of them — if not all of them, were and are wrong.

For more proof of the falseness of any Christian religion, you only have to look at the various creeds, dogmas, doctrines, articles of faith, confessions, canons, catechisms, liturgies, fundamental truths and theses of these various religions. As an example of the tremendous complexity of these man-made works, you only have to look at the book (in three volumes) by Philip Schaff

6

— *The Creeds of Christendom Volume 1* deals with the history of creeds. *Volume 2* considers Greek and Latin Creeds and their translations, and *Volume 3* is on the *Creeds of Evangelical Protestant Churches*.

For more proof of the folly of mankind in trying to define and describe its Christian religion, check out also the three-volume work *Truths We Confess*, by R. C. Sproul. *Volume 1* deals with and is subtitled *The Triune God*, *Volume 2 A Layman's Guide to the Westminster Confession*, and *Volume 3 The State, The Church and Last Things*. In addition, there is the 400 page book by G. L. Williamson titled *The Westminster Confession of Faith for Study Classes*.

There are more, all proving only the importance to man (the religious, anyway) of the man-made words, man-made deeds, man-made doctrines, and man-made creeds to prove or make up the so called "truth" of the Bible and of religious thought and belief. It is an attempt to prove that "my religion is better than yours" and that "my beliefs are better (or truer) than your beliefs."

Ultimately, it is that area of superiority, self-righteousness, and condensation to others for which Christians are widely known. But it is all man-made. Different religious and theological councils or writers could just as easily come up with totally different concepts of belief that would be no better (still man-made) but totally foreign from the beliefs of the past and of today for the Christians. All of these creeds merely build one concept on top of another, and all are lies or made up thoughts.

As one famous saying goes, "A lie is as good as the truth if you can get someone to believe it." That Christianity is a lie, and that its various creeds are only designed to extend and embellish the lie is without question. The Nazis of the Third Reich did the same thing starting in the 1930s by spreading horrible lies about the Jews, originating with their Catholic leader, Adolf Hitler.

Perhaps the earliest of these widely known Biblical and religious creeds is the Nicene Creed, formulated and modified from earlier creeds by the First Ecumenical Council of Nicaea in 325 CE and called for by Emperor Constantine as a result of his conversion to Christianity in 312 during a battle. This council met specifically to deal with the various differences of the various man-made aspects and Christian beliefs of different views.

The primary function of this council was to formulate a so-called "correct belief" of Christians so that there would be a baseline of doctrine for the future. It was also to correct the controversy over Arianism which declared that God had created Jesus and thus was more divine than Jesus. This conflicted with the concept of the Trinity of God, Jesus and Holy Ghost. The Nicene Creed affirmed the divinity of Jesus making the three in the Trinity almost interchangeable. Various other creeds — the 381 version of the

Nicene, the Athanasian Creed and the Apostles' Creed — all had different explanations for this, again proving that the man-made writings of any creed of belief change with the winds.

The creeds continued, hundreds of them through change and modification, with the Apostles' Creed and the Westminster Confession of Faith of 1646 to be the ones known by most Christians today. The Apostles' Creed was so named because religious lore has that each of the twelve apostles contributed one of the twelve articles. It was first discovered in a letter from a Council in Milan to Pope Siricius in about 390 CE.

The Westminster Confession of Faith largely used by Protestants was again a man-made fabrication from earlier philosophy and religious thought and again to prove a law of religion, a document of correct worship, doctrine, government and discipline of the Church of England. It has been modified further by various denominations and sects throughout the world. But the fact remains that it is still man-made from 1646 and Calvinist philosophy, yet formulating what MUST be believed by the faithful of any of the various Christian religions to be called Christian. Don't believe and you are immediately drummed out of the club.

The same thing would undoubtedly apply to the interior of the church although some would argue this with references to the Jewish temples of the Old Testament. By the same token, to my mind, much of the furnishings of the more ornate churches look tacky rather than traditional, more ridiculous than respectful. This includes the bright, seemingly gold plated candle holders, bowls, chalices, plates, dishes, and goblets on the altars of Catholic churches where these special furnishings look more like oversized gold-plated plastic Christmas tree ornaments from a dollar store than objects of respect or veneration.

Clothing is another aspect of religion, with the uniform designed to separate those of the church from those of secular interests. Thus everything, from the wimples of nuns (those tent-like headdresses, often unique to a given order of nuns) to the collars of clerics, is part of a uniform designed to presumably elicit more respect, honor and awe from the secular faithful of each religion. This is used more by the Catholics, but some of the Protestant religions such as Episcopalians, Lutherans, and even some of the other more fundamentalist religions, also use collars and other symbolic wear. In addition there are also the capes, robes, sashes, and such that are again most ornate with the Catholics but also used to a lesser degree by the Protestants.

You do not find any of this in the Bible (other than in the Old Testament where some priests of the Levi or priestly clan of Israelites are involved in religious acts). Most telling is that you do not find any elaborate clothing or artifice in Jesus in the New Testament. Were Jesus living today, and still of his carpenter training, he would be most likely be wearing construction clothing including perhaps a tool belt and hard hat, and be more welcome in a Home Depot than a church.

Equally outlandish are the man-made aspects of baptism, the supposed symbol of being reborn into the religion and a copy of the baptism of Jesus by John the Baptist. In some Christian denominations infants are baptized, within a specified time period after birth, and in a short (usually private) religious ceremony involving the child's family and extended family of grandparents, aunts, uncles, perhaps close friends. The child has no choice in this; it is done even through the child at this time is an atheist. Babies and children have no knowledge of a god, God, Lord, Jesus, Ganesh, Shiva, Buddha, religious beliefs or religious rites. It is only as they grow and are miss-taught and brain-washed about religion by their parents and others in the parents' church or Sunday school are they deceived and deluded into the fairy tale of religion.

In some cases the man-made aspects of the Christian religion could fit as well in Chapter 7 on Biblical Physical Impossibilities. The specific question here is about the Eucharist and the transubstantiation of wine and bread used in communion. In almost all Protestant religions, this religious rite is seen as a symbol of communion with Christ, communication with his religion, or a representation of his last supper with his disciples. The wine or grape juice and the bread or cracker used are merely symbolic. In the Catholic Church, both the Host (bread) and the Wine are according to Catholic catechism really the real, true biological body and blood of Christ. The fact that the Catholic theologians and hierarchy could in all seriousness write this into a catechism or believe it to be true is no different (perhaps worse) than early alchemists trying to convert base metals such as lead into pure gold.

The simple fact is that when considering what parts of Christianity are man-made, the answer is that everything is man-made. The Bible was written by man and we don't even have originals of that document to see if what we follow today is accurate from the original of those ancient times. In Christianity and all other religions, you never hear a booming voice from the sky dictating God's wishes or demands. You never see controlled experiments proving that prayer works. You never see any miracles of any type as a supernatural phenomenon occurring, you never see healings of any type. You never see truly good people who have died being raised from the dead. You never find amputees with their arms and legs rapidly and completely painlessly re-growing. You never see bad acts confronted and defeated by God. You never see proof of heaven or hell. As the Greek philosopher Epicurus (341–270 BCE) said: "Is God willing to prevent evil, but not able? Then he is not omnipotent. Is he able but not willing? Then he is malevolent. Is he both able and willing? Then whence comes evil? Is he neither able nor willing? Then why call him God?"

But — is there really a cure for Christianity?

CHAPTER 5. WHY PEOPLE BELIEVE WHAT THEY BELIEVE

The author Guy Harrison wrote a book entitled 50 *Reasons People Give for Believing in a god*." He certainly hit the majority of the reasons people give for their belief, but surely there are many others in the minor leagues that could be added to any such list.

For most people of all faiths and religions, religious beliefs in a god or God come from our parents and grandparents. We are inculcated into these beliefs at an impressionable age. In some churches, you can find not only baby care for infants so that their parents can go to church, but also Biblical classes and religious instruction beginning as early as classes for two- to four-year-old babies.

This is of course an age when babies — all of us and any of us at that age — are completely dependent upon our parents for everything in life. We look to them for food, clothing, shelter, care, protection, cleaning, health care and gradually but emphatically teaching us about all aspects of life. In teaching, we depend — even if unknowingly — on parents teaching us correctly. We believe, if only for a while, their stories about Santa Claus leaving presents for all the children in the world on Christmas Eve, and the Easter Bunny leaving us colorful eggs for an Easter Egg Hunt. We later learn and believe the various Bible stories told to us by parents or in Sunday School classes. Of course, later in life we are told that the stories about Santa Claus and the Easter bunny are fake, while the stores about a flying Jesus, a resurrected Jesus and Jesus walking on water are all real, honest and really, really did happen. After all, these "real" stories are examples of God's miracles and his love for us.

Of course, for children, learning these Biblical tales at an early age, much of the impossible is thought of as possible. At an early age, we are susceptible to thinking that a snake can talk, that a woman can be turned into a pillar of salt, that blowing trumpets can cause a stone wall to fall down, that there is an ill-defined heaven somewhere in the sky, and of course, that a human god can be born of a virgin. It is and was all very confusing for children as it should be for adults. It leads to slogans such as the following:

- Christmas and Santa Claus are tricks that adults play on children. Christianity and Jesus are tricks that adults play on adults.

- If you could reason with religious people, there would be no religious people.

- "That which can be asserted without evidence may be dismissed without evidence." (Christopher Hitchens)

There also seems to be no limit to which the religious will stoop in their effort to confuse their children and insert religion into their early brain washing.

A classified and general information circular of a local non-denominational church had an ad as follows: "Do you have a heart for children to know Jesus? Women in the Word's children's ministry Kids in the Word has a great way for you to serve God. We need caregivers & teachers for our classes. Detailed teaching material, supplies & training are provided. Consider signing up with a friend!" It follows with dates, times, a contact name and phone number.

I visited the lobby information area to find out more about this notice. I was particularly interested in the "little ones" and their brain washing introduction to Christianity. The lady to whom I was directed first asked, hopefully, if I was interested in volunteering for this teaching class. Nope, not me — you have the wrong pig by the ear.

I told her that I was just interested in the program.

"Oh," she volunteered, "they might be in the range of about two years old to five years old. After that they would be going to school on Thursday." One would hope so.

"They get a nice lesson first and they are there with their Moms. After this first lesson, they play games and have fun and get a snack to eat."

"What are the lessons on?" I asked, forgetting prepositional grammar for the moment.

"Oh," the nice lady countered, "they are Biblical stories, stories of the Old Testament, stories about God's creation of the world."

"Do you include Charlie?" I asked, using my nickname for Charles Darwin.

She confused my question with someone in the church.

"No," I countered, "Charles Darwin." A dark look passed over her face. "No, we leave him out of all this."

Naturally. Why preach the truth when you have all those nice fables and fairy tales of the Bible to teach and use to indoctrinate and confuse children? I've been there myself, although the indoctrination apparently did not work on me.

She was quick to point out that children would not be able to understand evolution and that the Bible provided a simpler answer. Simpler, certainly; and certainly wrong.

I would not expect for two- to five-year-olds to receive a thorough explanation of fossil finds, Galapagos finch bill evolution, earlier Lamarckian theories on evolution, the role of Huxley in all this, the researches of Darwin on his five year voyage on the ship Beagle and the role of current DNA studies in confirming past studies by Darwin. After all, DNA studies confirm that we are 50 percent identical to a cabbage. I would not expect information on primates and how we are about 98.5 to 99.5 percent DNA identical to chimps and closely related to other great apes — gorillas, bonobos, orangutans. I would assume that teaching would not include the fact that our ancestors probably involved sea urchins and slime molds and that chlorophyll of plants and hemoglobin of animals are identical except that hemoglobin contains iron while chlorophyll contains magnesium.

I would expect a very simple little preview of evolution and how over millions of years, one wonderful species led to other wonderful species, each adapted to the time, climate and habitat in which it lived.

In short, I would have expected what we all expect in life — honesty, truth, facts, fairness, and sincerity. Realize that these Sunday School classes are not designed to be factual or truthful. They are concerted efforts to brainwash children as young as two years old and up through the age of five into the fairy tales and fables of the Church and the Christian religion. When this was done to small German children with their raised-hand "sieg heil" salute to Hitler and the Third Reich, wearing their swastika-adorned shirts and carrying small swastika flags, we thought — and still think — of this as being awful. It was and is awful. But no similar thought has been given to filling Christian youth with false tales and fables as they carry their cross-emblazoned Bibles and the little girls proudly wear small gold crosses on delicate chains around their necks.

They — and Christian churches throughout the country and world — are brainwashing children about religion when they are as young as two years old. At that age they don't know about death, would be horrified about crucifixion, and don't know the difference between reality and "make believe."

If adults were to have regular open weekly classes for children on witchcraft, palm reading, alchemy, astrology, Tarot cards, numerology, the flat earth "theory," tea leaf reading, spontaneous generation of animals, the philosopher's stone, geocentrism of the universe, giant people living underground, alien abduction, UFOs, and similar false ideas, most people would be upset. People would try to legislate against it. There would be calls to Congress, the White House, vehement anger on radio talk shows, legislation and protest marches. Yet, since religion is covered under free speech in the First Amendment, there is no way to prevent the prevalent psychological scars caused by teaching the myths of the past and the fables of faith. Parents and churches are free to brainwash children with lies and fairy tales as they see fit.

There is also another problem. Early childhood religious training and instruction for most of us is sort of like malaria or perhaps herpes — once you get it, you never quite get over it, and you can always have a recurring bout of it. Logical thinking along with skepticism and a longing for truth, science, facts, and proof must be maintained to have a peaceful life, a content existence and an honest existence.

The point is, do you want to have a false belief or believe in a religion or doctrine — regardless of the origin — that fosters a total acceptance of something for which there is no proof and which flies in the face of logic, truth, facts and science? Do you want your children — of any age — to be imbued with ideas which cannot be substantiated in any way or those ideas formed by facts, truth, established knowledge or science? With the carrot and stick of heaven and hell, do you really, really want to scare the living daylights out of your kids? Do you really want to encourage your kids learning "bible stories" that are patently false?

Some Christian fundamentalist Internet web sites emphatically state that if there is a conflict of Biblical "truth" vs. facts, science, evidence, knowledge or other information, you should ONLY believe and ONLY accept the Biblical truths — never the facts that provide a truthful or scientific view. If people learned of this charade and trickery, we would not have Christianity lasting past next Thursday.

Early exposure is by no means a guarantee of what religion or belief you end up accepting, but it is a very strong indicator. This does not mean of course that you will stay in that religion. In fact, a 2009 Pew Forum research study showed that about half of all American adults have changed their religious affiliation at least once, sometimes even more often. But among Christian and Jews (Jews up to a certain point, that point usually being just short of the New Testament), the Bible fiction and fables stay the same regardless of religion.

All babies are born atheists. They would remain atheists for all or most of their lives except for the immediate teachings and constant brainwashing of their parents and others who bombard them weekly with the idea that the fairy tales and fiction of the Bible are true. They are taught that there is no other way of looking at these fairy tales other than the slant of their parents or Sunday School teachers or the deliberate lies of their ministers.

Figures show that in the last twenty years, the number of those in atheist or agnostic positions has grown from about eight percent of the adult population to about sixteen percent now, or about perhaps 30 million adults in an adult population of about 200 million of the 330 million of us in the US. If we measure against the total population of 330 million, there are about 45 to 66 million who are atheists, agnostics, non-believers and I-don't-carers.

Another reason for belief by adults is that we do not want to be separated from the things that we once "knew" were true. We want to continue to hold onto the so-called truths of the past, and to not consider the possibility that some of those "truths" might be wrong, or have to be modified or considered as made-up fables rather than historical truth.

This is covered in the article *"The Malleability of the Human Mind"* by Jason Long in the book, *The Christian Delusion*, edited by John Loftus, a one-time evangelical preacher who became an atheist and who has written extensively on religion. This psychological effect is when you do not want to disbelieve your learned and cultural religion since you are afraid of what you might change to and how it will affect you.

To think other than that your belief is absolutely correct and that your religion is the one true religion among the thousands in the world past and present might — just might — send you to hell. If you for one day, one hour, one minute or one second question your religion and your pastor, priest or minister. God will find out and deny you entrance to his heavenly afterlife. How sad to think this way. How foolish to believe that searching for truth — using your brain and thinking — is going to somehow condemn you to an everlasting hell. How terrible to think of a god — any god — who would deny you use of your brain and your intelligence and thus place you in a permanent purgatory or a holding tank of hell.

None of us like to do any of this, and few of us consider switching religions. Another argument given for belief is that it is better to believe in something than to believe in nothing, as do atheists. For this same reason, statistics have shown that the religious generally accept those who have a faith — any faith — completely differently from their own over those (such as atheists or agnostics) who have no religion.

The idea is that it is better for people to believe in something, even if they are only occasional or casual church goers, than to believe in nothing. The argument goes along with and follows Pascal's Wager. This argument by the French philosopher Blaise Pascal (b. June 19, 1623–d. August 19, 1662) is sometimes used as an argument for belief in God. The wager is that if you at least act as if you believe in God, you have nothing to lose. If you are right and there is a God, then because of your belief you will go to heaven and get all the benefits of religious belief. If you are wrong and there is no God, then you will die, crumble to dust and be nothing as will atheists and agnostics with their lack of belief in God. You can't lose!

There are two things wrong with this, one of them obvious, the other more subtle. The first is that you can't fake belief. If there is a God, God would know your thoughts. Knowing that you are faking it, God knows that you do not really believe but are "believing" only as a bet against being wrong. It is fire insurance against hell. And if you fake belief or just use this as assurance of a life after death, then you do not have a real belief and anything that you think is suspect and not real.

A more subtle argument against Pascal's Wager or anything similar is that, by believing or faking belief, you are living by the standards of Christianity, including not only the good stuff but also the nonsensical aspects. Thus, you are robbing your life by spending totally unnecessary time in church, Sunday School, Wednesday night prayer meetings, Bible study, church picnics, religious outings, mission work and evangelism. And time is the most valuable thing in life. You are also robbing yourself and your family of money by contributing in any way to the tithing con of churches to be in line with the so-called teachings of the Bible. (Many theologians today, according to reports, do not agree that tithing is particularly Christian or necessary in this modern religious world.)

Similar to this is believing because we want to make Mom happy, even if we had serious fears or doubts about the religion of our parents when we were young. Some people change religion or change churches for business reasons. In essence, it is sort of a Pascal's Wager, but with a benefit here and now in this life, rather than the bet on an afterlife. Early in my life when teaching at the University of Maryland School of Medicine, Anatomy Department, I knew a professor who did this, switching from one Protestant religion to another denomination church in a better part of town, a "higher class" of parishioners and with members more to his liking who were in the university educational system They were possible pawns, sycophants and confidants for any advancement opportunities that might come his way. He was happy, although how well it worked for him I do not know. I do know that he had to drive farther to church each Sunday.

Some believe in a Christian religion (any will work) because of the NDEs (Near Death Experiences) that people have reported, going to heaven and then coming back to tell the rest of us all about it. There is one problem with this. It ain't true. Near Death Experiences are called NDEs for the simple reason that no one died, no one went to heaven, no one came back. There is no more evidence for this than for the reality of the dream that you had last night. Check Chapter 14, *Eternity And Heaven* — for more details on this.

The Bible tells us to believe in Jesus and an afterlife through Bible verses such as John 3:16. In John 3:16, we read (as quoted by Jesus), "For God so loved the world that he gave his one and only Son, that whosoever believes in him shall not perish, but have eternal life." The problem with this is that it is a circular argument.

"You must believe in what the Bible says about God."

"Why?"

"Because it is in the Bible!"

"Who wrote the Bible?"

"God wrote the Bible or dictated it to humans as God's word."

"What does the Bible say?"

"The Bible says that the God of the Bible is our God and that Jesus is part of the God/Holy Spirit Trinity and that we must believe in him to be saved."

"We have to believe in God to be saved?"

"Yes. That's what the Bible says."

"But who wrote the Bible?"

"God wrote the Bible silly — I already told you that!"

There are other ways of gaining the ridiculous beliefs that many of us continue to have today and that almost all of us are taught as youths. In some cases, it can be a simple scare in life in which we end up promising "God" that we will do something special, or build a church for him or devote our lives to the ministry and to God if only "god/God" will do something for us or spare us from something.

That is probably how we got Martin Luther, first a Catholic and then as the stalwart of the Protestant Reformation and through him, the split with the mother church, Catholicism. When Martin was on his way to school at the age of 22, a lightning bolt struck near him. He was afraid, and uttered, "Help, Saint Anna! I will become a monk." The lightning strike was responsible for Martin Luther's acceptance of the Catholic religion, later his disgust with priests selling indulgences, and of his hammering his 95 theses to the Wittenberg church door in 1517.

Having been close to being struck by lightning on three occasions (once ending up with a numb arm and elbow) I can appreciate his fear but not his conclusion as to how to deal with it. When these three things happened to me, I did not think of God, Jesus, religion or an afterlife — not once. Of course, I had the benefit of living some 450 years after Luther and thus being privy to more general knowledge about lightning and the forces of nature than Luther would have had in his youth.

But the ultimate concern is not so much how we became to be religious, if we indeed did, but why we continue to be religious and "believing" in the face of overwhelming evidence against anything close to a religion. I can see "believing" in Santa Claus and the Easter Bunny for all of us when we are very young and gullible, but we should grow out of fairy tales — including religion — as we get older. We grow out of sleeping with our Teddy Bears or for girls perhaps a doll as a make-believe companion and friend. We ultimately grow out of carrying around a worn and ragged patch of baby blanket.

The problem can be serious. It is not serious for me. It is a problem for you only if you are a serious believer in any religion. As Socrates said when quoted by Plato, "The unexamined life is not worth living." If you have not seriously examined your religion, your faith, your belief, then you really do not know what you believe or why you believe it. You are lost in life, wandering through the world without a clue as to what is real because you have been told lies by your parents, grandparents, a pastor or priest, a loved one or esteemed friend.

Without examining the truth and value of your belief, you have no belief. You have nothing by which you can convince me or anyone else the value of your thoughts, your "truths," your religion. After all, in most cases, you did not choose your religion that you hold so dear. You were forced into it by not wanting to disappoint your Mom and Dad, by the fear of an angry vengeful God who would condemn you to hell forever if you did not believe. And that is sad.

Chapter 6. Miracles

Dictionaries define a "miracle" as something that occurs outside of the laws of nature. Thus, it is the occurrence of something impossible, or seemingly impossible with our current state of knowledge about the laws and rules of physics, chemistry, biology, and the universe. My Webster's New World Dictionary defines a miracle as: "an event or action that apparently contradicts known scientific laws and is hence thought to be due to supernatural causes, esp. to an act of God." If that is the case, we all ought to be pretty careful about using the word "miracle" and use it only when appropriate. We wouldn't want to offend God or Jesus.

Secondary dictionary definitions are a little weak, as per: "a remarkable event or thing; marvel." If we want to talk about "marvels," that's one thing. If we want to talk about "miracles" as per the prime definition in a dictionary, that's another. Marvels exist throughout the world. Birds flying and fish swimming are marvels. So are cheetahs running at 65 miles per hour, sailfish swimming at 60 miles per hour, North American butterflies migrating annually to Central America and ocean salmon swimming hundreds of miles back to their natal streams to spawn.

But you can define "miracle" in several ways, according to my critically thinking friend Tom Kirkman of North Carolina. But he does offer some explanation of his thinking on this as follows. "I do not offer it as any sort of proof that there is no God of some sort, but rather that the workings of the universe are more random and outside the consideration of humans, particularly those who find a religious connotation in everything. If we are going to ascribe wonderful miracles to a loving God that bends or suspends the natural and physical laws in order to protect and save an individual, who for whatever reason has found special favor with such a God, then scenarios where the outcome is opposite that of what most consider miraculous must be attributed to a vengeful, hateful God who rains tragedy upon those who have angered 'him.' Or, we can simply accept the fact that random things happen and the outcome, whether beneficial or disastrous to the individual/s involved, is not the determining factor as to whether something is or isn't a 'miracle.' A coincidence remains a coincidence, regardless of the outcome. Therefore if a person wants to believe in miracles, they must accept miracles as being two-way streets. I think a simpler way to put all this is, '[stuff] happens'."

Kirkman notes that a hiking and biking trail (New River Trail in Virginia) near his home in High Point, NC, is a popular place for recreation and used by tens of thousands of people each year. This trail is along a river in a mountainous area of the Southeast. One year, a solitary female biker was peddling through this area when a huge boulder on the uphill side of the trail dislodged, rolled and bounced down and instantly killed her. As Kirkman said, "it is a miracle." Initial thoughts would be — hey, let's wait a minute here — nothing good happened that would be ascribed to God — there is no miracle here. But it is or was a miracle by our currently popular definitions, and that is Kirkman's point.

Had the rock fallen just ahead of her or just behind her, or if two or more rocks had fallen to bracket her position without harming her or a single spoke on her bicycle, people would be quick to claim a Godly miracle. But as per our definition above, a miracle would be "an event that apparently contradicts known scientific laws and is hence thought to be due to supernatural causes, especially an act of God."

Why would miracles have to be good all the time? An airplane crash in which some of the people aboard were saved is characterized as a miracle. But that same crash also killed people and has to be part of the same event, if it is indeed a miracle. The fiery wrath from God on Sodom and Gomorrah killed people, but was considered a miracle because God had two angels usher Lot and his family out of the city just in time. The killing of all the people and animals (the animals all innocent and perhaps amoral but certainly not immoral) with the flood during Noah's time had to be a miracle, according to the religionists.

Thus the tsunami of 2004 Christmas that killed 250,000 or more people in Indonesia would be a miracle. So would Hurricane Katrina of 2005 which killed 1800 in New Orleans and caused $81 billion in damages. The terrorist attack by Taliban members on the New York World Trade Buildings would also be a miracle, although none of these or so many others would be good or ascribed by the religious as Godly miracles. But you would get a completely different point of view about the World Trade Buildings and Pentagon terrorist attacks from some Muslims. They would consider as martyrs the 19 zealots on the four planes, as highly religious and devoted followers of Islam. After all, according to them and those who applauded their acts, they were fighting against the "infidel" — the Christians and the Christian world and nation.

The list — or lists — could go on forever. The fact remains that almost all of these are in the realm of established commonplace events (births, and animal senses of smell and vision), facts learned through science and experimentation (earth spinning on its axis and revolving around the sun and vaccinations for disease), understandings of biology (DNA, genetics, brain chemistry), anatomy, genetics, embryology, physiology, surgery, and all the other "-ologies" and fields of endeavor and study. Who survives and who does not in accidents or events occurring around the world — or who is injured and who is not — is a matter of circumstance or coincidence, not anything involving God.

As Richard Dawkins says in his book, *The Blind Watchmaker*, "Coincidence means multiplied improbability." Take, for example, a flight on a plane which unfortunately crashes on landing. A passenger in question may have had to fly at the last minute for a business meeting or family problem. That's an unexpected improbability. Once boarding the plane and seated, he is asked by the stewardess to switch seats on the full flight so that a husband and wife can sit together in his row of seats. He does. That's another unexpected improbability.

Suppose that during a crash landing, the husband and wife in his assigned seat are killed while he in the switched seat walks away unscathed. That's a third unexpected improbability. You could add more improbabilities or unexpected events if you like. Suppose the man who switched seats upon being asked was a hit man for the Mafia, returning from a "job"? Suppose the couple killed in the seats were both doctors, medical missionaries returning to the US to visit friends and family after five years in the field to help others in impoverished countries? Would this change your Godly thinking about why God saved some, or almost all, and killed others?

Sure, someone about now will pick up on the phrase "almost all." Certainly not all cures and repairs by man are in the realm of the knowable. As stated before, there are — rarely — spontaneous "cures" and spontaneous remissions of disease. For example, we know that some children with autism will in time grow out of this affliction and become normal or almost normal — as we lamely define "normal" — as adults.

We do not know why some partly or completely "recover" and others do not. There are theories and there is continuing research, but no definitive answers as of this writing. That does not mean that those who grow out of autism in time are "miracles." Thus, just because we do not yet know the answers as to how or why this happens, does not mean that any result in this area is a miracle or that it is a result of God or praying or any religion or religious practice. We also do not know why or how autism happens to develop in some individuals and not in others. Hopefully, that information will be discovered in time from serious medical research and also result in more research and understanding of this devastating disease and early life condition.

We do not yet know the answer to spontaneous remissions. The fact that the cause for remission is unknown does not automatically lead to God. The other possibility is that there are hundreds of thousands of so-called "miracles," although to call them that countermands the true meaning of the word. Most if not all of these are marvels, awesome, wonderful, beautiful, inspiring, wonders. Most of these marvels are in several categories, but none of them fall into the "supernatural" category or as "an act of God" and outside the basic physical laws of the universe.

Real miracles, if indeed they were real are those events such as Jesus being resurrected (both from the dead and also flying away), walking on water, floating ax heads, a talking snake, a magical fruit, a worldwide flood and all the activities of Noah connected with this, Daniel in the lions' den, Daniel's friends in the furnace yet not burning up, a talking donkey or the sun standing still for Joshua.

These are myths. They did not happen — they couldn't have happened — they are beyond the laws of nature and physics. There is no proof of them any more than there is proof of any other Greek, Roman, Norse, Egyptian and far eastern myth or god involved with these myths.

There are many examples of marvels that are thought to be miracles or pseudo-miracles. Often the birth of a child is cited as a "miracle." Nope, in the strict dictionary sense it is not, regardless of the wonder that we feel about it and the wonder of two humans creating a new life. It is a part of the basic evolutionary basis of life, of the duplication of cells, of mitosis, of X and Y chromosomes, of eggs and sperm, of DNA, of embryonic development. It happens all the time with all sorts of creatures, small and large, vertebrate and invertebrate, in many of the various classes, phyla, families, orders and genus of life.

You can look on a microscopic level at the fertilization of a sperm and egg of a sea urchin and find it not much different than the process involving two humans. You can find both asexual reproduction and sexual reproduction throughout nature. You find plants with sexual reproduction. The typical egg/sperm sexual process is not only in humans, but also in dogs, whales, eagles, spiders, toads, elephants, mayflies, shrews, bees, dragonflies, and millions of other creatures.

Sometimes the religionists refer to medical miracles. "Oh, the operation was so delicate and so rarely done that there was only a 30 percent chance that he would survive it on the operating table! We prayed — the whole church prayed — and our prayers were answered! He not only survived the operation but now, two weeks after the surgery, he is doing fine and will be coming home from the hospital in another week. Our prayers have been answered! God saved him! God is so good! God is so loving! God cares for us! God knows our needs! God is in control! He is a loving God!" Note that there are seldom similar thanks for the surgeon, his or her skills, knowledge, training, alertness and experience in this delicate operation. There is little appreciation of the surgical staff who surely contributed to the success of the operation. Little thought is given to the hospital which allowed this surgeon to continue to learn and practice and flourish in his or her surgical skills. There is no appreciation or thanks for earlier surgeons and medical teams who previously developed and in time perfected the delicate operation that saved this supposed patient. There are no thanks given to the medical school and staff which provided the chief surgeon the four years of basic training plus the following one to two years of an internship and up to five years of a surgical residency.

The other part of the thanks should go to the part that chance makes. The understanding in this hypothetical set-up was that the operation, based on past experience, allowed only a 30 percent chance of the patient surviving, yet he survived. Thus, he fell into the category of the 30 percent who live, not the 70 percent of those who undergo the same operation and who tragically end up in the hospital basement morgue.

Medical marvels can include everything from the operation on our hypothetical patient listed above to the development of vaccines such as the annual flu shots, the separate shot for the H1N1 swine flu, various shots for tetanus, pneumonia, measles, diphtheria, mumps, rubella, smallpox, polio, and even rabies for those bitten by a wild animal suspected to be infected.

These vaccines are not from God or gods. They are not miracles. They are expansions from the early experimental work of Jenner and Pasteur to inoculate patients against the disease of anthrax, rabies and subsequently other diseases. Since then, other doctors and experimenters have developed and perfected the vaccination process for a wide range of human and even animal diseases. Thus we not only have vaccines against human diseases, but also against our pet's distemper, bordetella (kennel cough), rabies, parvo, para influenza, and other diseases, with similar vaccinations for diseases of cats, cattle, pigs and ferrets. Vaccines save lives, both animal and human. They are the result of knowledge resulting from experimentation, not supernatural miracles. The fact that cow pox was and is similar to smallpox allowed

Jenner to use this to inoculate humans against the once-deadly scourge of smallpox. That these vaccines are marvelous in that they save lives is without question. That they are God-ordained in saving these lives is certainly unmitigated nonsense.

The word "miracle" has become a word that I hate. Or at least I hate the cavalier way it is used by so many, including people who should know better. You find it in the regular news media, either in print in newspapers and news magazines as well as on the air. It is used as an erroneous substitute for different, unusual, odd, strange, rare, or offbeat situation, circumstance, event or people.

The problem with thinking about miracles and ascribing miracles to commonplace occurrences — or even rare occurrences — is that many people want to ascribe any unusual good thing or occurrence to God. Note the use of "good thing or occurrence." A plane crashes and some few people in some seats live or perhaps are not hurt at all or suffer only minor injuries. Those who live through such a horrible occurrence are "miracles," saved by God, according to the religious types and Christians.

Somehow, God gets all the credit for saving some for whatever purpose God wants, but God gets none of the blame for killing the rest which might include young marrieds on a honeymoon trip, a mother with her baby, a husband coming home from a sales trip or a college student going home after graduating with honors.

It seems strange — indeed impossible — to many lacking religious beliefs that God can and will "save" some and "condemn" others to death. Of course, you can't ever get the Christians to think that a plane crash and the results of life and death have nothing to do with God. Equally, they will never believe or ascribe causation by God to those who die, are horribly injured, lose homes, businesses or families. You have to only think critically and use common sense to realize that a tragic plane crash is nothing more than a crap shoot, a roll of dice, as to who lives and who dies.

A recent TV story showed a woman who was supposedly saved by God at the last minute from being placed into a gas chamber at a Nazi concentration camp. The reason? The gas chamber was stuffed so full of so many other unfortunates that when they added her, the door would not shut. Naturally, the door had to be shut for the poison gas to kill those inside. For this one woman, it was a "miracle." The end of this story was about God's grace in letting her live, about her having been blessed in this regard, and the fact that she alone was left to tell this particular story about the Holocaust to others.

What was not mentioned was the fact that dozens or hundreds or thousands of people died, day after day, while she lived; and that this was certainly not the only one such session of packing and cramming the gas chamber full to kill as many as possible. What was not mentioned was that while God supposedly "saved" this one woman, he did nothing to save the others. If God could save one, could he not also have saved tens of thousands? How come God is being praised for a "miracle" instead of being condemned for allowing so many others to be killed? And of course, realize that this mass killing by the Nazis was largely of Jews, who were and are listed as "God's Chosen People." They can't be chosen people if God is asleep at the switch or off doing something else when his people really, really need him.

I have had Christians with no thought or critical thinking skills ascribe to the power of prayer (and God) any event for which they prayed and for which the outcome was exactly as they prayed. Was it God? Religion? Was it a miracle? Was it their particular belief system and adherence to one particular religious cult? Nope. It was a chance, an improbable, a coincidence that by Dawkins' definition is the multiplication of improbables. Naturally, all these same praying people immediately dismiss those times during which they prayed and nothing happened or when the outcome was the complete opposite of what they desired and for which they prayed. These believers are really just like Las Vegas slots gamblers. Those slots gamblers remember the time that a quarter got them a return of ten dollars, but forget all the many, many times that they continually slipped quarters into the machine and got nothing.

What then would be a miracle? That is relatively simple to answer. Since by definition a miracle is something outside the ability of nature, the laws of nature, physics or chemistry to do, it is something that could only be defined and accomplished by God, gods, or some supernatural force or being. Naturally, anything like this would have to be proven under the laws of science, with an experiment or controlled test, or under conditions that would obviously rule out any possible but improbable event, trickery or fraud.

Thus, for someone to levitate for a few minutes six inches above the ground would be a miracle. For someone to fly around, as Jesus supposedly did after his resurrection, would be a miracle and defying the laws of physics and nature. To re-grow the leg of an amputee (as has been suggested by Sam Harris in his comments on prayer) would be a miracle. To easily lift a 2,000 pound car, the equivalent weight of which can be lifted easily by an ant, would be a miracle. To hold your breath underwater for 15 or 20 minutes or longer as a whale or seal does routinely would be a miracle.

It would be a miracle to have a small baby that was accidentally squashed like a ripe pumpkin under the double tires of a heavily-loaded 18-wheeler brought back to life, as per the mouse Mr. Jingles in *The Green Mile* movie. In this, the huge black man, John Coffey (played by Michael Clarke Duncan) restores life to the small mouse, (a pet of another death row inmate), that was squashed flat under the foot of a sadistic guard. Do that with a child, or for that matter even a mouse, and you have the makings of a miracle.

The idea that there are miracles or that there have been miracles in the past is ludicrous. If you can't make a reasonable argument for a miracle today, then there is no reason to think that anyone could have done this 2,000 or 3,000 years ago, or that miracles occurred independently of anyone or any physically possible event.

Chapter 7. Biblical Physical Impossibilities

The Bible, as all Good Book-pounders and fundamentalist Christians know, is the inerrant word of God. The Bible has no mistakes and the Bible cannot lie. God cannot lie. We will get to the lying, contradictions and mistake parts later, but for now let's just accept and work with what the born-againers believe.

We also know through this inerrant word of God that we are all descended from Adam and Eve, and that through their foul up with the fruit in the Garden of Eden we are all destined to be like them, to die, to sin and do other bad things. Adam and Eve were bad, so we have to be bad. That's what the Bible says and that's what the preachers preach.

We also have to look at how we descended from Adam and how Adam and Eve came into being. God, blowing air into a pile of dirt made Adam and Eve (Genesis 1:27), according to one of the two different accounts in Genesis. In a second account, Adam was made and then Eve created from Adam's rib as a companion to him. This whole idea was part of a conversation with two Jehovah's Witnesses who wandered up the driveway one fine summer day to convert me to their particular brand of delusion. Playing with them on the Genesis story, and acting dumb, I asked them about how Eve was formed and how this physically affected Adam. "Well," I ventured, leading them on as a minister works up to selling the idea of Jesus and the concept of tithing, "since Eve was formed from Adam's rib, and since all men are like Adam as a result of the fall, does that mean that men today, descended from Adam, are missing one rib? Does that mean that they have one less rib than women?"

"Yes," they enthusiastically assured me, confident that they had found a kindred spirit who would become a head-bobbing sycophant of their famed fables and false faith. "Yes, that is why men today are missing one rib. Adam was the precursor of us today and what happened to him also happens to us," they concluded happily. It was, I assumed, sort of like the Christian story of original sin. Adam and Eve had original sin, so we inherited it. I cut to the chase to lessen the pain and time involved. I explained to them that men have exactly the same number of ribs as do women and that there is no absence of ribs or any other bones or connective tissues in the male human body. And yes, I do know — I used to teach human anatomy in a medical school.

Part of these improbabilities of rib numbers between male and female are a result of a continuation of a series of ridiculous beliefs from the Bible, never mind the facts that various sciences have discovered and since proven. Many such examples abound.

For example, Archbishop Ussher in 1650 "discovered" the age of the earth by counting backwards the ages of early prophets and from facts of various historical events. He also worked backwards from all the begetting that was going on in Biblical times. He found out that the beginning of Creation, as per Genesis 1:1, occurred on October 23, 4004 B.C. Others have added to this by stating that this beginning of creation began at 9:30 a.m. No mention was made of the time zone in which this was figured. That is about 6,000 years ago, or about the time that the Samarians were inventing glue and developing cuneiform writing methods and also about the time that Babylonians were starting to brew beer. It is 5,000 years after religious and secular obelisks and pillars were created in Turkey.

In this Godly creation, it would be like spontaneous generation, later finally disproved in 1859 by Louis Pasteur (b. December 27, 1822–d. September 28, 1895) after similar introductory experiments by other earlier scientists such as Francesco Redi (b. February 18, 1626–d. March 1, 1697).

There is more. If Adam and Eve's children were the only offspring on earth with this creation of man and his wife, then Cain (Abel was gone — killed by Cain) and Seth would have to "marry" or have sex with their Mom Eve or their sisters, the sisters later described briefly in Genesis 5:4. That's not an impossibility, but it is highly questionable from biological and genetics (and eugenics) standards to say nothing of ethics and morality as we think of it today.

This of course ties in with another magical impossibility, the fruit, often called the apple in modern parlance. We know from reading the Bible that God did not want Adam and Eve to eat the fruit from the tree of the knowledge of good and evil.

Otherwise, God would have wanted to educate mankind or make these two prototypes — Adam and Eve — able to eat of this "knowledge tree" and become smart for their own good and for that of future generations along with making us all better people. But it seems that we have no "good gene" or "God gene" to keep us on the straight and narrow. How neglectful of God! Apparently God did not want that, according to this part of Genesis. Or was God just trying to prevent some smarts in mankind so that God could maintain control over all of us?

Moving on to the fable of Noah's ark, there are lots of problems. First, this echoes the similar flood fable found in the Epic of Gilgamesh and some earlier myth/creation stories. The Epic of Gilgamesh was written at least about 800 years prior to the recounting of the flood of Noah's time. This whole story of Noah's Ark is ridiculous, to say the least. Expert ship builders state that it would be impossible to build a totally wood ship of the dimensions of 450 feet by 75 feet wide by 45 feet high (300 cubits, 50 cubits and 30 cubits).

Second, if the boat were built like a barge or shoebox, square on all sides for maximum room, it would have a total size of 1,518,750 cubic feet. But that would be charitable, since ships and boats are not built square, although some barges are built that way. Second, this total 1-1/2 million cubic feet does not allow for the space lost in building the three decks described and the various bulkheads necessary to keep pairs of animals separate. You can't have a lion being a roommate with an impala. Third, any remaining open space (there really would not be any) would not be nearly large enough to hold all the animals on earth along with their food.

Today, scientists do not even know how many animal species we have. Estimates, including water creatures (which Noah obviously did not include) are at least a few million. Expert estimates are that we have from 5 to 100 million species, many of them smaller than flies. A good generally accepted number of species would be about 10 million.

In flies alone we have 157,000 species. Bees number 20,000 species; ants about 20,000 species; beetles well over 350,000 species and still counting. There are 200,000 species of butterflies in the world, 3,000 species of mosquitoes, 35,000 species of spiders with a total of about 950,000 insect species worldwide. Total figures for land animals also include 10,000 bird species and 10,000 species of reptiles.

In vertebrates alone, we have worldwide 62,000 species. This includes the ocean foraging 18 species of penguins, and the marine iguanas living in the Galapagos Islands off Equator. Other than the occasional sea snake, and the obvious whales, porpoise and dolphins and such, they all require land as a base of operations.

This presents an insurmountable problem for those believing this Noah's Ark fable. If Noah and his crew were to load a pair of animals (one species) per minute, and work 24 hours a day, seven days a week and 365 days a year, it would take them one year to load 525,600 species, or two years to load the first million. With estimates of well over 2 million land species of creatures, it would take four years to get a full load on the ark. If we went with the scientifically accepted 10 million species of animals, then it would take over 20 years for Noah and crew — again working to load one species per minute, working around the clock 365 days a year with no breaks — to load all the animals. With two million pairs of species alone, and 1.5 million cubic feet based on the Biblical description of the Ark that would only allow for three-quarters of a cubic foot for each pair of animals. That would be a little hard for the elephants, hippos, giraffes and rhinoceros. And that does not include the space necessary for food for these two million or more species of animals.

Food is a problem and not just because of the physical space necessary to store it. Some ant colonies constantly need fresh leaves to carry back to the nest to feed fungus that in turn becomes their food. Much vegetation for all herbivores would become stale, moldy, mildewed and rotten in the 150 days of the Ark floating around after the 40 days of rain, the four years of loading the animals, the many days for the water to subside and the time to offload animals.

Many animals are carnivores, including lions, tigers, wolves, hyenas, cheetahs, bears, shrews, fox, mink, even anteaters, aardwolves and such. They eat meat — not vegetation. True, tigers might eat wild boar and aard-wolves eat termites (aardwolves are insectivores), but both are still carni-vores. And you would have to figure on bulk food items. After all, aardwolves alone can eat up to 250,000 termites a night (times two aardwolves). Figure that food supply for a long voyage and what the termites have to eat!

And no, you can't substitute vegetation or an early form of Purina dog chow. The gastrointestinal systems, stomach and digestion of carnivores vs. herbivores are completely different.

For shrews you have to include food of mice and insects. Lions and cheetahs would require impalas, gazelles and other small game such as the springbok and dik-dik. And even though Noah would not care about fish (we'll get to that in a few minutes) he would have to carry fish and frogs. These and other aquatic creatures and insects are the food for water voles, anacondas, otters, and mink living in or on the banks of an aquatic habitat. Thus watertight containers to hold fish, crayfish and frogs for up to 200 days or more would be a must.

And not all herbivores eat grain and leaves. Herbivore hippos eat river water plants, as do moose. Giraffes eat the tip tops of trees while sheep and goats scour plains plants down to the roots. It is not like feeding dogs where you just wander over to Wal-Mart or Pet Smart and pick up a bag of Purina. Overall, this food problem is a big, big, really impossible task!

Don't forget also the problems of transportation in dealing with this worldwide flood that reached 29,055 feet (twenty feet above the highest mountain — Mount Everest at 29,035 feet height). In this, Noah had to get all the creatures from all over the world, from all of the various continents. "You are to bring into the Ark two of all living creatures, male and female, to keep them alive with you. Two of every kind of bird, every kind of animal and of every kind of creature that moves along the ground will come to you to be kept alive. You are to take every kind of food that is to be eaten and store it away as food for you and them," said God in a direct quote from Genesis 6:19-21. God should know.

Thus, bison from North America, penguins from the Antarctic, polar bears from the arctic, civet cats from Asia, reindeer from the north, Tasmanian devils from Australia, tapir from South America, Amur tigers from Asia, red deer from Europe, blue tailed skinks from the American Southwest, along with tens of thousands of other species all from unique environments and specific habitats, are necessary for this boat ride to fulfill the dictates of God. It goes without saying that this would be absolutely impossible. How do you get a South American sloth to move that fast? Admittedly some sloths can race along at about a mile a month, but that still creates (especially with an ocean to cross) an impassable and impossible problem. And that one mile a month is awfully fast for a sloth — about 176 feet per day for a creature that often seems to barely move.

One answer from the creationists is that the earth at one time had all the various continents melded into one large land mass — a supercontinent — today called Pangaea by scientists. It was only later than the continents separated to make the distinct continents we know today.

The theory then would be that all animals could travel back and forth over this large land mass and thus easily (?) get to Noah's Ark in time for the sailing date. This of course assumes another fanciful tale that animals would be able to travel the thousands — or tens of thousands — of miles to get there in time, and that they could somehow survive, even with different food and habitat requirements of each species for the chosen routes. It also presumes that a few pairs of animals at least would know of God's plan to kill everything on earth and thus as species representatives were being paged to the mid-east so that their species would survive through them.

Of course, all that would be impossible. You can't contact one pair of pronghorn antelope; they travel in herds. Similarly, passenger pigeons of North America only flocked, nested, mated, and reproduced in large flocks and thus one pair would not work for reproduction of this species after the cessation of the flood. We as the "smart" species did not recognize this in time to help this magnificent bird, and thus the last one died in the Cincinnati Zoo September 1, 1914.

What is equally impossible is the idea of the separation of Pangaea to make the separate continents in the time frame allowed by the Bible. We know that the rate of continental drift, depending upon each continent and drift rate, is somewhere between 0.78 and 5.9 inches per year. That's not a lot. Thus, if an original Pangaea were to allow animal movement, and the Atlantic today is widely separated from Africa and Europe, it would take a lot of time. The width of the Atlantic Ocean is about 1700 miles between Brazil and Liberia, and about 3,000 miles between the United States and North Africa. If we look at the continental drift at its speediest of almost 6 inches per year, and if we do the math, the 3,000 mile distance would take almost 32 million years. If we use the figure of 1700 for the distance from Brazil to Liberia, the time frame would be almost 18 million years.

Of course this would mean that evolution was in full effect, despite what creationists hallucinate about, and that Noah would have to have built his ark and sailed his ship sometime before Pangaea started moving around — this so that all the animals could crowd onto the ark. For the creationists, that presumes evolution occurring far faster than it would and could really occur and far faster than any evolutionist has even suggested. It also suggests continental drift occurring at a rate of about a mile a year, something obviously impossible and not within any geographical model. In addition, it throws out the idea of the earth being about 6,000 years old and beginning at 9:30 a.m., October 23, 4004 BCE. Creationists have to reframe their geology math for that one.

In addition, for some species it would take more than a pair to repopulate the earth once the waters subsided. The instructions were also to take seven of every kind of clean animal. The two (one male and one female) only applied to all other animals. This still would not be enough for some animals to mate.

One other problem is with fish. Since the flood would be rising to a height of 29,055 feet above the current ocean level, freshwater and saltwater fish would be mixed together. Since the rain and the welling of waters from the ground would all be fresh water, what would happen to freshwater fish and mammals with this mix of the two water types? Would this not increase in salinity to a brackish water state along the coastal areas? What would happen to truly pelagic ocean species such as bluefin tuna?

Further, how would all these separate and distinct saltwater and freshwater fish and mammals get back to their proper habitat once the flooding stopped and after the waters remained level but high for hundreds of days before subsiding? This would not only involve fish and mammals getting into the right kind of watery habitat (fresh water or salt water) but also at the right latitude. Tropical saltwater fish cannot live in the icy waters of the

Baltic Sea. Freshwater pacu and tucanare of jungle rivers in Brazil are not interchangeable with the freshwater Arctic char of Hudson Bay. High mountain golden trout cannot survive in the sea level river waters of the Nile perch.

It gets even worse with getting land creatures back to their native and necessary habitat. Bighorn sheep need rocky (and Rocky) mountains. Camels need sandy (Sahara) deserts, water voles need riverine areas, moose need watery woodlands, tigers need jungle and cheetahs need grasslands. Then again, Noah would somehow have to get that New World two-toed sloth back across the ocean and to his tree-top South American home where he could race around again at a mile a month.

In addition to the impossibilities listed above are the specifics about the flood itself. For example, we know that the rains came for 40 days and nights and the ark floated around for 150 days. We can also calculate that the rain would have to have fallen or the ground water spring up at a continual rate of 30 feet 3 inches per hour, 24 hours per day, for 40 days to reach the top of the highest mountain in the world, Mount Everest at 29,035 feet. The flood rose to 20 feet above the highest mountain. Check Genesis 7:18–20.

That pretty well slams the door on the idea of covering the whole earth, as the Bible states and as the Judeo-Christians like to waffle about. Many religionists like to tell you that the story only covers the flooding in one little valley. Not so, unless you want to juggle and jiggle with Bible "facts" and jimmy the Biblical "truth." You don't want to juggle with this inerrant word of God, do you? You are not calling God wrong, are you? You are not saying that God or his scribes made a mistake, are you?

In 2 Kings 6:4–7, you find floating axe heads made of stone, brass, bronze or iron. These materials do not float. Yet in this 2 Kings story, an axe head is made to float so that it can be retrieved from the water. Of course, this is not possible. It is pure pixie dust. Or another way of looking at it is that while God wanted an axe head to float, he could not save the iron Titanic, in which 1,577 lives — men, women and children, passengers and crew — died. Strange, isn't it?

Jesus flies, also, as per the resurrection story listed in the four gospels in the New Testament. This is 40 days after his death on the cross but without the winged horse (Buraq) that Muhammad enjoyed. You have to ask yourself — why is the notion of Muhammad on a winged horse wrong, stupid, dumb and ridiculous, yet Jesus without a horse — winged or otherwise — is believable, miraculous and worthy of our fervent belief, total acceptance and constant worship? Does any of this make sense?

We also have Jesus walking on water, something else completely impossible by the laws of physics for anyone, anywhere, anytime, anyway. It defies physics as does the flying Jesus story.

And just think. According to the Christians, who created the laws of physics? Why, God did, silly! Everyone knows that! God made all the natural laws. If that is the case, then why is God or Jesus breaking those laws of physics, or allowed to break or violate laws of physics?

There is more — healing the diseased, restoring a withered hand, raising the dead after four days and curing lepers. Unless this all occurred through some sort of magic trick and showmanship stage-type legerdemain (and thus a true trick), it did not happen. And if it happened through magical trickery and legerdemain, it also did not happen, since we know that magic is not real. We know that is all sleight of hand or illusion. All these events are also obvious impossibilities.

Jesus feeding the thousands is another impossible fairy tale from the Bible. In the first of these two tales (Matthew 14:13–21) Jesus finds thousands of people with him at mealtime, but he and his disciples have only five loaves of bread and two fish. In a later tale (Matthew 15:32-38) Jesus and his disciples, walking along the Sea of Galilee, find themselves late in the day with thousands following Jesus and again with nothing for them to eat as the mealtime hour approaches.

They count their food resources and this time find seven loaves of bread and a few small fish. The food multiplied mysteriously, and it fed all the people. In the first tale, the available food fed five thousand, and in the second four thousand. In each case this did not count women and children (who were also fed), since none of them counted for much of anything in ancient times anyway.

There are two possible explanations for these tales of feeding thousands. One of these would involve a miracle which is impossible (see Chapter 6). The other possible explanation is the very real probability of "nail soup." Nail soup comes from an old folk tale concerning cooking a delicious repast using only a nail. It has been attributed to Sweden, but there are also versions from other Scandinavian countries, Portugal, Mexico, and China. Basically, it is about a tramp or traveler seeking both a place to stay and a meal, and offering to make "nail soup," also variously called "stone, wood, button, or axe soup."

The simple plot includes dropping a nail into the pot of boiling water to make a soup. The secret is in asking the lady with the boiling pot, and other ladies or bystanders, for just a few additional items to thicken the soup, add a little more flavor, add some texture, add some bulk and add some color.

In time, the tramp gets and adds to his nail soup items such as flour, barley, milk, potatoes, salted beef, spices, vegetables and herbs, all while boiling down the original water to thicken the soup.

Since most people carried much of their belongings along with necessities for eating and sleeping (there was no Motel 6 with the light on for you in the first century) it would not be unheard of for people to combine their food supplies into a more varied and substantive meal. It would be an Israelites version of the nail soup story.

Was Jesus pulling a con? Was Jesus performing a real miracle? Were the people that gullible back then? The answer to the questions are respectively "yes," "no" and "yes." The answer to the third question is "yes" or "very likely" since there were lots of uneducated and illiterate people. Most likely, Jesus and his disciples were illiterate also, able to read and write little more than their names, if that. Acceptance would have been easier for them and also more likely with large numbers of people feeding both literally and figuratively on the food and the con.

Check with Joshua 10:12–14 for something else that ought to peak our curiosity and skepticism about the facts of the Bible and the impossibilities of the Bible. This is the famous scene taught in Sunday School classes everywhere when Joshua asks God to extend the day, to make the sun stand still, so that Joshua and the Israelites can defeat their Amorite enemy in Gibeon.

Naturally, as little kids in the middle of religious brainwashing, most of us were astonished and amazed that God can stop the sun. That, after all, is some pretty heavy-duty magic. We — most of us anyway — were impressed. I was impressed at the time. But as we know from Galileo in the early 1600s the sun does not really revolve around the earth.

The earth revolves around the sun and also rotates on its own axis. For the sun to "stand still" in the middle of the day as stated in the Bible, the reality is that the earth would have to stop spinning on its axis for the sun to stay in place. The earth and the rotation on its axis would have to come to a screeching halt. That would create problems. Big problems. For example, our day and night combined is 24 hours. That means that the earth spins on its axis once per day — once per 24 hours.

Our earth is about 8,000 miles in diameter, or 25,901 miles in circumference at the equator. Do the math and our earth is spinning at the equator at a rate of 1037 miles per hour. Naturally, the closer you get to the poles the slower spin rate. Stand at the true pole and all you do is turn around completely — 360 degrees, kind of like a pig on a spit at a North Carolina barbeque — in a 24 hour period. At roughly 30 degrees latitude, where Israel is located (along with our Jacksonville, FL and Houston, TX), the spin rate is about 906 miles per hour.

Next, think what happens to a car when it hits a brick wall at 65 mph. Here with the "sun standing still" we are thinking of a speed of 15 times that of a car wreck. People, horses, armies, houses, wild animals, huts, temples, warehouses, domestic cattle, uprooted trees, sandy beaches, water out of rivers, beds, home furnishings, tents, cooking pots, loose rocks, camp fires, river banks, fish, rats, mice, zebras, elephants, wolves, camels, dust, dirt, stumps, gravel, and more would all be flying off into space tangentially to the curvature of the earth.

They would be flying at an initial rate of 906 miles per hour from Joshua's camp. And that says nothing about the damage that would result to habitats, the environment, etc, left in the hot sun for a full day as described in this Bible, this so-called truthful, inerrant word of God.

Is this one more little tidbit of information and a "fact" from the Bible about which we should be skeptical? There is no skepticism here, since it is laughable to even postulate about this. The stopping and starting would be impossible. If it did happen, it would cause most living things, including humans, to fly off into space before falling back to the earth, dead and dying, broken and brain dead. It is just a flat-out, ridiculous, physical impossibility. Since God was dictating the Bible to humans, does this mean that God flunked the 6th grade?

These are just a few of so many impossibilities of which the Bible is full. You can check about Shadrach, Meshach and Abednego thrown into the fiery furnace. Despite the furnace being heated to "seven times hotter than normal" (whatever normal is), the three men were not harmed. This of course is physically impossible when you consider the heat of other stars and planets, some of which are so hot that molten iron falls as does our watery rain.

These tales go on through the Bible, in both the Old and New Testaments. These are all physically impossible, thus they are all ridiculous in so many ways and on so many levels.

Chapter 8. Biblical Immoralities

We get our morals and ethics from the Bible and from God, don't we? That's what ministers, pastors, priests and rabbis would like you to think. One of the biggies in the ethics of Judeo–Christian belief revolves around the Ten Commandments (covered later in chapters 12 and 13).

When it comes to morals, there are two divergent views. One is Godly and the other is common sense. We all know that there are morals, ethics, mores, memes and folkways in societal activities that include parts of the Ten Commandments. Morals and ethics define what is right and what is wrong and, hopefully, doing what is right. That makes it moral.

The morals, ethics, mores and folkways of the Ten Commandments — in many cases laws and regulations — in society are pretty good, although they do fall into major and minor categories. One of the biggies included in the Ten Commandments is the prohibition against killing. But this can vary also.

Some religions, such as Jehovah's Witnesses and Quakers, are of the belief that they try to strictly honor this Biblical Commandment and thus never kill in any circumstances. They remain conscientious objectors or neutral in war, willing to do other tasks for the benefit of soldiers and the fighting force but not willing to carry a weapon and engage other troops with the intent of killing people. In addition, the commandment against killing does not specify what should not be killed, only that "thou shalt not kill" or, as some translations say today, "Thou shalt not murder." Whether or not killing for defense or country in time of war is murder is a subject for a long philosophical debate. It all boils down to the possibility of so-called justified killing vs. unjustified killing.

In addition, this morality or prohibition against killing could be a prohibition against killing animals for food or sacrifices. It seems clear that this is not the intent; otherwise there would not be the many killings for food or sacrifice mentioned in the Bible by the Israelites, usually under the direction of God.

The seventh commandment is "thou shalt not commit adultery." We all know that to be a no-no that has been around for thousands of years and is a basic tenet along the lines of other commandments including those such as "thou shalt not steal, thou shalt not bear false witness, thou shalt not murder." Adultery is usually thought of as extramarital sex, when one or both of the parties are married to another person. It does not usually apply to premarital sex or non-marital sex by those in which both parties have never married, or those which are divorced or widowed.

We "know" — or think that we know — that this edict against violating the marriage vows comes from thousands of years ago, from the beginning of the Bible and Adam and Eve and the one man, one woman rule about relationships and marriage. The one man, one woman concept and faithfulness in marriage is a biggie among the fundamentalists interested in preserving the family and also fighting against the supposed horrors of homosexuality and how it can ruin the world.

But even the Bible fudges on this. Take for example those bastions of the early teachings, Abraham, "father" of the Israelites, and Sarah. These two — according to the Bible — formed the beginnings of three of the world's religions — Judaism, Christianity and Islam.

For starters, Abraham and Sarah (formerly Abram and Sarai) were related (same father), and thus were half siblings (Genesis 20:12). That's not exactly what we would consider proper today, biologically or culturally, as either dating or marriage partners. Also, the Bible considers half-siblings the same as full siblings. You must not marry or have sexual relations with either your full or half sibling.

That Abraham married his half-sister Sarah is without question; it's found in Genesis 11:29 and Genesis 20:12. Even though Abraham was married to his sister Sarah, on two occasions he also pimped out his wife, first to the Egyptian Pharaoh and then again to Abimelech, king of Gerar. In the first case, (Genesis 21:11–20) Abraham was afraid that because of Sarah's beauty, he as her husband might be killed so as to make her legally available for marriage to the Pharaoh.

By claiming that they were brother and sister (half true, as half-brother and half-sister, even though married), he would have a chance of staying alive and they would both find favor with the Pharaoh. They became wealthy until God exacted revenge on Egypt and upon which the Pharaoh found out the truth and sent them packing.

The second time (Genesis 20:5–7) Abraham did the same thing, with Abimelech. Here, Abraham pimped her out the same way, with the same story as for the Pharaoh. Sarah was complicit with this plan, saying (lying) that Abraham was her brother (partly true) but not her husband (a lie).

In both cases, the sister/brother relationship was only half right and both Abraham and Sarah left out the one little detail that they were also married to each other. In these two cases both lied and both agreed upon an adulterous scheme to fool others for their own benefit. It also seems that this was a true man/wife sexual arrangement, at least between the Pharaoh and Sarah. Genesis 12:10–20 states pretty clearly that the Pharaoh "took her to be my wife." (Genesis 12:18-19). This arrangement of marriage between the Pharaoh and Sarah lasted for some time, since it would have taken time for Abraham to acquire his wealth in sheep, cattle, donkeys, manservants, maidservants, and camels, as outlined in the ensuing weeks, months or years in Genesis 12:16. Thus, the Pharaoh and Sarah were living in a sexual union as man and wife for some time, even though Sarah was married to Abraham at the time.

What is also vehemently inexcusable, immoral and evil is God creating and favoring a "chosen people" particularly in light of the plan of Christianity to convert the whole world to the faith and thus make God and particularly Jesus the god or both of them the gods of all people.

This God did, right from the start of Genesis when making Adam and Eve as the first two people — according to the inerrant Bible — in the Garden of Eden. This follows up with many passages through the first several books of the Bible and following about how God will protect his people, protect and guide the Israelites, serve as a "shield" for these tribes. Basically, you can't have a "chosen people," regardless of who they are, without making the rest of the people outside of the "chosen" group "unchosen," discriminated against, second class citizens and thus unworthy and with bias against them. Women today were once "unchosen" by not being able to vote and in earlier times, to own property. Blacks were unchosen by being bought and sold as slaves. American Indians were unchosen by having their native ancestral lands stolen from them.

This selection and discrimination comes to fruition in the book of Joshua in which Joshua and the Israelites condemn, attack without provocation and conquer at least 31 cities (more suggested in the Bible) in the land of Canaan, the land of the innocent Canaanites. These unwarranted attacks on cities in Canaan are the subject of the whole book of Joshua, but nowhere more evident than in the attack of Jericho (Joshua, chapters 5 and 6) with the statement in 6:21 where "They devoted the city to the Lord and destroyed with the sword every living thing in it — men and women, young and old, cattle, sheep and donkeys." The simple statement is bad enough. Other references in the Bible mention the Israelites killing not only the Canaanites, but also the Hittites, Amalikites, Perizzites, Moabites, Midianites, Syrians,

Ethiopians and others. One Internet sites (www.godlessgeeks.com) counts up 2,270,365 people killed by God or on orders from God, but this is probably an underestimate.

The facts about this inerrant word of God, when you think about it, are horrible and make Hitler, Stalin or Pol Pot look like pikers when it comes to killing innocents. It becomes worse with you think of all those innocents killed. They were not just innocent soldiers defending their city and it's peoples from attack, but also old infirm men, weak aged women in their death beds, the sick, the injured, innocent children playing in the streets, babies not yet able to speak or walk, innocent teenagers just reaching for adulthood, pregnant women, wives and young women. That's absolutely evil — and it was on direct orders by God.

You can find a small but very similar evil tale of horror of innocents being killed in the aftermath of the tale of Daniel thrown into the lions' den. In this (Daniel 6:24), those administrators and satraps under King Darius, were all thrown into the lion's den for plotting against Daniel. But with them, their wives and children — presumably all totally innocent — were also thrown into the lion's den to be crushed, torn apart and killed. How and why did the wives and children of these men have anything to do with the punishment of Daniel? They were innocent. How can this be anything but evil?

Those who follow TV and movies know the name Woody Harrelson. He played the hapless and helpless bartender on Cheers and has been in many movies. Those who follow actors closely may know that Woody's father, Charles Harrelson, was a freelance contract killer who in 1979 was tried and convicted for killing federal judge John H. Wood, Jr. Charles Harrelson spent the rest of his life in prison, dying in 2007.

Should Woody Harrelson be executed or imprisoned for the crime of his father? The answer is obvious and the question ludicrous, ridiculous and shameful. Of course not — Woody Harrelson had nothing to do with his father's criminal activity.

You can find similar stories of unbridled evil and punishment of innocents in such tales as that of David's census of Israel in 2 Samuel 24:1–17. In this David was asked by God to take a census, but David did not do it "correctly." The result was that God gave David choices of three punishments. Ironically, any one of these three would have not affected David, but would have — and did — harshly affect his Israelite people. The choices were to endure three years of famine, three months of fleeing from enemies or three days of a plague. David chose the plague and as a result (2 Samuel 24:15) seventy thousand Israelites died. "So the Lord sent a plague on Israel from that morning until the end of the time designated, and seventy thousand of the people from Dan to Beersheba died."

A similar act of evil occurs during Passover when God instructs the Israelites to leave Egypt and that as punishment for not allowing the Israelites to leave, God will visit death upon the first born of all in Egypt. This is to include the first born of Pharaoh, along with the first born of every Egyptian in the land including young and old and even all the livestock including cattle, sheep and donkeys.

Sadly, this is taught as a great Biblical lesson in Sunday School of most Jewish and Christian faiths. This is the Passover time of the Jews and used by Christians as an example of God's goodness to the Israelites — his chosen people — and an example of God's punishment to the Pharaoh and Egypt.

Sadly, no one ever looks upon this as unbridled evil by a baby-killing, innocent-destroying God in ruining much of an entire country by killing innocent people. By placing lamb blood on the lintel and sides of the door frame, God will "pass by" or "pass over" that house and kill only the first born of all other houses. Of course, this whole scenario is ridiculous — sad, evil and despicable — but still disgusting. With God being omniscient, God would know all his chosen people and they would not have had to slaughter a lamb with the blood sprinkled on the tops and sides of the door frame or anywhere else to protect the Israelites. God as "God the Omniscient" would also know all the first born of Egypt with or without the bloody lintel, and he could have chosen those innocents he was to kill. Demographers estimates are that 250,000 lambs were killed for the approximately 2,500,000 Israelites who left Egypt.

This becomes more ridiculous and evil with God killing — by whatever means — the first born of everyone in Egypt. After all, it is the Pharaoh who is not doing God's bidding — not his son (who died) and definitely not the first born of those throughout the rest of the country. Think about this. Suppose that we in the United States had a terrible president (you pick, or you can substitute governor, congressman, mayor, business CEO, as you like) who has through an act of stubbornness or other awful act in international relations or public office, caused some similar act of evil in the country or in the world. Perhaps an equivalent would be not letting blacks return to Africa or enslaving blacks again or not allowing Mexicans and Central Americans go back to their countries.

That might be on the same par — or worse — with the Pharaoh not allowing the Israelites to leave Egypt. How is the death of that president's child — his first born — along with the death of all first born citizens going to correct this or be in any way a fair and proper punishment for the crime of one government official? It is twisted logic, an abomination of justice and infliction of evil.

The sad thing is that Jews and Christians buy into this same error-filled song and dance every year. The Jews look at this as an example of God's deliverance from bondage by the Egyptians. Christians look upon this as an example of God's love for "his" people — his Israelites. Both groups look at these acts of killing innocents as exemplary, godly situations in which God is caring for "his" people. If you or I were to do this with our children or pets, and if it were known, we would be brought up on charges of homicide, child abuse, cruelty to animals or all of these.

The important thing to realize is that our morals, ethics and justice do not come from the Bible. Based on the above, perhaps that is a good thing. The Code of Hammurabi existed long before the writing of the Ten Commandments in the Bible. This was in about 1700–1800 BCE or 300 or more years prior to the writing of the Bible and Ten Commandments. And this code of Hammurabi was not the first written in history. It references earlier unknown and lost dictates of law and order as promulgated by those early societies just out of the Stone Age. For example, the laws of Ur-Nammu of Samaria are similar to those of the later writings of the Ten Commandments and Leviticus.

Note that the Code of Hammurabi would not make it in the society of today, since the 281 laws then were pretty brutal also, as are the laws and dictates found in Leviticus and other early Bible books. (Note that 282 laws are listed in the Hammurabi code, but that there are only 281 laws, since there was a void for number 13. The number 13 was thought to be bad and evil. Superstition has a long history.)

The important thing to take away from this chapter is that evil, horror, killing, slavery, maiming, subjugation, stealing, degradation, and other violations of human rights of the past and the present were accomplished by God, or by mankind under the strict direct orders of God. God does not get off of the hook. If we were to believe the Bible as the inerrant book of God and word of God, innocent mankind is wrongly killed and punished for evil things never done by mankind or groups of people. The evil does not come from the innocents but from God, in his evil acts against innocents.

Chapter 9. Biblical Contradictions and Errors

"Do not answer a fool according to his folly, or you will be like him yourself." (Proverbs 26:4)

"Answer a fool according to his folly, or he will be wise in his own eyes." (Proverbs 26:5)

Those two quotes are especially intriguing to me, since they are right next to each other in the Bible. And each one completely contradicts the other. These are very minor contradictions, but their placement next to each other is interesting and particularly hard for Christians to explain.

There are of course, contradictions and errors throughout the Bible. Most of these contradictions are separated by at least a few verses, many by being in a completely different part of a given book of the Bible.

In some cases errors and mistakes can be picked up from a sentence or two in the Bible. Take for example the one day traversing of the Israelites across the parted waters of the Red Sea (Reed Sea) as Moses led them from being slaves in Egypt and took them out of Egypt with the army of the Pharaoh following them. This, according to the Bible, occurred in one day (Exodus 14:30) "That day the Lord saved Israel from the hands of the Egyptians, and Israel saw the Egyptians lying dead on the shore."

However, Numbers lists the population of the army of men twenty years old and older at 603,550. "The Lord spoke to Moses in the Tent of Meeting in the Desert of Sinai on the first day of the second month of the second year after the Israelites came out of Egypt. He said: 'Take a census of the whole Israelite community by their clans and families, listing every man by name, one by one. You and Aaron are to number by their divisions all the men in Israel twenty years old or more who are able to serve in the army." The Bible then lists by tribe all the men twenty years old or older, with the numbers ranging from a low of 32,200 for the tribe of Manasseh to a high of 74,600 for the tribe of Judah. The total was 603,550. (Numbers 1:46)

Biblical scholars have calculated the total Israelite population at the time to be about two to three million, based on population dynamics and family groupings of the time period. Scholars have also calculated that about 600,000 cattle accompanied them. This population of perhaps two million or more, marching ten across would be a column about 200 miles long, perhaps longer.

Do the math. Two million people marching ten across would make a column of about 200,000 people in length. If on average each person was five feet in front or behind another person in this stylistic but informal column (1,000 per column length in this one mile of marching), there would be 10,000 people per mile (10 X 1,000) or about a total column length of 200 miles (ten thousand per mile divided into two million people.) Further calculations show that with hard marching, it would have taken them at least a week — probably longer — to cross one point, or to pass through the Red (or Reed) Sea. Most likely it would have taken far longer, since women, children, those carrying some household goods and cattle cannot travel at a rate of 25 miles per day as listed for passage of the two to three million Israelites.

References in Exodus (Exodus 14:19) state, "Then the angel of God, who had been traveling in front of Israel's army, withdrew and went behind them. The pillar of cloud also moved from in front and stood behind them, coming between the armies of Egypt and Israel. Throughout the night, the cloud brought darkness to the one side and light to the other side; so neither went near the other all night long."

In all of this, the Bible refers to this as a one day and one night event. Everybody — according to the Bible — got through the Red Sea in this one-day time period as referenced by the Bible. In Exodus 14:30 find "This day the Lord saved Israel from the hands of the Egyptians, and Israel saw the Egyptians lying dead on the shore." Note that the time was "one day."

Would not the Pharaoh's army have caught up with them in two weeks or more? Considering as previously calculated that a column of ten across would be a column 200 miles long and that it would take two weeks of traveling, and more like four weeks for a sensible and reasonable rate of about 7 miles per day for women, children and cattle. Would not the cattle alone have muddied the river bottom to muck, mud, manure and mire, making both human and cattle transport almost impossible? Would the entire army of 600 chariots of the Pharaoh been in the river with the waters parted when Moses once again stretched out his hand to cause the waters to again fill the Red Sea. Thus, the suggestion of a Charlton Heston (as Moses) march of a few thousand film extras people in the movie *The Ten Commandments*, is a total farce.

But there are other examples of errors and mistakes. For some prime examples of these, look at the birth of Christ and also the crucifixion of Christ. First, on the birth of Christ we have nothing on Christ's birth in Mark or John. Both begin later in Jesus' life with John the Baptist and continue from there. Only Matthew and Luke have anything about the birth of Christ. This might be because Mark was the first gospel written, about 30 years after the death of Christ and before the writings of Matthew and Luke, both undertaken about 60 CE. Of course the real question is why do Matthew and Luke have something on the birth of Jesus, when Mark — acknowledged to have been written earlier — has nothing on this?

None of the four gospel writers knew Jesus. The first possibility is the most likely and the one most accepted by Biblical scholars. None of these Gospel writers wrote anything about Jesus until well after his death. It is a little strange that both Mark and John would ignore the birth of Christ, especially since tales of this event were known prior to the writing of their Gospels. However, we can pass on that for a moment. Many writers, writing about the same subject will start in different ways, cover only parts of a subject and write in every possible style including narrative, first person, third person, straight chronologically and flash-back.

The two stories of Christ's birth are completely different and mixed up as follows. In Matthew, it happens in 6–4 BCE during Herod's reign as king. In Luke, it occurs ten years later during the time of Quirinius when Caesar Augustus orders a census in which everyone must return to the city of their forefathers to be counted. That's in 6 CE, ten years after the Matthew account. After Joseph and Mary had presumably settled their mutual concerns about the virgin birth of Jesus, and Jesus had been delivered in Bethlehem, Magi or wise (or wealthy) men appeared (Matthew), seeking Jesus as king of the Jews. Three wise men are understood, but no actual number is mentioned in the Bible. They had traveled together to Jerusalem from the east where they saw the guiding star to lead them. No one has explained how the celestial star seen in the east caused these magicians to travel west. Then this "star" changed directions 90 degrees from moving west to Jerusalem to almost due south to Bethlehem. The family, including Jesus, was living in a house, as recounted in this tale in Matthew.

The magi or wise men then presented the baby Jesus with gifts of incense, gold and myrrh. Both the magi and the family of Jesus left. The magi escaped to a place (probably Persia) where Herod could not find them; Jesus and his family west to Egypt. Herod then had all Bethlehem boys under the age of two murdered, thinking that he would also kill Jesus — the King of the Jews — in this broad swath of execution.

Note that in this Matthew story there are no shepherds, no manger or dwelling or inn for the birth delivery, no census of the people. There was one angel to tell Joseph of the virgin birth and one to warn them to escape to Egypt.

A big contradiction occurs with the star in the East. In Matthew 2:2 it says, "'Where is the one who has been born king of the Jews? We saw his star in the east and have come to worship him.'" In some translations, this would be written as "the star when it rose" obviously rising from the east.

In any case, were the magi looking east when they saw the star (as described), following logic, the Magi would be traveling towards the east to follow the star — not traveling to the west to Jerusalem as in the Bible. In addition, stars in the sky are dim and distant and any star that would specifically be over one house in contrast to any other homes in the area would have to be no higher than an Interstate road light or a traffic helicopter. At that height, it would have burnt to a cinder anything below it on earth. Low enough to identify the house and it would incinerate the house; too high and it would not differentiate Jesus' house from any dozens or hundreds of others around it.

Contrast this with Luke, where Joseph went to Bethlehem for a census, since he was of the line of David (he was not, had no biological role in the birth of Jesus as is covered elsewhere), and had to return to the city of David, who reigned 1,000 years prior, for a census. This of course is patently ridiculous, since it would be like you having to return to the city of your ancestors of the 11th century, sometime in the early 1000s. And there was no star in the east or anywhere else mentioned in this story. It seems funny that such an important part of the Matthew story should be non-existent in Luke, and with nothing at all of this birth in Mark or John.

Here (in Luke) the story differs in that Mary clothed and wrapped her son and laid him in a manger, essentially a food trough for animals, because there was no room in the inn. The angel talking to the shepherds (no Magi here) was also suddenly joined by a "great company" of angels. The other stories and translations view this as him being delivered and kept in a normal home. Here there are shepherds but there is no star in the east and no Magi.

What follows is a story of the circumcision of Jesus eight days after his birth, naming him Jesus (Matthew 1:25 suggests that Joseph named Jesus immediately), taking Jesus to Jerusalem as according to the Law of Moses, the acceptance of Jesus (in Luke) by Simeon and also the prophetess Anna as given by God to save the Israelites. In this, there is no escape to Egypt, no Herod trying to kill Jesus, with Jesus and his parents returning to their home of Nazareth in Galilee where Jesus grew from a baby into a man.

This is quite a mix-up for a couple of writers/historians/recorders writing about this seminal event in history. The point is that there should be one story with the bare basics and no major contradictions concerning a star in the East, shepherds and/or Magi, gifts or no gifts, a couple of angels or a whole heaven filled with angels, Herod trying to kill Jesus or him not even being mentioned, Jesus living and growing up in Nazareth or Galilee or escaping to Egypt for 30 years.

Even more contradictions of the gospels occur in the death and resurrection of Jesus. In this case, all four gospels are involved and all four cover this event which signals the beginnings of Christianity. Let's take these one at a time, looking first at those women who followed Jesus to the grave and following up with the angels who met them there.

In Matthew 27:57–28:4, the only two visitors to the grave are Mary Magdalene and the "other Mary" after the Sabbath and at dawn on the first day (Sunday) of the week.

In Mark 16:1-5, the visitors at dawn on the first day of the week were Mary Magdalene, Mary the mother of James and Salome. All three went to the grave.

Luke 23:49–24:5, mentions no names, but only "the women who had followed him (Jesus) from Galilee." Later on, in Luke 24:9-10, you find these women identified as Mary Magdalene, Joanna, Mary the mother of James and "the others with them."

The description in John 20:9, indicates that only Mary Magdalene visits the grave and later on in John 10:18, sees Jesus but at first does not recognize him.

A similar mix-up occurs with the accompanying text as to men, people or angels at the grave and the condition of the grave at the time that the women visited it. In Matthew 28:2-8, an angel came down from heaven and rolled back the stone covering the entrance of the tomb and sat on the stone. His clothes were white as snow and like lightning, as per Matthew 28:3.

In Mark, the women were wondering who would roll back the stone or would be able to roll back the very large stone covering and protecting the tomb entrance. But when they arrived at the tomb in Mark 16:4-5, the large covering stone had already been rolled away (no indication how or by whom), and as they entered the tomb, they found a young man dressed in a white robe sitting on the right side in the tomb.

Luke describes in Luke 24:2-4 the women finding the stone rolled away from the tomb entrance, and two men in white clothing "that gleamed like lightning" on either side of them.

The description of this scene in John 20:11-12 describes Mary as going to the tomb and presumably finding the tomb empty. She was crying, and when entering the tomb found "two angels in white, seated where Jesus' body had been, one at the head and the other at the foot."

Thus, there are four different descriptions of those in or at the tomb, respectively one angel dressed in clothing white as snow; a young man dressed in a white robe inside the opened tomb; two men in gleaming white clothing; and two angels in white inside the tomb. Can't these writers get their act together and their descriptions to coincide?

The whole story of the resurrection is the inception and purpose of the Christian faith. Part of this is the story of Judas betraying Jesus and the subsequent outcome of Judas. The outcome is simple — and again, contradictory. We all know about the acquiescence of Judas in betraying Jesus, and of his accepting 30 pieces of silver from the priests who wanted Jesus put to death. We also know of the signal to the armed guards to identify Jesus when Judas kissed Jesus in the Garden of Gethsemane. In Matthew 27:3-6 is the story of what happened to Judas after Jesus was betrayed. In Matthew 27:5 you find: "So Judas threw the money into the temple and left. Then he went away and hanged himself." This also implies that he did it right away, or almost immediately after the arrest of Jesus, since the following text is of Jesus being presented to Pilate and the beginning of the judging of Jesus.

But there is a completely contradictory story in Acts, thought to be written by the writer of Luke. There is nothing on Judas in the other three gospels of Mark, Luke and John. In Acts 1:18, following the story of Jesus being taken up to heaven, you find: "With the reward he got for his wickedness, Judas bought a field; there he fell headlong, his body burst open and all his intestines spilled out. Everyone in Jerusalem heard about this, so they called that field in their language Alkeldama, that is, Field of Blood."

Thus, between the two contradictory stories, we have contradictions on several levels. First is a time differential. In Matthew, Judas threw away the 30 pieces of silver almost as soon as he got them, and before or as Jesus was brought before Pilate. In Acts, he had to retain the silver for as long as it would take him to find a piece of land for sale and to be able to finalize an agreement or contract for him to buy this land. This probably took at least several days, and could have taken weeks or longer.

Second, in Matthew, Judas was seemingly immediately regretful about his act of betrayal and thus never used the payment, instead throwing it away or back into the temple where the priests probably paid him. In Acts he was using the money to buy something and bought land for whatever use he planned for it.

Third, Judas hanged himself in Matthew while in Acts, threw himself down hard enough to cause his body to burst open. Just how high this was is difficult to determine — and checks with the Centers for Disease Control and Prevention reveal no definitive statistics as to the required height of a person's fall to cause abdominal cavity bursting. The point is that Judas's purchase had to be hilly or mountainous land. It had to have a cliff by which he could commit suicide by dry diving off it and hitting the ground hard enough to burst his skin open and spill his organs and intestines.

Fourth, reading the Bible literally, it is completely obvious in Matthew that Judas committed suicide, since it explicitly states that after throwing the 30 pieces of silver into the temple, he "went away and hanged himself." In Acts it only says that "Judas bought a field; there he fell headlong, his body burst open and all his intestines spilled out." This does not say whether this fall was deliberate or accidental. Judas might have been quite happy with his betrayal of Jesus and his payment of 30 pieces of silver and thus out survey- ing his new land purchase when he fell from a high cliff. Or he might have wanted to commit suicide. We just don't know.

One serious contradiction is in the genealogy of Jesus as listed in both Matthew and Luke. This is in the section in both books about Jesus being of the line or genealogy of David of the Old Testament. Through this twisting of facts, the early Old Testament prophecy is fulfilled. In Matthew, the listing begins with Abraham and continues through David and then to Jesus. In this however, there are 27 men — ancestors — listed in the genealogy, including David and Jesus.

In Luke, in a recounting of the genealogy of Jesus in 3:23-38, the total genealogy from Jesus to David is 43, not the 27 ancestors of Jesus listed in Matthew. In addition, the names are completely different in the two lists, making it look as if Matthew and Luke had two different conflicting stories of names seemingly made up as they went along.

In addition, if either were right, this still would not cover the necessity and prophecy of the Old Testament as to Jesus coming from the line of David. For this to happen, Jesus' father would have to have been Joseph and not the Holy Spirit. His mother would have to have been from God, God in human form, or some other configuration. But only Jesus as the true biological son of Joseph would preserve the desired line of genealogy from David.

An evangelical minister tried to explain all this to me in an e-mail in the following way. The Bible, he said, is without error or contradictions, and the genealogy of Jesus goes like this:

> Now in terms of Luke's genealogy, based on the previous facts, Luke's genealogy must list Jesus' ancestors through his mother. Jesus was the natural son of Mary, who conceived by the Holy Spirit. Con- sidering the fact that by the Jewish tradition women are never listed in the genealogical links, it is biblically consistent that Luke lists Joseph instead of Mary (as he was the "father" of Jesus) and thus Luke names Joseph as the son of Heli. But how can this be, Boy [sic — misspelling of my first name, Boyd]. Can you tell me this? Heli had no sons. So how could Joseph be listed as Heli's son? Heli had only daughters. Well,

you need to do some investigating and when you do you will find that Jesus, through his blood relationship with his mother and her ancestors demonstrates His fulfilling all of the criteria for being the Son of David, who was prophecied [*sic*] as occupying the throne forever, and for being the son of God. Jesus also often referred to Himself as the Son of Man.

It should be noted that this minister had known me for several years, thus his reference to "Boy" several times in the letter could be looked upon as forgetfulness, early dementia, or deliberately planned as an insult. It appears to be a deliberate insult, using a part of my name in a pejorative, insulting, demeaning and condescending term that in the past was used for blacks of any age, especially in the Deep South. Reminiscent of that time and terrible prejudice, it was then and is now an insulting term. This minister grew up in the deep south of Georgia.

The important thing is that while this minister and supposed student of religion refers to daughters of Heli, there are no daughters of Heli listed in the Bible, nor are any daughters listed anywhere in the two genealogies of Jesus. Matthew follows the genealogy from David to Jesus, referring each time to an Israelite as the father of the next Israelite in this genealogy as "David was the father of Solomon. . ." This finally lists "Jacob the father of Joseph, the husband of Mary, of whom was born Jesus, who is called Christ."

In Luke, the reverse takes place with the listing, "He [Jesus] was the son, or so it was thought, of Joseph, the son of Heli, the son of Matthat. . ." Thus, Jesus' grandparents do not even match between the two gospels and there are no daughters listed anywhere. If nothing else (and there is a lot) there is a contradiction here as to the father of Joseph, the husband of Mary. It is also a deliberate lie to me by this ordained minister, along with him referencing me in an insulting way. He lied, and I caught him in this lie.

There are also contradictions in Genesis as to the formation of the earth and order and creation of animals and man, and also on the method of the creation of man. In Genesis 1:25 you find, "God made the wild animals according to their kinds, the livestock according to their kinds and all the creatures that move along the ground according to their kinds. And God saw that it was good."

In Genesis 1:26 you find the reverse order of creation, as follows. "Then God said, 'Let us make man in our image, in our likeness, and let them rule over the fish of the sea and the birds of the air, over the livestock, over all the earth and over all the creatures that move along the ground.'"

In Leviticus and in Deuteronomy you find a listing of birds that are appropriate to eat and those that are an abomination to eat. In Leviticus 11:19

and Deuteronomy 14:18 you find among the abominable birds of stork, heron, and lapwing the inclusion of a bat. A bat is a mammal, not a bird.

The religionists will argue that the people of that time did not know what a bat was or that it is not a bird. Perhaps they would be right. But that is no excuse. This book, this Bible, is according to many, the inerrant word of God and written by God or by men under God's absolute and infallible direction. Thus, God, being omniscient, would have known that a bat is not a bird and would have directed such in writing this book, even if the scribes of the time were not knowledgeable in this area of biological taxonomy.

The same thing can be said about Leviticus 11:6, referencing rabbits chewing their cud, and having a divided hoof (or any hoof). They are listed as "unclean" even though they do not chew their cud as do cattle and as the required description in this passage.

Leviticus 11:20-23 also lists those insects which can be eaten and those which are unclean. Following this listing of good and bad insects, it also lists those that are unclean and to be avoided, as "But all other winged creatures that have four legs you are to detest." Of course, insects have six legs, not the four legs listed for both good and bad insects in this section. God should know better.

Either a contradiction or error can be found in Genesis 3:14. In talking about the snake who gave Eve the magical fruit, God condemned all snakes as follows. "You will crawl on your belly and you will eat dust all the days of your life." This first sounds as if the snake was originally a lizard of some sort and with legs removed by God after the Eden incident was then forced to crawl along with no legs. Also, no snake eats dirt. Nothing eats dirt. Snakes are basically carnivores eating small mammals, insects and other inverte-brates, fish, reptiles, amphibians and even birds and eggs. At the very least, this edict from God is a contradiction of basic biological facts. Snakes must eat as do all living creatures. Dirt is not food. God was wrong.

You find errors in the Bible as early as Genesis 1:3. In these first verses, you read, "And God said, 'Let there be light," and there was light. God saw that the light was good, and he separated the light from the darkness.

The point of all this is the statement that "God saw that the light was good,. . ." is important. Since we know from your lessons and Biblical read-ings that according to this inerrant word of God, that God is not only om-nipotent (all powerful), but also omniscient (all knowing of past, present and future). Thus, if God really was omniscient and all knowing, he would already have known that the light was good. Similar statements of God "knowing" what he already knows by being omniscient follow throughout the Bible and particularly Genesis.

In Hebrew, the word for "young woman" was alma or almah, with a different word — bethulah — for "virgin," with all the meaning that this word contains.

Realize that while a virgin is usually (not always) a young girl, a young girl is not always a virgin. Thus, the use of alma/almah did not specifically mandate that this prophecy of the mother of the messiah from Isaiah be a virgin, but only that the mother would be a young girl. Had they wanted to insist on a virgin as the mother of this king of the Jews, the Old Testament passages, particularly Isaiah, would have used the Hebrew word Bethulah, which specifically means "virgin."

When almah — young woman — was translated into Greek and used by Luke, the word for "young woman" was translated as "virgin" — which is wrong and which was not in the original Isaiah. The word almah was translated as parthenogenesis (Greek) meaning virgin birth.

Thus, an entire aspect of Christianity — especially Catholicism — has been developed around an erroneous or at least somewhat spurious translation early in the church from an early book of Isaiah to the books of the New Testament, not written until about 50 CE (Paul), 60 CE (Mark), 80 CE (Luke and Matthew) or 90–100 CE (John). This contradiction from an early prophecy to a modern Christian religion resulted in a whole dogma of religion as to a "virgin birth" being certainly questionable if not wrong or totally in error.

Perhaps the ultimate in contradictions comes from the New Testament. Much of the New Testament along with parts of the Old constantly harangue us with the idea that God loves us, that God is love, that Jesus preaches love, that Jesus heals us and practices love to us all, that God will take care of believers, that God will take care of his chosen people.

But for a different viewpoint, check out Luke 14:26. This is a direct quote from Jesus. It is in red type in "red letter" editions and translations of the Bible where the precise words of Jesus are in red type to contrast with the black type of the rest of the Bible. It is also in quotes — quotation marks — in many versions and translations of the Bible. And it is very clear what it says with no wiggle room, taking anything out of context or misinterpretation.

It says: "If anyone comes to me and does not hate his father and mother, his wife and children, his brothers and sisters — yes, even his own life — he cannot be my disciple."

Do you love your parents? You do? Do you love your husband or wife? You do? Do you love your children? You do? Do you love your brothers and sisters? You do? Sorry, you have to step aside from this Christianity thing and wait for the next new religion to come along. Jesus says so. Maybe the next religion will be the real thing — but I doubt it.

CHAPTER 10. PRAYER

Prayer is one of the basics of many, perhaps all, religious beliefs. Prayer especially seems to be a vital force in Christianity. Foremost in the Christian and particularly Protestant religions, this often involves bowing of the head, closing the eyes, and then "talking" to God to ask that a particular request be fulfilled, that a particular favor is granted or maybe just giving thanks for "God being there" or for some aspect of life in which God is involved.

It can vary from the casual daily prayer of some Christians, to the day-long meditations and prayers of various orders of nuns and monks, to the rolling on the ground ecstasy of holy rollers, to speaking in "tongues" by some fundamentalist sects, to spinning Tibetan Buddhist prayer wheels, to the candles wafting prayers to heaven in many Catholic churches or the similar effect of prayers to heaven through kites of some Japanese faiths and the prayer flags of Buddhist Bhutan.

The Ambrose Bierce definition of prayer in his book *The Devil's Dictionary*, is as follows: "Pray — To ask that the laws of the universe be annulled on behalf of a single petitioner, confessedly unworthy." Bierce, always economical with words, has perhaps the best brief description of prayer, although several slightly longer but similarly based versions are also available, as follows: To ask that the laws of the universe, physics and chemistry be modified, altered or changed, all to satisfy the supplications of one individual and for the benefit of someone who is decidedly unworthy of any such request.

It would be highly unlikely if not impossible to find even one small, tiny prayer granted that would not be a curse or disservice to someone else. That is assuming of course that God would grant such a prayer if it could be easily granted or proven to have been granted by God. And of course, if there is a God.

An example would be group of Christians praying to God for a beautiful, bright, sun-filled spring or summer day. This could be for a Christian group outing, a church event, a church picnic, a Sunday School class, an outside wedding or an outside baby shower. The prayer can be expressed so that the group has a fine time during that day in question. This sounds like a worthwhile, laudable and certainly simple innocent request.

Let's suppose that from this prayer or collection of prayers, a particular group gets its prayer granted and does enjoy a beautiful, rainless, windless warm spring day and thus reverently thanks God for granting its prayer.

But there might be another side to this story. Suppose that in the same county where this rainless, windless beautiful day occurs for this church group, there is also a school-wide kite festival, a regatta for a sailing club on a nearby lake, a local airport glider competition, a hot air balloon show, or similar wind-oriented events. The prayer to stop the wind for a wedding so that a few dozen or few hundred people will not have veils, hats, wedding cakes and plastic silverware blowing around can change or stifle the plans of others for wind-oriented events. Thus, God would be making a choice between the goodness and value of a windless wedding and the choice of wind desired for another event. Is God that capricious? Is God that patently unfair to one group? Does God care at all? Should he care? Why would he care? Is there a God?

As the bumper sticker says, "Fifty-thousand children in the world died today from disease and starvation. Why should God care about your prayers?"

Worse, let's suppose that there has been no rain for a long time but that these petitioners' request for another day or weekend without rain is granted. This is a request for just one more day — one more day or weekend — without rain. The prayer is granted (let's say by God — to keep the theme going) and the appointed day is a beautiful. This could, in our little hypothesis, be the final day with a lack of rain that would completely dry up and destroy the crops of a small local farmer. It might lead the farmer to visiting his bank on Monday to complete the foreclosure paperwork of his farm or to see his lawyer to begin bankruptcy proceedings. A lack of rain in this hypothetical case could be final drought to kill the farmer's crops and to destroy the farmer's livelihood.

The fact remains that the beneficence of one simple prayer request for something seemingly pleasant and happy for one group can lead to something ranging from discontent to an outright tragedy for someone else or a different group with different interests

Additionally, let's suppose that there are several farmers and many farm workers, and that they are all praying for rain. With some standard of equality, let's suppose that there are an equal number of farmers praying for rain as there are church members praying for no rain. Sounds like a stalemate. What is a Jesus or God supposed to do? How can a God or Jesus slice this Gordian knot?

After writing this, I again came across again "The War Prayer" by Mark Twain, published after his death, since he thought at the time that it would be too inflammatory to be published in his lifetime. It is sort of a reverse of my thoughts above. Part of this short book on war and prayer involves the above thoughts, albeit in a slightly different way. To quote:

"If you would beseech a blessing upon yourself, beware! Lest without intent you invoke a curse upon a neighbor at the same time. If you pray for the blessing of rain upon your crop which needs it, by that act you are possibly praying for a curse upon some neighbor's crop which may not need rain and can be injured by it."

One additional problem with prayer is that it can be so diffuse, so widespread, so varying in request that it is difficult to wrestle into manageable form for discussion. Most religions eschew prayers that are for an individual thing or a specific outcome that they deem is materialistic rather than religious. For example, prayers for a new car, a beach vacation, high grades in high school, or a winning lottery ticket are generally frowned upon. This is not really true of course, since you can always find the newspaper headlines about nuns on their knobby knees praying to Jesus for a win by the Notre Dame football team in some late fall sports conference or regional playoff. It seems to the nuns at least, and also interpreted by the country, that God and Jesus would certainly favor the football team of a good God-fearing, God-loving (do we have a contradiction here?) Catholic University over the football team of some Jesus-hating, God-ignoring, atheistic, secular, non-religious, non-Christian, Bible-disbelieving presumably Satanic state school also fighting for football dominance.

Other types of prayers are really just quickie one-way streets. They are one-way streets, because like the example above Christians never examine the other side of the coin. And as Dr. Phil says, no matter how flat the pancake, there are always two sides. For example, often there is only a quick prayer of thanks to God by those who have seen, heard about or even been involved in (but not hurt by) a car accident, a burning home, an airplane crash, a drive-by shooting, a sinking boat, a tornado-torn house, or similar disaster. Or, it can be as simple and unimportant as the happy result or conclusion for a lost set of car keys, a pie that was burned in the oven, an overcharge on tube socks at Wal-Mart, a flat tire.

"Thank God!," "Praise be to God!," "Praise God!," "God is good," "God cares for us," "God is in control," "God has proven his power once again," "See, this proves that prayer works" or "Thank you Jesus!" are the usual quick responses on everyone's lips to thank a deity or "The Deity" for saving lives or preventing other damage, destruction, injury, loss of life, finding car keys or preventing a burned cherry pie.

But then you have to ask questions about a God that controls the weather, as most Christians believe. Why did the Indonesian tsunami of December 26, 2004 end up killing approximately a quarter million people — 240,000 to 300,000 lives? (Remember — God controls the weather.)

Why couldn't God have arranged for those tectonic plates to slide a little more gently or slowly to eliminate or lessen the tsunami destruction? Why couldn't those tectonic plates slide around on another day when there would be no people on the beach or likely to be involved? Why couldn't God have changed by a second or two the release of that bullet so that it would miss that small child running down the street for his home and away from the shooting area? Why? Why? Why? Why? Why? Could it be that prayers do not work and are good for nothing? Could all these events just be circumstance and coincidence? Could it be that prayer — all prayer — is a sham and a failure?

Does prayer help? Is it necessary in life? Capt. Chesley "Sully" Sullenberger, pilot of the US Air flight 1549 with a bird-dysfunctional engine, had to land in the Hudson River. He noted (when asked) in later TV interviews that he did not pray during that critical time. He was a little too busy landing the plane, he said, trying to keep the wings level, trying to slow the plane to just above stall speed, trying to hit the water nose up. He did it, and he did it right, saving all 155 people on board, even without prayer. Amazing! No loss of life in this remarkable feat of flying and landing where you are not supposed to be able to land. And he, and his second officer, with the help of the whole flight crew, did it without any acknowledged prayer!

Prayers are good for something, but it makes little difference who or what you are praying to or praying for. Prayers are basically good in several ways, but not in the ways that Christians would want, expect or in which they believe. First, prayers help those who are praying, provided that they believe what they are praying, why they are praying and for whom they are praying. It makes little difference whether they are praying to the God of Abraham and Moses, to Jesus, to Allah, to a McDonald's Happy Meal or to a John Deere tractor.

In all cases, however, it would have to reverential, honest, sincere and heartfelt. That is perhaps less possible with a Happy Meal or John Deere tractor than with an invisible Deity. That reverential prayer could be harder to do honestly when praying to a McDonald's Happy Meal. It would have to be the thought and sincerity rather than just the words or the chosen Happy Meal of the day or some other deity. The bottom line is that in all cases of sincere prayer, it will make the praying person feel better. In this fiction of prayer and religion, it makes the praying person feel as if he or she is "doing something," helping as it were, by keeping the thoughts of someone or some condition or something in his/her mind, and hoping for the positive outcome which the believer desires.

Prayer is not unlike various other beneficent acts by humans, through various thoughts and actions that are designed to help others — at least in spirit — and make us feel good in the process. A donation to an animal shelter can make anyone feel good in that they are helping to care for pets — cats and dogs — that are unwanted, abused, abandoned and lost. That is positive, at least to the animal, assuming that the funds are used correctly. Such funds can provide food for animals for another day to prevent them from being euthanized, to pay for ads to find happy homes for abandoned pets, to help collect strays to prevent them from being injured, starved or used as an unwilling sparring partner prior to an illegal and immoral dog fight.

Volunteering at a hospital does not involve money but does involve time to help the hospital expand services to patients. Giving time to restore a home for Habitat for Humanity helps in the same way. It gives the home recipient a warm comfortable place to live and the workers a warm fuzzy feeling of having helped their fellow man or society. It is why Salvation Army kettles and someone ringing a bell appear in front of most businesses, department stores, and shopping malls at Christmas time when everyone is thinking — or supposedly thinking — nice religious thoughts, thoughts (even though miss-timed) of the birth of Christ, and feeling in a giving, happy, loving, mankind-helping mood.

It is also why massive donations always occur after some major disaster in the world. Pick a tsunami, huge tornado, Katrina-type hurricane, massive 9/11-type disaster, war in Africa, starvation in the Sudan, civil war between tribes in Rwanda, and you immediately have outpourings of help, however, usually with United Way, Red Cross and others there to remind those of us not touched by disaster how much help is needed and how much we need to give — to them of course. Giving might be considered a form of prayer, or certainly an expression of a desire to help.

The bottom line is that doing something — almost anything in some cases and for some causes — leads us as a society and as collective individuals to feel better about ourselves. It shows that we do care about other people, even those whom we do not personally know. Physical evidence for this flawed but understandable reaction can be seen in the massive piles of flowers, gifts and written prayers piled around sites of tragedies. This often coincides with private or public displays of praying for those lost, praying for the dead, praying for the family members left alive, praying that such situations never happen again.

Second, such prayers, if they are known about by the recipient of the prayer, generally also make that recipient feel better. It is a different type of warm and cozy, fuzzy and friendly, since the recipient is no longer the giver of this good feeling, but the one receiving it from others. Since we are pack animals and social beings, we like the fact that people care for us and about us. We like it that people think of us during our bad times and that hopefully they are wishing for better times for us.

Just think how much such prayers mean during an illness, sickness, injury, bereavement from the loss of a family member. Realize also that this expression of concern does have a psychosomatic or psychological affect on a person and that in turn can help reduce the time of illness, shorten the time necessary to get out of the hospital. It has nothing to do with religion, or Christianity or God or Jesus, but does have a lot to do with and say about our connection to our fellow man and to our mental capacity to heal ourselves.

On both the giving and recipient end, praying makes one feel good — and can help as per above — but does little as far as changing or alleviating the tragedy or discomfort that occurred. As stripper Gypsy Rose Lee said, "Praying is like a rocking chair — it'll give you something to do, but it won't get you anywhere."

There are several other types of prayers in addition to the above in which you are praying for a named, known individual who also knows that you are praying for him or her. These additional types of prayer are principally first person and intercessory prayer, both with many variations. First person prayer is praying for yourself. If you believe in God or a god, this can be beneficial. This can be prayer in the traditional sense, but just for yourself or for your own betterment, moral improvement or physical healing rather than for someone else. It can be a feeling that "God puts his healing hands upon me," or some such thinking.

It also does not have to involve prayer as to God or a god. It can be nothing more than an epiphany or a realization that each day that you wake up is a new day and one in which you can change, be better, excel or change the direction of your life. It can be a new day in which to start treating family, friends and people better. It can be a day in which you treat yourself better and try harder to succeed in life. It can be a day in which to excel. In short, while prayer is perhaps nice for those who believe and want the prayer for themselves, it ultimately boils down to each of us as individuals to make our lives and each day into what we want and what we desire for ourselves and others with whom we deal on a daily basis.

Studies have shown that at these times, prayer can result in lowered blood pressure, certainly a positive thing for most of us. Of course, serious studies have shown that you can achieve the same result by getting a pet dog. But a pet dog equaling to prayer is not what Christians would want to admit.

For believers, however ridiculous it is seen by the rest of us, such prayer almost seems to be a self-fulfilling prophecy. If anyone was predicting results, those engaging in first person prayer are expecting a good effect, psychological or physical. That they get a good result, or that they have a patient and stoic acceptance for any result that occurs, is to be expected. In short they have convinced themselves — or deluded themselves — into the belief that the result that they got — physical or psychological — is the one that they deserve for their condition and which has been delivered by their god. Prayer, you might say, is just a substitute for or expression of a good positive feeling about yourself or others. In essence, prayer is talking to yourself. But wait a minute — talking to yourself does not accomplish anything, for you or anyone else. Also remember that if you talk to God, that is considered praying. If God talks to you, that is considered schizophrenia.

CHAPTER 11. PRAYER PROBLEMS AND PRAYER THOUGHTS

Intercessory prayer breaks down into several modalities. Basically, it is praying for someone else, or a group of people, or a situation rather than praying for yourself. It is interceding for another person or situation in hopes that a prayer or request to God will be granted and bring some good, some relief, some healing to that person or groups of persons or that God will upon your request change or aid a certain situation about which you are concerned. It can be praying for a person or persons or a desired outcome for a situation. Of course, then you can run into the sunny-day-vs.-rain scenario and resulting conflict as earlier mentioned in discussing prayer.

A prayerful situation can involve praying for an end to all war (general), to an end of war in Iraq (more specific), to an end to the loss of life in the war in Iraq (even more specific), to keeping safe without injury or death an individual (highly specific) or a squad or platoon of soldiers on that Iraqi battlefield (also selective and specific).

It could also be prayer for an end of famine or disease or illness. It can include praying for a person, such as praying for a known friend or family member. This prayer can be for that person or object of prayer to find a job, to become a Christian, to stop drinking, to stop using drugs, to study harder in school, to get well from a debilitating disease, to gain strength from a serious injury, to find a job quickly, or to just have a happy day.

There are other aspects of prayer worthy (perhaps) of some future study. Is prayer more forceful and efficacious if ten people are praying for the same outcome instead of just one person? If one hundred are praying, or a thousand, or a million or more? Do one hundred church members praying for no rain and a sunny day outweigh one farmer praying for rain to save his farm as in our earlier scenario? Does quantity of prayers by many improve the chances of the prayer request being granted? What effect does frequency of prayer have on the end results? Do convent nuns praying everyday carry more weight with God than city trash collectors praying only occasionally on weekends? Does praying three times per day create better results than praying once a day or once a week?

Does the relationship and knowledge of prayer between the praying person and the prayer recipient affect the result? Is that result good or bad? Does the recipient of the prayer know or not know that he or she is being prayed for and how does this affect the results? Assuming the efficacy of prayer for a moment, which would be more powerful — a church group praying for a sunny day or a farm family praying for rain? Further, a person praying may know the person being prayed for, but not have any personal experience with that person or know him or her in the sense that we know friends and family. The prayer recipient may not know at all the person praying for him.

In addition, prayer could be for those with whom we disagree, such as a family member who is an atheist, of a different faith than the particular brand of Christianity of which the prayer believes, planning to vote for someone with whom we disagree, or planning to marry someone not of the family faith. It could also be a prayer for a just-out homosexual friend or family member to eschew their homosexual desires, since this is anathema to many churches and Christians and almost all of fundamentalist leanings.

Does rote prayer such as a standard Protestant Westminster confession, Lord's prayer or Catholic Hail Mary work better or as well as a heartfelt, original prayer? It would seem that original prayer would work best, since the thinking and honest concern of the praying individual about another person or situation would seem to carry more weight than a simple recitation of words said by rote either once or repeatedly. Catholic candles, Tibetan prayer wheels, Bhutan Buddhist prayer flags and Japanese prayer kites work to get unthought prayers to God or heaven. For believers, they work or can work 24 hours per day sending prayers heavenward. Or so the devout believe. Do they work? Are they as good as a heartfelt prayer from the mind of a believer?

Whether believing or not believing in the effectiveness of prayer, there seems to be much confusion about it and many inconsistencies concerning it. Chief among these is the one time acceptance and now prohibition of publicly pronounced prayer in school and the way that Christians get such a twist in their knickers over this terrible flaw, as they see it, of "prohibiting prayer." To be sure, when I was a small boy in a public school, prayer, along with the pledge of allegiance to the American Flag, was a part of each school opening day.

If you were in elementary school, you said both of these as part of the morning exercise of announcements. (Back then, we said the Pledge of Allegiance without the "under God" clause, which was added by the insistence of intolerant and demanding religious groups in 1954.) The present pledge is as follows: "I pledge allegiance to the flag of the United States of America and to the republic for which it stands; one nation under God, indivisible, with liberty and justice for all." The original as written by Baptist minister and socialist Francis Bellamy in 1892 was without the "under God" as follows: "I pledge allegiance to my flag and the republic for which it stands: one nation indivisible with liberty and justice for all."

Bellamy also developed a "salute" to be used during this recitation. This salute was identical to the "sieg heil" salute (first with the palm up and then quickly changed to the palm down) of the 1930s Nazis, the SS and Gestapo of the coming World War II. This was fortunately changed to the right-hand-over-the-heart by Roosevelt and Congress in 1942.)

Today, all that has been changed with no more public recitation of school prayer allowed. Most strident fundamentalists vehemently attribute this to avowed atheist Madelyn Murray (or later, O'Hair). Most people forget that it was the US Supreme Court that finally decided to slice this Gordian Knot by an 8–1 decision. It was hardly close for these justices.

Unfortunately, no one seemed to realize — then or now — that anyone at any time can think anything that they want — pray, wish, blaspheme, joke about anything, desire silently, pray reverently to Jesus, make up bad and disgusting jokes about Jesus, or anything else, in their head. On the bus going to school, you can pray pious thoughts. You can also think "unclean" thoughts. Walking into school, sitting quietly at your desk, going to the bathroom, walking the hallways, during lunch, before lunch, after lunch, during class breaks, during recess, during gym class, on the way home on the bus, during a break in school athletics, and a whole bunch of other times, you can pray. Prayer is just a way of thinking. It can be thinking about or expressing thoughts to God, a god, examining different philosophies learned in school, and thoughts of fellow classmates.

It is not the time to pray when you are supposed to be paying attention to the teacher, but silent prayer is possible any other time. It would seem that those adults who were or are most interested in their children praying would know this. There seem to be two answers to this. Either the parents do not know this, which means they are stupid and/or ignorant (probably both), or they are afraid that their little darlings will forget about what their parents, pastor, priest, rabbi, Sunday School teacher, or others have told them about prayer or how to be good and pray to keep Jesus and God happy.

Another aspect of Christian prayer is the act of praying in public, often specifically before a meal in a public place such as a restaurant, fast food shop or cafeteria. Norman Rockwell painted a famous scene of this featuring

a small child and grandmother at a table in a restaurant. They are praying before their meal, something seemingly anathema to the others in the painting.
Through the restaurant window looking outside, it is obvious that this is a
rough, seedy, industrial side of town, a view seconded by the views of blue
collar working men in the restaurant, two of whom are seated at the same table as the child and grandmother, presumably due to mealtime crowding. It
is a wonderful human scene, a slice of life as only Rockwell could do so well.

Many families, particularly of the fundamentalist, evangelical faiths, follow this today, praying before each and every restaurant meal, or public
event, thanking God for their blessings, their life, thanking God for their
meal. That's fine — if you want it — when home or in private; not so good
when out in public or at a restaurant, according to God's inerrant word, the
Bible. Scenes in real life as per the Norman Rockwell painting are contrary to
Christianity as some few (very few) thinking pastors will tell you. Certainly
praying in a private place, home, in your parked car while eating a sandwich,
or in other places prior to a meal is approved by the church and also — sort
of — by the Bible. It is not a public display or showing off.

Apparently, none of these religious types has ever read Matthew 6:5–8.
Here you can find the following quote from Jesus: "And when you pray, do
not be like the hypocrites, for they love to pray standing in the synagogues
and on the street corners to be seen by men. I tell you the truth, they have
received their reward in full. But when you pray, go into your room, close the
door and pray to your Father, who is unseen. Then your Father, who sees
what is done in secret, will reward you. And when you pray, do not keep on
babbling like pagans, for they think they will be heard because of their many
words. Do not be like them, for your Father knows what you need before
you ask him."

The problem seems to be that Christians do not carefully or critically
read their own Bible. Ever. That's sad. The other end of this stick is that the
easiest and quickest way to create atheists is to have them critically read and
examine the entire Bible. One careful and critical trip through the Bible is
often enough to cure Christianity; two trips a virtual guarantee.

Perhaps the earliest study to determine the efficacy of prayer was made
by Francis Galton in England in 1872. His hypothesis was that if prayer is effective, we should see definite intercessory results that would demonstrate
this. His study was of the general population vs. the Royal Family, since in
England at the time (perhaps now also) hundreds of thousands, perhaps
more, prayed every Sunday for the well being of the British Royal family.

His study compared the life expectancy of the Royal family with that of
the general population. His reasoning was that the effectiveness of prayer, if
true, should be shown by a longer life span of the Royal family when com-

pared with the general British population. Using statistical tables, he found no real difference in longevity. That is in spite of the fact that the Royal family would or should have had far longer life due in part to better, more consistent medical care, healthy living, and more frequent check-ups than received by the general population. They would then and now have absolutely the best physicians, hospitals and medical advice.

His specific studies of 1872 state this in the area of his dissertation: "An inquiry of a somewhat similar nature may be made into the longevity of persons whose lives are prayed for; also that the praying classes generally; and in both these cases we can easily obtain statistical facts. The public prayer for the sovereign of every state, Protestant and Catholic, is and has been in the spirit of our own, 'Grant her in health long to live.' Now as a simple matter of fact, has this prayer any efficacy? There is a memoir by Dr. Guy in which he compares the mean age of sovereigns with that of other classes of persons. His results are expressed in the following table. The sovereigns are literally the shortest lived of all who have had the advantage of affluence and presumably better or the best medical aid. The prayer has therefore no efficacy, unless the very questionable hypothesis be raised, that the conditions of royal life may naturally be yet more fatal, and that their influence is partly, though incompletely, neutralized by the effects of public prayer."

The table shows the following, for the **Mean Age Attained By Males** of various classes who had survived their 30th year, from 1758 to 1843. (Deaths by accident are excluded.)

Category	Number	Average Lifespan
Members of royal houses	97	64.04
Clergy	945	69.49
Lawyers	294	68.14
Medical profession	244	68.14
English aristocracy	1,179	67.31
Gentry	1,632	70.22
Trade and commerce	513	68.74
Officers in Royal Navy	366	68.40
English literature and science	395	67.55
Officers of the Army	659	67.07
Fine arts	239	65.96

Note that the royal family, which was prayed for all the time by the English population of that time, had about two to six years less life span on average than all the other professions or nobility listed.

Various results both slightly proving (slightly and rarely) and disproving the efficacy of prayer can be found in the literature. A report of a double blind test by the Mayo Clinic (2001) revealed no statistically significant difference in recovery times between people for whom prayer had been said (unbeknownst to them) vs. patients who received no prayer. A similar study by Duke University found no difference in patient results of cardiac procedures as a result of prayer or lack of prayer. A recent major test of the efficacy of prayer was reported in the American Heart Journal, Vol. 151, Issue 4, April 2006. Titled "Clinical Investigation Study of the Therapeutic Effects of Intercessory Prayer (STEP) in Cardiac Bypass Patients: A Multicenter Randomized Trial of Uncertainty and Certainty of Receiving Intercessory Prayer." With fifteen researchers and doctors authoring it, the test sought to solve the question of the effects of intercessory prayer in the degree and number of complications after cardiac bypass surgery and grafting.

Various churches were involved in praying for patients who were divided into three groups of approximately 600 each. The patients and their groupings were chosen from six US hospitals. The churches were given the name and surname initial of each patient so that they would know specifically for whom they were praying. In one group of approximately 600, all received intercessory prayer after being told that they may or may not receive it. A second group did not receive any intercessory prayer after being told that they may or may not receive it. All of a third group did receive intercessory prayer after being told that they would definitely receive prayer. The prayer for those groups designated to receive it was started on the night before the bypass graft surgery and continued daily with each person for a total of 14 days.

The test for the effectiveness of prayer was the presence or absence of any complications within 30 days following surgery. The results were fairly definitive. The group that did receive prayer after being told that they may or may not receive it had a complication rate of 52 percent. Those that did not receive any prayer had a complication rate of 51 percent, minimally less but not a statistical difference. Thus there was no difference and no measurable positive effect from prayer between those being prayed for and those not being prayed for — when they did not know if they were or were not receiving prayer. The interesting fact of all this is that the group that did receive prayer and was told that they would definitely receive prayer had a complication rate of 59 percent — about 20 percent higher than the other two groups. Other similar medical results including mortality were uniform or similar with all three groups. The final statement of the abstract on this study sums it up nicely. "Intercessory prayer itself had no effect on complication-free recovery from CABG, but certainty of receiving intercessory prayer was associated with a higher incidence of complications."

The larger the number within reason in such a study, usually the better you would expect the results. Where the praying takes place could also be considered a factor — in a church, while resting in a backyard lawn chair, in school (guess what? — they can't prevent you from doing it silently), during a long walk, at work or drunk in a bar. Would God care about the belief or religiosity of the prayee? Thus, if I were being prayed for, God might decide that I am not worth a bucket of warm spit and thus deny any healing powers.

The irony of all this is the degree to which Christians DO NOT WANT or DO NOT INSIST upon testing and experimentation about something that is so deeply rooted in their religion, their faith, in their text (the Bible), in their rites and Sunday services, in their arguments for prayer in schools and other public institutions, in their belief in their Christianity. If they are so sure of the efficacy of prayer, you would think that they — or at least some particular denominations — would insist on a test that would by their thinking prove them right. But give them the results like those of the above and they will not believe it anyway, coming up with some fanciful delusional answer about "other prayers," "too vague," "you can't measure prayer," (they just did), "I am faithful and don't believe it." Part of this might come from Deuteronomy 6:16. "Do not test the Lord your God as you did at Massah."

However, in today's modern world with Galileo's pronouncement as an early but important fact of the world as we know it, and with biological follow ups on other questions by Darwin, Pasteur, Jenner, Redi and so many others over the years and decades, we should realize that to test something is the only way that we can assure the efficacy and safety of aspirin vs. arsenic or sugar vs. strychnine. Just ask the FDA, NIH or the CDC.

Usually when tests have been done with the Christian community involved, the tests do not come out the way that already-convinced Christians think that they should. Thus, they then complain that there were not enough subjects, there were too many subjects, the subjects were not chosen properly, the test was not done properly, the researchers were ungodly, the experiment was ungodly, science is ungodly, we can't know the purpose of God, God does not allow testing of his rules and edicts. In short, they change the rules, move the goal posts, pick a smaller or larger ball, or have other objections to keep them in the game without really being in the game, once the results are in and the score tabulated.

Often what the Christians seem to want is a general softball approach to any such test that will not be hard core, will not prove anything except what their side wants to prove. That's not an experiment — that's a futile fuzzy exercise with a fuzzy result, subject to fuzzy interpretation and unfuzzy, definite rejection. Or, they look upon one result as a "test" instead of real-izing anything at all about the scientific method. "We all prayed for Aunt Lizzy and she got well, so there you have it. That's absolute proof that prayer works." Not so quick, Bunky. It only proves that you are ignorant of or not at all familiar with the scientific method of testing.

Testing — true testing — is something that we insist upon when buy-ing a car with a newly designed engine, when undergoing a surgery that is relatively new, that involves purchasing a grocery store chicken to make sure that it is not laced with salmonella, when buying a newly designed light bulb. You don't check with your minister, priest, or rabbi to see if your chicken, your Ford, your Bayer aspirin is safe or your light bulb efficient and workable and properly tested for your use.

For these and hundreds of other things small and large in life, we insist upon tests and verification by the FDA for food and drugs and Underwriters Laboratory for electric and electronic products. It is what we expect and demand from the Department of Transportation and the Federal Aviation Administration for our protection when involving trucks on the highway, trains on rails and planes in the air. It is something that Christians insist upon in real life and yet happily leave out and neglect as to any prayer "stud-ies" or worrying about their eternal life or how Aunt Lizzy really got well.

It has been reported that during exchanges between Our Lady of Fatima and Lucia Santos, the girl who first saw Mary in 1917 in Fatima Portugal, the Lady (Mary) asked for a novena prayer that Russia would convert to Catholicism. Also asked for by Pope Pius XII and John Paul II, millions were instructed and presumably did pray for several years for the conversion of Russia. The end result? The falling of Russia in 1989. To the religious, that was attributed to prayer. It was a "miracle," even though it took 72 years to accomplish.

To expert economists, it was attributed to market and economic forces in the world and unsettling socioeconomic situations.

The point is that the Christians can't lose a "test" such as this, because it is an untestable situation. To be a true test, you would have to repeat the same test a number of times under the same conditions, something clearly impossible. To know that prayer works, you would have to have provable results, beyond the area of circumstance, coincidence, luck, or Aunt Lizzy being prayed for.

During this writing, a one-hour TV show has been repeated several times seeking money to help volunteer doctors surgically correct hare lips and cleft palates in children a half a world away in Southeast Asia where there is no good medical care or funds for same. These presumably laudable efforts are to gain money to help contributing surgical teams go for a few weeks at a time to these countries to help bring some aspect of normality in facial features to children who did not ask to be born and who had no control over their lip and palate deformity.

If prayer is so effective, why not a massive prayer campaign to "cure" these children from their deformity and to restore to them in an instant normal lips and palates? Certainly God — God the Omniscient, God the Omnipotent, God the Omnipresent, God the Omnibeneficent — could do this. It is easy — stupefyingly easy for a god to do this. Where was God when these innocent children needed him to make their lives better? Where was the prayer to help them? Why was not a prayer team convened? Why didn't the Pope ask for this? The reason is that nothing would happen, there would be no repairs of cleft lips and palates, there would be no proof of God. A massive effort like this would make people realize that God is just a piker when it comes to the prayer and healing department and that there is no God.

The atheist Sam Harris once suggested a simple experiment that should satisfy everyone in every way, except for the Christians for whom the outcome would not be of their liking. Or they would strongly object to setting up a prayer test such as this.

"Get a billion Christians to pray for a single amputee. Get them to pray that God re-grow that missing limb. This happens to salamanders every day, presumably without prayer; this is within the capacity of God. I find it interesting that people of faith only tend to pray for conditions that are self limiting."

CHAPTER 12. THE TEN COMMANDMENTS — FOUR UNIMPORTANT ONES

George Carlin had a funny shtick in which, with his typical irreverent and caustic style, he discussed the Ten Commandments. With his off-center logic and example, he whittled the Ten Commandments down to two. The two end up being as follows:

1. Thou shalt always be honest and faithful, especially to the provider of thy nookie.
2. Thou shalt try real hard not to kill anyone, unless, of course, they pray to a different invisible avenger than the one you pray to.

Forgetting for the moment the sexual aspect of the above, he worked his way down through the Ten Commandments from his little boy Catholic background. These vary only slightly from the Protestant version. The Protestant version separates out the "no other gods before me" and the "no idols" part while including all coveting (wife/wives or goods) into one commandment. The Catholic version lumps together "no other gods" and the "no idols" parts and separates out the "coveting thy neighbor's goods" and "coveting thy neighbor's wife." Together they both say the same thing, albeit in slightly different arrangements.

Of course, these commandments are not the only ones in ancient literature, despite what the Christians might tell you. These were written about 1440–1200 BCE. Earlier codes of social and religious conduct can be found in the 1700 BCE (300 years earlier than the Bible) in the Code of Hammurabi, which covered the 282 rules of conduct of the King Hammurabi of Babylon. (There are really only 281 rules, since while the number "13" is listed, there is no rule after it. Apparently the number "13" was an "evil" superstitious number several thousand years ago, just as it is today.)

Even older — back to about 2100–2050 BCE — is the code of Ur-Nammu, an earlier king of an earlier Syrian civilization, which included 50 rules, some 40 of which have been preserved; the remaining lost. Ironically, the first three of these are that there are prohibitions of killing, stealing and kidnapping. In a broad sense, these can be equated to the Ten Commandment numbers six, eight and ten — respectively killing, stealing and coveting or stealing, if kidnapping can be broadened (as some Christians do) to taking or wanting (coveting) property.

My logic was to break down the Protestant Ten Commandments into three parts — those that are strictly from an egotistical and insecure God with poor self-esteem issues (the first four commandments), those that are minor and unimportant and which could have been supplemented or added to with a whole bunch of other very minor dictates (two) and those which are relatively good for societies to follow to avoid anarchy and societal self destruction (four). These last four incidentally, were adopted by primitive societies long, long before the writing of the Ten Commandments. Check out the Code of Hammurabi, for example. The Catholic version of the Ten Commandments, as I understand it, would have had three for the egotistical and insecure God, three that are minor dictates and four that are pretty important for all societies.

Using the Protestant version with which I am more familiar, let's take them in order and see where we go.

1. Thou shalt have no other gods before me.
2. Thou shalt not make or worship any idols.
3. Thou shalt not take the name of the Lord in vain.
4. Thou shalt remember and keep holy the Sabbath.
5. Thou shalt honor thy mother and father.
6. Thou shalt not commit murder.
7. Thou shalt not commit adultery.
8. Thou shalt not steal.
9. Thou shalt not bear false witness against thy neighbor.
10. Thou shalt not covet anything belonging to your neighbor.

(1) The first of these — thou shalt have no other gods before me — is the first of four that are a result of a fearful and insecure man writing and trying to keep his God on top of the god-heap. If written by God as the Bible says and as the devout believe, then it was written by an insecure God — perhaps one of many — who is not sure that he can hang onto first place in the Mr.

Universe god contest. He (the god — not the man writing it for God) — if the Bible is correct and truthful — should have no problem. After all, this is the God that (again according to the Bible) is conducting miracles such as creating the universe, talking snakes, parting the Red Sea, causing a bush to burn but not burn up and be consumed, causing plagues, turning sticks into snakes (and snakes into sticks), causing a bunch of plagues and finally the three days of Passover in which all the first born (or first born sons) of Egypt were killed. There are lots more.

With those kinds of miracles, if they really occurred, it would be hard for another god to mount a "can you beat this?" counter ploy in the miracles contest. Other miracles are described throughout the Bible but these in the time of Moses, Exodus and the Ten Commandments seem particularly germane.

Thus, this Commandment about not having any other gods seems to be axiomatic in that if one God can do all of the above, plus make the whole universe in one week, along with the other Biblical miracles, then there is no need for any more gods. It is insisting that the god writing this document (the Bible) is the Big Cheese, the Great Poo Bah, without other cheeses or Poo Bahs around who can match skills of this god.

(2) Thou shalt not make or worship an idol. An idol, as defined by a dictionary, is as follows: An image of a god, used as an object or instrument of worship; sometimes said of any heathen deity; any object of ardent or excessive devotion or admiration.

But realize that the "heathen god" as an idol mentioned in the dictionary definition is your god by those worshiping the thousands of other gods and deities out there in the world. In short, it is a thing being worshiped, rather than the "real" god. Of course there are/were about 10,000 religions around the world and each of them has its own "real" god or gods; and to others, your Christian God is just one of many pale imitations, fakes or feeble god representations. Your cross, with or without an image or idol of Christ hanging from it, is just one more idol god to be shunned and ignored by adherents of other religions. This is particularly interesting with the three Abrahamic religions of Judaism, Islam and Christianity.

This is a difficult area. Protestants often accuse Catholics of idolatry with their use of the cross, including the image of Christ, along with the various religious medals, and the seeming veneration of pictures and objects of Mary. The heavy involvement of Mary seems to particularly vex most fundamentalist Christians. There can also be similar accusations with other possible idols involving a host of other religions. But there are problems in that both Catholic and Protestant religions use the cross, Jesus, and sometimes even other symbols (Mary for the Catholics) to show their religion or as reminders of their constant devotion to God and Jesus. Ironically, the cross often becomes a typical small pendant on a light chain necklace for white Anglo-Saxon protestant (WASP) girls along with Catholic girls. Catholic girls may also sport a chain with the cross and a small, appropriately-sized Jesus hanging from said cross. Lenny Bruce, the irreverent comedian of 65 years ago, once said that it's good that Jesus was not killed recently, otherwise Christian girls would be wearing a chain featuring a small electric chair pendant.

The Protestant argument against Jesus on the cross would be that the simple cross is a plain symbol — and symbol alone — of faith, while the Catholic cross with the image of Christ hanging on it becomes — or can become — an idol. Protestants would think the same thing about an image of a saint, such as the commonly used Catholic St. Christopher medal or the dashboard figurines of Mary, mother of Christ. With Protestants, the cross can be in a church, outside of a church, outside or inside of a church during Easter celebrations, a visible sign at any Christian camp or retreat, as a small symbol hanging or placed in a home, or a piece of jewelry. In these, they state, the cross itself is not being worshipped or venerated, but instead serves as a constant visual reminder of the Christian Protestant religion and of Protestant faith.

The same could be said for the Catholics with their symbol of Christ on the Cross, used everywhere the Protestants use it. Both faiths also argue that other aspects of life can become de facto idols. These can be ways of making money, hobbies, sports, symbols of success, cars, homes, boats, go-carts, stamp or coin collections, disposable money or income. A current TV ad for a discount pricing company shows a ball park when talking about religion. That ball park could be an idol.

Those involved with individual participatory sports such as hunting, fishing, kayaking, hang gliding, rock climbing, skiing, hiking and swimming could also be accused of this if the hobby and dedication to it becomes excessive. The same applies to those with hobbies such as chess, gardening, model railroading, quilting, stamp collecting, model plane flying, coin collecting, knitting, jewelry making and scrap booking. It would be particularly true if any of these — sports, participatory activities or hobbies — interfered with paying for the basics of life — or were excessively demanding of time to the point of interfering with normal relations with spouse, children, parents, siblings, friends or work.

There are also other items that become objects of veneration and worship with these primarily found in the Catholic or very fundamentalist Protestant faiths. These are the apparitions of an image of Jesus or Mary (most often) found in the aluminum siding on a bank, the glass window of a gas station, on a potato chip, toasted bread, an oil spot in the highway. (Such images are also found that some people think look like Nixon, Elvis, Obama or other notables.)

There is one big difference between those of religious or recent political/ other background. We know what recent notable figures look like. If you see a potato chip that looks like Richard Nixon or a street oil stain that resembles Nancy Pelosi, you at least have a real picture or mental representation to go along with your imagined object of curiosity, veneration or hatred. We have absolutely no idea if the current artistic renderings of Jesus or Mary look anything like the originals, since there are no pictures of from the Biblical era.

My suspicion has always been that Jesus, being a Jew and living in the area that is the Middle East today, could well have looked like the late Palestinian leader Yasser Arafat — short, swarthy and stocky.

There are other things that can become and probably are by most analyses, idols. One example is the recent shipment from the Vatican to Australia of the Jesuit relic of the supposed forearm of St. Francis Xavier. This 506-year-old treasure, traveling with its own ticket in a glass reliquary, shows the bones of most of the forearm along with the wrist bones and fingers. It went on a 23-city tour of Australia, with the faithful (or the duped and dumb — take your choice) lined up to see what otherwise would be no more than a medical curiosity in the Anatomy Department of some medical school.

Another aspect of this can sometimes be interpreted, depending upon the Bible translation or edition being used. In the King James Version, this section reads as follows. "Thou shalt not make unto thee any graven image, or any likeness of anything that is in heaven above or that is in the earth beneath, or that is in the water under the earth." This simple statement alone initially refers to a "graven" image. As per a dictionary definition, this would mean some image engraved, as engravings have been done in the modern world, imprints on a copper plate. But it could also mean any drawing or image, whether on a flat stone or tablet, a lithograph, or anything that would resemble something of which we as a human species are familiar. The next section refers to making "any likeness of anything that is in heaven above or that is in the earth beneath, or that is in the water under the earth." This could be an admonition against any likeness of any person, a stylized person or any animal or object that would be recognized by people in general as being a likeness of that object. Using this definition, you could not make a drawing, painting, sketch, etching, or photograph of a fireplace, tree, dog, Uncle Sydney, a landscape, the Brooklyn Bridge, Statue of Liberty or anything natural or man-made. You could not watch TV.

In any case, none of this is really a big deal, although it seems that way for some Christians. Mostly these are Christians who are seemingly interested in and likely to point their fingers at others to point out their flaws, rather than looking at themselves and their own way of life or morality and ethics lapses.

(3) Thou shalt not take the name of the Lord in vain. This would be to blaspheme, such as saying or writing "Goddamn it," or just "Goddamn." It could also be used past tense, such as "that Goddamned boss of mine," "that Goddamned computer printer just broke!" It could also be an outburst of "Jesus Christ!," "Jesus H. Christ," or a similar expletive let fly when someone is startled or upset about something.

In any case, in present tense it would be calling down or suggesting a curse from God or Jesus on a particular situation, person or thing. And, according to the Christians, we have no right to do that. We are not God, only puny mortal people occupying some small space here for a short time.

But Christians are wrong in thinking this way. To say "God damn Boyd Pfeiffer" is no different than saying "God bless Boyd Pfeiffer." Sure, it has a totally different meaning, but from a standpoint of grammar, syntax, semantics, linguistics and any other aspect of grammar and speech, the two statements are equal.

In essence, both of these are in the form of a prayer or request to God. They are asking that God perform a specific request, in this case either blessing me or damning and cursing me. Both statements have a subject (God) a verb (bless or damn) and a predicate or object (Boyd Pfeiffer).

If you use the past tense, as in "That Goddamned Boyd Pfeiffer," then that is using God's name in vain and a violation of this part of the Ten Commandments as Christians understand and use it. In using the past tense, you suggest that you know that God has, in this case, dammed or cursed me. You can't know that, and thus this is blasphemy. It would also be blasphemy to say, "That God-blessed Boyd Pfeiffer." It is still assuming something about God, in that, in this case, he blessed me. Suggesting that we know God's wishes or acts is blasphemy.

But you also have the term "God" used in a variety of ways in English, and presumably in other modern languages as well. For example, you never hear a devout Christian voicing "Goddamn" or "Goddamn it." At least you won't hear it with anyone else around. You will occasionally hear them in a tight-lipped voice and with obvious malice in their speech saying something such as, "God bless this . . ." with the rest of the exclamation referencing something, someone or some situation about which they are particularly vexed. It is an obvious curse veiled as a blessing, perhaps hoping that the "blessing" to God will really be a curse from God agreeing with them that this particular person, thing or situation should be condemned in some way by the Great Poo Bah or Sky Guy.

You also hear Christians and those of other similar religions referring to "GD or G.D." or something like that. Naturally we all know that "GD" is just shorthand for God Damn or God Damned. In addition, Christians might not say something, but express it in their minds. I would assume that God knows about this (if there is a God), and thus would still chastise those thinking this way, even if they keep it to themselves.

Also, casual and unthinking youth in particular constantly utter an exclamatory "Oh my God!" with the emphasis and/or pause between words in this phrase dependent upon how they feel at the time. It can also be an "OhmyGod!" or, in the favorite dialect of the teenager (texting), it can just be "OMG!" Or, it can be just a "God!" exclaimed loudly and excitedly about something new, awful or different in their small lives.

In any case, "Oh my God!" is an incomplete utterance, since technically it requires an ending, although it can be just a single statement expressing the ultimate surprise or shock. "Oh my God, what?" "Oh my God, that's great!" or "Oh my God he's so cute!" would be a few examples of this; but they are all blasphemous since they are said as a euphemistic substitute for a curse or interjection that in a frivolous way invokes God.

And this is blasphemy by any measure. In addition, for the youth or others who use the "Oh my God!" statement, it can be a weakening of the language or loosening of standards, since it can and often is used when a more thoughtful or appropriate comment — or maybe no comment at all — would be better. The irony is that the suits in the media of TV and such will for prime time TV usually censor a use of "Goddamn Boyd Pfeiffer" or such which is not blasphemous and yet allow the use of "Oh my God" in its various iterations, which is of course the use of God's name in vain and in a frivolous or casual manner. That's blasphemy.

Realize that anything about God that is used in a frivolous way or manner is blasphemy. That's what "vain" means. Go ahead, look it up in the dictionary. "Lordy, Lordy, Lordy" said after some event? That's blasphemy. "Lord love a duck." Blasphemy. "Thank God It's Friday" as per the restaurant chain. That's blasphemy. Why should God care if it is or is not Friday? (This comes into a little bit of an amorphous meaning, since both "God" and "Goodness" have been used with the chain.)

The question is whether or not earlier references are blasphemy. The interesting point is that if a non-believer or I-don't-carer says "Goddamn" or a phrase including that, and a Christian is around, often the Christian will confront and condemn the non-believer. Often it comes down to a phrase such as, "If you damn or condemn God or use his name in vain, he will condemn and damn you." Oh yeah? Prove it! Of course, this is meaningless to the non-believer. If there is no god or God, then obviously that non-entity can't condemn you or do anything else because he/she/it does not exist. He can't even shine your shoes. It is as if a Christian were to be damned with something similar with a curse or saying involving or invoking Zeus, Apollo, Baal, Achilles, Minerva, Odin, Mithra or other now out-of-work gods.

Certain words, such as the "Goddamn it!" statement can be used deliberately to irritate some people, even though not blasphemous. For example, were an atheist to use this repeatedly in front of company or in company with highly religious Christians, it would be — and should be — considered an act of defiance and deliberate disrespect. I would hope that all atheists would have higher moral and ethical standards (they usually do — check Chapter 3 God and gods — Monotheism and Polytheism) than to engage in such a practice, regardless of how they feel about the delusions of dogma and doctrine. Fortunately, most do.

Sometimes we change words in spelling and or pronunciation so that it is not as bad as the original. From a Christian's standpoint, "Goddamn it" would be bad — very bad. The watered down version of this as in "goldurn it," "gosh-darn it," "gol-durn it" or "gosh-dang it" and variations of these would be saying the same things, just as a watered down version of God (gosh, and golly) and "damn" (durn, darn, dang, drat) or similar milder words.

Many of these words developed in the late 1700s as ways to safely use the terminology of damn, God and various combinations in swearing or cursing, which were then punishable offenses. Saying "Goddamn" could get you in the stocks for a time, or subject to a hefty fine. "Gosh" as a substitute for God comes from 1757, "dang" for damn from 1793 and "darn" for damn from 1781. Thus, to say "Gosh dang" (or "Goshdang") is to use a slightly euphemistic combination of words of "Gosh damn" from 1757 and 1793. To use "Gosh darn" or "Goshdarn" is to use expressions from 1757 and 1781. It still means "God damn." Similar expressions are "dad burn it," "dad gum" and similar voicing of exasperation and awe, with the first letters of the two words switched, presumably to further confuse those of a high religious order to whom any substitution or suggestion of the terrible "God damn," "Goddamned" or "Goddamnit" would be anathema.

Many of these probably continued in usage as a way to avoid the wrath of the Christian right of the time while continuing to express disapproval or disgust with something or someone. Some expressions are more recent, such as "dag nabbit" or "dag nab it," an inverted or "Pig Latinized" version of Goddamn it, but presumably also influenced by Elmer Fudd of the 1940s Bugs Bunny movie cartoons.

The interesting thing is that some dictionaries point out that by using this expression, many people know that it is a euphemism for God damn or God damned and thus are knowingly saying this blasphemy, but really lying since they know the real meaning of the word. It would be sort of like saying "fudge" when you know what you really want to say — and are saying.

For Jesus, you have "geeze" or perhaps the odd "geezie peezie" or something similar as a substitute for cursing with the word "Jesus" involved.

Similarly, one could use blasphemy in his or her mind without ever voicing it in public. Thus, one could be thinking various blasphemous words and curses of, by, for and to God, but never say anything and thus appear to be completely circumspect to the surrounding people. This would not be the case with an all-knowing omniscient God who would obviously know what is in one's mind.

(4) Thou shalt remember and keep holy the Sabbath. Strictly, this means no work at all on the Sabbath. Of course, which Sabbath you honor depends upon your religion. For Muslims, this is Friday. For Jews, it is Saturday. For Christians, it is Sunday. For Jehovah's Witnesses there is no specific Sabbath, since all days are considered holy. Of course, all of this is a man-made construct, since in nature there is no difference in days. There is only a difference day by day as what humans call seasons gradually manifest their changes of weather and daylight variations. Also, for the religious of any stripe, the stipulation of "no work" on the Sabbath varies somewhat with the sect and belief of each religion, and with those worshiping within that sect.

When my mother was very little, she was paid each Saturday evening to visit her Jewish neighbors and turn on their lights, then to come back later in the evening and turn the lights off. In the eyes of those orthodox Jewish neighbors, flipping a light switch on and then off constituted work, and they would not do any work that would violate their Jewish precepts and beliefs. They did not cook, and only ate meals prepared the day before. As a nice Jewish lady told me recently, the Jews are thus responsible for creating the first crock-pot cooking, since they would often cook a meal on a very low heat — perhaps a stew or casserole — the day before the Sabbath and then eat it on the Sabbath — Saturday — with no cooking or stoking fires involved.

You find the same thing today in many Jewish communities. A New York catalog supply house of photo, video and electronic goods closes at about 2 p.m. on each Friday in the winter, since its Hassidic Jewish owners, managers and workers by religious dictum have to be home by sundown, which arrives early in the winter (by 5 p.m.) in New York. They are of course always closed on the Jewish Sabbath of Saturday, and also on all religious Jewish holidays. You have to admire their adherence to their faith, even though from a practical business viewpoint it is perhaps questionable.

Similarly, Chick-Fil-A, the franchise fast food chicken establishment with 1,600 shops, is owned by a devout Christian who initially insisted that all of his shops close on Sunday, the Christian Sabbath. (This changed in 2014.)

And the punishments for infractions of this "no work on Sunday rule" of the Bible used to be pretty severe. Take for example the man gathering wood for cooking or heat on the Sabbath as outlined in Numbers 15:32. "While the Israelites were in the desert, a man was found gathering wood on the Sabbath day. Those who found him gathering wood brought him to Moses and Aaron and the whole assembly and they kept him in custody because it was not clear what should be done to him. Then the Lord said to Moses, 'The man must die. The whole assembly must stone him outside the camp.' So the assembly took him outside the camp and stoned him to death, as the Lord commanded Moses."

Christians also often cite the problem of working on the Sabbath, Sunday in their case. Once with my wife at a Sunday luncheon of a devout member of a Christian church, it was noted that another church member couple could not be there since their employer required that they work on Sunday. This fact was bemoaned with a lot of hen-like clucking on the part of the Christians at the luncheon. This was not against the couple working who, it was agreed, had no choice in the matter, but the fact that employers would require — actually require — employees to work on a Sunday when the store in question was open. The nerve of that store!

This might be excused, except for a couple of things. First, they all drove to the luncheon, thus violating the precepts of faithful Jews about driving being work on the Sabbath. Of course, you can argue that they were Christian, not Jewish, and thus not subject to the strict rules of Orthodox Judaism. Second, they all had to cross the Chesapeake Bay Bridge from the Annapolis area to the Eastern Shore, and thus had to pay a toll to a toll taker — a person — at one end of the bridge. For them to get to the luncheon, a toll taker had to work, or else allow everyone to drive free over the bridge, or close the bridge down for the Sunday. Third, while at the table eating lunch at a private home, several commented about buying gasoline on the way home since at the time gasoline was cheaper on the Eastern Shore than in the Annapolis area. They also talked about buying some groceries and snacks for Monday work while on the return ride. Thus, they were overtly planning to deliberately violate a strict interpretation of the "no work" rule of their Bible, for their own convenience or cheap prices of gasoline.

Naturally, others would have to work to sell them gasoline, snacks, drinks or convenience items. Also, you would expect that there would be some gas and electric company workers at power plants and emergency crews who would be working on Sunday to keep the utilities on for lights, heat/air conditioning and cooking in this and other homes. And naturally, we always have to have emergency personnel and crews standing by for us, including police, fire departments, EMT crews, doctors, hospitals, traffic control, fire boats and Coast Guard. Do Christians practice what they preach?

The no work and for that matter no fun rule used to be in effect, both legally and supposedly morally, back in the early part of the 1900s. Then, there were "blue laws" that prohibited most stores from being open on Sunday, although these laws, conventions and such varied in time and also in the state or area in which they were in effect. Some still exist to this day and vary widely by state or county.

Most of these laws have some sort of religious background, and some go back to the Puritans in New England or some 1624 laws in Virginia. Most were done away with over time, but they made a resurgence in the early 1900s with Prohibition and the staunch religious fervor of the time. There is a returning interest in them now with the rise of the religious right and its effort to impose its constricting Christian religion and religious beliefs on the rest of humanity.

Just as with religious views on idols, one god, and blasphemy, these are individual views of two religions (Christianity and Judaism) and thus should not be imposed on others in society. In fact, if you look at the fact that the Muslim Sabbath is Friday, the Jewish Sabbath is Saturday, and the Christian Sabbath Sunday, with everyone respecting differing views, this tolerance would have to be practiced in other areas of life and religious doctrine. If we were to close down everything on the "Sabbath," being respectful of the several religions in this country, we would at least be closing down the country from Friday evening through Monday morning for the Jews and Christians alone. If we similarly respected the Muslims, we would be closing major businesses, perhaps all businesses, for at least a few hours on late Thursday also.

Chapter 13. The Ten Commandments — Four Important Ones and Those Left Out

The Fifth Commandment — Thou shalt honor thy mother and father — is one of those minor unimportant commandments. This does not mean that we should not be respectful to our parents, those in authority or others. We should be respectful, honoring, honest, faithful and dutiful in dealing with parents, friends, family members, teachers, police officers, clergy of any type, co-workers, employees, employers, children, and anyone in life in general. That's a given and following that rule would result in a far friendlier, quieter, less violent, more peaceful society than what we now have.

By the same token, a specific dictate to honor your mother and father, in face of the biggies such as not killing, not stealing, not lying, and not committing adultery is patently ridiculous. Yet, there are families where this fifth commandment has and does hobble relationships due to the fact that a son or daughter continues to insist (or be told emphatically) that as a result of this commandment he or she MUST honor parents, even through those parents are not worth any attention or respect at all. You should honor a father who beats his son weekly for some minor infraction? A girl should honor a father who sexually molests her? You should honor a mother who invites various "uncles" home when her husband is working the night shift? You should honor a father who drinks and gambles all his earnings so that you as a child have to move in the middle of the night all the time and never have clothes, new shoes or food? Obviously, these are parents not deserving of disrespect, but rather deserving of a divorce by the son or daughter to remove forever this thorn of poor parenting from the lives of these children.

To suggest honoring a mother and father is akin to doing your homework, taking care of the dog, going to bed on time, using good telephone manners, not driving while drunk, working a full day, changing the oil in the car, and similar admonitions of good honest skills and attributes in family and society that we should all practice. It is – or should be – more of a Dear Abby or Emily Post courtesy than religious dictate.

Another interesting aspect of all this is that Jesus in Luke 9:59 — 62 admonishes his potential followers to shun this fifth commandment and to not adhere to it. Luke 9:59–62 says, "He (Jesus) said to another man, 'Follow me.' "But the man replied, 'Lord, first let me go and bury my father.' "Jesus said to him, 'Let the dead bury their own dead, but you go and proclaim the kingdom of God.' "Still another said, 'I will follow you, Lord; but first let me go back and say good-by to my family.' Jesus replied, 'No one who puts his hand to the plow and looks back is fit for service in the kingdom of God.'" Thus, Jesus if not condemning this particular Commandment, is at least discounting it as an important part of the big Ten.

(6) The Sixth Commandment states that thou shalt not murder (or kill). That is a biggie, and something that we as individuals and society in general should agree on and follow. The exception to this is killing in war to protect our collective selves, something that all societies in at least our recorded history have agreed upon. Individual killing and murder is wrong, killing under the auspices of our government to protect our country, region, state, city or community is, if not right, then approved as a version and condition of self defense. Some religions are also against this, such as Jehovah's Witnesses who are against not only blood transfusions, but as with Quakers are also against participating in war.

(7) "Thou shalt not commit adultery." This should remain, at least in the western world and hemisphere where various forms of Judaism and Christianity are followed and practiced. It was not stringently true in the Old Testament, where polygamy, adultery, and various combinations of sexual joining were not only accepted but prescribed. Sex with animals was out, but not much else. For example, in Genesis 38:8, you find the following passage: "Then Judah said to Onan, 'Lie with your brother's wife and fulfill your duty to her as a brother-in-law to produce offspring for your brother.'" Similar requirements to marry the widow of your brother, should she be childless, can be found in Deuteronomy 25:5–10, Ruth 4:5 and Matthew 22:24. This requires a man to marry his deceased brother's wife if she is without children so that he can have sexual intercourse with her and produce children — or a first child — that will be considered and named as a part of the deceased brother's lineage. According to the Bible, this in turn allows your brother's widow to become pregnant (adultery, as we today would look at it), and

thus, in the parlance of the Bible and thinking of those days, leave children of the deceased man.

Similarly, you have Sarah, wife of Abraham, giving her husband Hagar, her servant, with whom to have sex and produce offspring, since Sarah at this point is barren. (Later in life, she has Isaac. Thus, there is adultery approved in the Bible, with Abraham) producing Ishmael with Hagar prior to producing Isaac with Sarah.

There are also the two times where Abraham allows and encourages his wife Sarah to have sex with or marry others, specifically the Pharaoh of Egypt and later Abimelech, king of Gerar. In the second case, Abimelech presumably did not have sex with Sarah, although it appears that Sarah and the Pharaoh did have a sexual relationship.

(8) The next commandment is "thou shalt not steal," is also one of the biggies that should be retained, since stealing can only lead to anarchy in society. Very few if any cultures throughout recorded history have approved of stealing, and these, if interpreted correctly, were primitive tribes for which stealing was little more than what we might consider unlimited borrowing back and forth, or a truly broad-based society in which communal usage of something was approved, rather than a crime against the individual involved.

Stealing can be accomplished in many ways, as in taking money from a person, stealing goods, stealing an idea as from an inventor who otherwise would hope to gain money from the development of his invention. Stealing ideas and laboratory procedures being developed to make a product or refine a raw material is also stealing (industrial or intellectual stealing), since the procedures when developed can be used to produce things and make money for the developing individual or company. It could also be stealing literary property, such as stealing a book, magazine article manuscript, music, songs or anything similar. It also suggests that it is done secretly, so that the thief is not known.

Stealing can also be accomplished in other ways, such as claiming that your 13-year-old son is under the child cut-off age of 12 when buying movie tickets, or asking for a senior citizen discount when you're 59 and the minimum age is 62. These are stealing since they are depriving the store or movie owner from the proper payment under his own rules. Most people who do this make the claim that "They charge too much anyway," "They can afford it," "I have overpaid all my life" or "They should change the age minimum (or maximum) anyway." That of course is not the point. The business sets the rules, which they have a right to do. If you do not like the rules, do not give your business to that enterprise, go somewhere else or stay home. Changing the rule yourself is stealing.

The term stealing can be also used in other ways, such an actor in a stand-by or subservient role "stealing" the scene from others in a play or performance and thus assuring good reviews and more future work. The term "to steal" is also used in accepted forms, such as to steal a puck in a hockey game, a ball in a lacrosse game or to steal a base in baseball. Despite the word used, these are legitimate and expected in the sports games.

The dictionary also notes other words that are used in various modified ways as a connotation for stealing, such as pilfer, filch, purloin, swipe, shoplift (you are not lifting it, you are really taking it out of the store), pinch, and even some slang terms such as the "five-finger-discount" to indicate taking something not yours rather than paying for it. In store and business usage, the antiseptic and euphemistic word "shrinkage" is often the term used for employee or customer theft.

The basic premise of all this is based on the work ethic — that what we work for and are paid for is a result of our work and payment for that work belongs solely to us. Others do not deserve ill-gotten gains of money or goods through stealing.

Harm to others through theft could be great or small. For example, a theft in a public place of an iPOD or coat might mean little in the total scheme of things. However, a theft of a coat on a bitter winter day, when the owner might only have one coat to keep warm, could lead to illness, pneumonia or death for that person, resulting indirectly in their murder. If money taken from a home is in the form of cash, it could be the grocery money to buy food for a family for a week or two, a payment for rent or a mortgage, payment for a needed utility bill, such as the gas and electric company to keep lights and heat on in the winter. It could in some cases, literally be the difference between life and death for individuals living on the cusp of basic survival.

Just how far you go with this is a subject for each society and individual. Certainly, the four words in this could not be more explicit — thou shalt not steal. However, we often tend to excuse certain "stealing" as accepted or of no consequence. For example, many companies often have supply rooms for their employees. Thus, for office workers, a supply room could carry company paper forms, blank paper, index cards, pens, pencils, computer floppy discs, CD discs, scissors, computer printer ink cartridges, paper clips, envelopes, tape and shipping supplies. A company such as a machine shop might have a store room with wrenches, metric tools, gloves, work aprons, abrasive soap for washing up.

All these things and many others could be used in the private sector or for school supplies each fall. Tools could be used in a home workshop for general handyman duties. Those workers taking home goods to work on company business in the evening, during holidays or on weekends are using those goods as planned — for the good of the company. Those company goods that end up in a school bag, garage workshops or kitchens are stolen, even if we're talking about nothing more than a simple wood pencil or single paper clip. While tacitly forbidden, it seems as if many in society consider theft from work or a workplace supply cabinet as approved or at least accepted or tacitly condoned, especially if taking the pen from a bank or from a Wal-Mart cashier stand.

You could also "steal" an extra fortune cookie or pair of chopsticks from a Chinese restaurant, take two of something in a "one per person" give away at a store. But basically, the prohibition against stealing should be taken seriously by society and is one of the biggies that is important.

(9) Thou shalt not bear false witness against thy neighbor is the Ninth of the Ten Commandments. This somewhat awkward wording basically refers to being honest and not lying. False witness is lying and neighbor refers to anyone with whom we have contact. False obviously refers to anything that is not real, as in a false drawer, false teeth, false pride. To witness is a statement, or fact or accusation, not just in a legal sense, but in any important discussion.

In a legal sense, lying — or bearing false witness — is a crime, since any lie in court can or could affect the outcome of that trial, whether it be a criminal trial against a person, a civil case involving money or property or any of the many variations of trials by judge or jury. Lying in such cases is called perjury. It is rarely punished, although there are laws in place for punishment against one who perjures. In a very broad and technical sense, a person who lies during a trial — whether ending up on the winning or losing side — has perjured him/herself. Lying could also apply to contracts or business agreements.

In some cases, we accept little lies, sometimes called "white lies." This term is used to distinguish them from "major" lies in which a person or situation can be harmed. A white lie is one on a trivial matter, and as the dictionary states, often said to spare someone's feelings. For example, people often answer basic questions in a way that is favorable to the questioner rather than being truly honest. "Does this dress make me look fat?" "Do you think that I have a good singing voice?" "Would you like to go to church with me this Sunday?" Honest answers to a wife, of "yes," "no" and "no" are not acceptable and do not make for a happy marriage.

There might be ways to phrase answers that are not lies or white lies but which will also approach the question differently. "Honey, I really like it when you wear that other patterned blue dress," "I love to hear you sing when you are happy and singing around the house," and "If I don't have any other plans, certainly I will go to church with you," are perhaps not completely honest, but they skirt the real issue and also avoid a simple yes or no answer. This also pervades other aspects of life, such as the question, "Did you go to church on Sunday?" You might lie and answer "yes" to your very religious boss to please him or her, even though the true answer for the past three months would be "no."

Even outside of the family you can get questions which seem to require a white lie or an oblique answer. "Fred, I think that my wife/girlfriend is really beautiful. Don't you think so also?" If you are Fred, you had better answer with a white lie or side-stepping answer, even if your friend's wife is as ugly as an old ox.

(10) Thou shalt not covet is the Tenth and last of the Ten Commandments. But coveting on a reasonable basis is basically good, since it is what keeps the economy running. It is an awareness of something that you see, would like to have and then hopefully save for and plan for to get your own through working and saving extra money for the legitimate purchase of the desired item or service. It could be a thing or a service, such as a flat screen TV, a very special fountain pen, or a day at the spa for a complete massage, facial and make-over.

It becomes bad if the desired item or service becomes such an object of desire that you steal (a violation of a previous Commandment) to get it. Thus, if a friend or neighbor has a flat screen TV and you covet it so much that you break in to his home to steal it when you know that they are on vacation, that becomes stealing. If you mug someone and steal their wallet to get the money to buy the flat screen TV, that is equally stealing (along with assault) and overstepping coveting.

In the usual sense of coveting, it is what makes the world go round. It is businesses creating new products for people to use. It is industry and invention, development and improvement. The huge plows of today pulled by John Deere tractors over thousands of acres are a far cry from the first plow that broke the earth several thousand years ago, or, I am sure, different from the plows of a few years or decades ago or the earliest offerings of John Deere. Without the "envy" or "coveting" that might come with a realization that a new product works better, faster, easier, more effectively or is more pleasing than current items, there would be little improvement in the situation of our lives. Color TV is better than black and white, cars and homes are better with air conditioning than without, ball point pens are less of a nuisance than fountain pens or chalk on a slate, dishwashers save time and effort, batteries to start cars are better than cranks, jet aircraft get us to our vacations faster than prop planes.

To look at the Ten Commandments in the above way is to realize that the listing is an uneven, unsettled document, with a lot of insecurities by the Great Poo Bah, some very minor and totally insignificant items and four that are important, but which were important since long before this Biblical writing. These four admonitions (thou shalt not kill, commit adultery, steal or lie), were around thousands of years ago. Apes and some monkeys usually will not steal from others in their clan, will not murder or take a life of their species unless unduly provoked. They also sometimes or often shun adultery. Since we cannot speak their language, we do not know about lying or "false witness."

Admonitions and laws like this certainly go back to the Code of Hammurabi, with its 281 laws that include all of the above in terms of killing, adultery, lying and stealing. And this dates back to 300 years or more prior to the writing of the Old Testament and the story of the Ten Commandments.

The sad thing is that there are several biggies of possible commandments that are never mentioned. One major one is or should be against slavery. Yet slavery was approved throughout the Old Testament and never disapproved of in the New Testament. It is the Commandment that is not there, but which should be there. In the Old Testament, you find slavery mentioned, but only in ways to buy slaves, treat slaves, not mistreat slaves, treat the families of slaves, how to sell your daughter into slavery, punishments for mistreating slaves, feeding slaves, trading slaves, willing slaves to your heirs, buying slaves from foreign tribes or countries.

Similarly, in the New Testament, slavery is completely left out. Jesus never mentions it, Jesus never condemns it, Jesus never describes the horror of owning another human being.

This, more than anything, proves the lack of good Godly rules for mankind. The Bible not only lacks any prohibition against slavery, but even has long passages on how to treat and use slaves. It is sadly the history of Michelle Obama, our first lady as this is written, about her ancestor Malvina, a six-year-old African girl who was a slave on a small farm in the South and who had a price tag of $475.00. Malvina was sold, ultimately impregnated by a white master, with the offspring the great grandfather of Michelle Obama.

What is surprising is how blacks have accepted and endorsed the Judeo–Christian Bible, despite the fact that the Bible accepts and approves of slavery. One would think that with a background of tribes and peoples being sold and traded back and forth, and ultimately black Africans being sold to Europeans and American slave traders to be taken as slaves to Europe and America, that slavery and anything or any document that endorsed or approved of it would be anathema to anyone with a black heritage. Apparently it isn't as evidenced by high church attendance among blacks of this country and the number of black Southern Baptist churches, missionary work to blacks in other countries and similar efforts to gloss over this aspect of Biblical history.

Similarly, incest is not condemned and in fact is tacitly approved, with a prime example being Abraham marrying his half-sister Sarah as per Abraham's answer to Abimelech when this king asked him why he was pimping out his wife. In Genesis 20:11 we find the following. "Abraham replied, 'I said to myself, "There is surely no fear of God in this place, and they will kill me because of my wife [Sarah]." 'Besides, she really is my sister, the daughter of my father, though not of my mother; and she became my wife.'"

Certainly we can reduce the Big Ten down further than my four or George Carlin's two. Naturally, you can reduce all of this to the Golden Rule, expressed in several ways, depending upon whether you are going by Jesus, Confucius or others. "Do unto others as you would have them do unto you." Or, "do not do unto others as you would not have them do to you." You can find some version of this in dozens of different world religions and early non-religious writings that predate Christianity. This would also cover the lack of Commandments against slavery, rape, incest and similar acts that are not covered in detail in the Ten Commandments.

"The law imprinted on the hearts of all men is to love the members of society as themselves." That is from Roman paganism, but other religions are similar as to the ultimate intent of this Golden Rule. Any of these will really take care of this concern as far as the basic four Commandments of killing, stealing, adultery and lying and those left out as per above. The rest of the Ten Commandments do not matter and in fact are fluff and nonsense.

Chapter 14. Eternity and Heaven/Hell

I was outside my home when the pair of evangelists strolled up the drive-way. You could tell that they were evangelists — nice casual clothes, smiling, seemingly enthusiastic, each carrying a black book (Bible) and some sheets of papers clutched in one hand. And they did not drive up into the driveway — they walked. They were not interested in sealing my asphalt driveway.

They were middle aged. That's one more signal that they were selling Jesus and not kiddies selling Girl Scout cookies. They were making the rounds of the small cul-de-sac of our neighborhood hoping to encounter someone who would talk to them and who might be receptive to their mission of selling Jesus.

Fine, I thought, without any hint of sarcasm in my mind. I liked these pairs, often Jehovah's Witnesses, Mormons, Seventh-Day Adventists or similar groups out to convert the world to their particular brand of delusion, cult or worship of Christianity. I felt like a cat with an approaching mouse to play with, except in this case I had two mice. They politely introduced themselves and the brand of the particular religious cult they represented and said that they wanted to talk about religion. I would not have expected less.

They wanted to start out by talking about eternity. They probably thought that with the concept of hell, they would worry me into believing their brand of fire insurance. That was fine with me. Eternity is a good subject as it relates to religion, heaven and hell and all that, where we go and what we do after we die here on earth. What with golden streets, singing choirs, meeting with Jesus and such, it sounds like a nice place for a two-day visit and a picnic maybe, certainly pretty b-o-o-o-o-ring for any longer period, particularly eternity, whatever that is. We just don't know much about heaven. And yet we have 606 or 662 (depending upon your translation) references to heaven in the Bible.

"Before we start, let me ask you a question," I said. "Sure," they replied in unison, happy that they seemed to have a willing subject, someone who actually had a question and who might make their task of converting one more soul for Christ quick and easy. They smiled with delight. They were undoubtedly hoping for that. They were wrong.

"Explain to me," I continued, "a piece of string with one end."

They looked at each other. They were obviously perplexed, confused, baffled. They looked at me and then back again at each other. They were puzzled, which was not surprising.

"Let's look at it this way," I explained, trying to help them out of their dilemma of not understanding the question and instead putting them into the dilemma of not knowing how to answer when there is no answer.

"We die — that is the beginning of eternity. Right?" Yes, they agreed, heads nodding. That was right. I was getting it, they thought. If you were saved through Jesus Christ and then died, that would be the beginning of heaven and of eternity in heaven. They were momentarily happy with my understanding of this.

"OK, that is the start of eternity for each person, just the way that a piece of string has an end. Right?" Oh yes, they beamed, confident now that there would be a wonderful salvation-laced answer that they could parrot at the end of all this to bring me groveling to Christ. One more soul for Jesus. Hooray!

"By its very definition, eternity never ends. Right?" Right, they assured me, both of them gaining confidence with each exchange. They were both moving around just a little, using body language that indicated that they were ready to pounce on this particular bait.

"Then explain to me a piece of string with one end — a piece of string that starts the same as eternity starts when we die and which continues on forever without any end or stopping. Explain to me a piece of string with only one end that goes on forever. Then explain to me how eternity never ends. That's an impossibility."

They fumbled around and you could almost see them searching for an answer to a question that had never before been asked of them. They looked bewildered, confused, bothered. They gave up. It was a good start for the three of us, particularly for me.

"What do you think?" they both asked, almost in unison.

"It is not for me to think or figure out," I replied. "You walked up here with your Bible and all the answers. I just have the questions. This is my question to you. You claim to have all the answers."

They gave up.

That's the problem with eternity. It is the impossibility of it all that would cause any thinking person to stumble over the whole concept of heaven, hell, eternity and such. It could also be — and is — a man-invented concept, nothing more than wishful thinking that is an idea and hope of all early civilizations and peoples. Ashley Montagu wrote a book on this, called appropriately enough, *Immortality, Religion and Morals*. It explained that as far back as we can go in recorded history, man invented, or at least had a concept of eternity, heaven and/or hell or the early civilization concepts of these ideas. The question of man-made or God-made continues to be a religious, academic and philosophical question. I go for man-made — and no scientific, definitive proof exists that I am wrong. And it is not my job to prove that I am right — it is the job of the Religionists to prove that I am wrong. I did not pose the possibility of heaven or hell. Those who did need to prove it.

Nothing will nor can last forever or have an eternal life or existence. There are exceptions, depending upon how you think of life and existence. The universe is about 13.7 billion years old. Beyond that, we just don't know the answer — or answers. The earth is about 4.5 billion years old. Life began to evolve on this earth about 3.5 billion years ago. But just because we do not have an answer does not mean that the answer for any of these questions is God, or heaven, or anything else. It just means that we don't know. We may never have an answer.

Ironically, Christians look upon heaven as a place almost like earth, but with no illness, no worries, no injuries, no disease, no fighting, no animosity, no one there but good people such as themselves. These are people who have accepted Jesus as their Savior. All of these people will be just as they are now, doing something, anything, that they like. Will they enjoy meals? Does heaven have flush toilets? Do you get sick in heaven?

Golfers will be in their arch angel-designed Madras golf pants, swinging a Holy Spirit-created club at a St. Paul inspired golf ball on a Jesus-developed golf course and going to the Moses designed club house once their round of Eternal golf is over, presumably with a score that is, of course, Gabriel perfect.

Fly fishermen will be on a beautiful stream wearing God-designed waders or hip boots that never leak and casting an apostle-processed floating line that never sinks, using a Holy Ghost designed fishing rod, a single action Gabriel fly reel in gold anodized finish, fishing of course, for large Eucharist trout, bred for strength and size in the Blood of the Lamb hatchery and released into the Stream of Life trout stream tributary for the pleasure of celestial fly fishermen. They will land their catch with a Galilee Landing Net before releasing their catch back into the Holy Waters Trout Stream. Of course, rain to harsh their mellow never occurs and thus raincoats are not needed.

Everybody will be happy, all the time, with Jesus, and with their family members. But wait, will we all be happy, and can we be happy, if in heaven and if a deceased loved one is not there with us? What about a mother waiting patiently for her three children, but knowing that when she died (or even later, if those in heaven can divine — no pun intended — the thoughts of those on earth) all three of her children were (or continued to be) atheists, agnostics or I-don't-carers?

Or suppose that, over time, her children died but, not being believers, did not ascend to heaven and are thus obviously in hell? Would that not make that mother unhappy, and thus not make it truly heaven for her? Would she accept that her children are in a burning, flaming, lake of fire, in hell forever, while she is in heaven? Don't we want our loved ones to be content and happy and not be in a place where their flesh is being burned off, melting away, charred continually, forever? How could we be happy?

Suppose, as one Christian postulated to me, that those in heaven know nothing about us on earth and thus are the equivalent of amnesiacs walking around with no knowledge of the recent, present, time (so they can't calculate when their children — if they remember them — would die). Would that not be a pretty miserable existence, not knowing any past, any earthly existence, early Christian thoughts or deeds, etc?

Could it be that people become spirits, only occasionally bumping into another ghostly spirit and not at all in a bodily form to be able to dance (but not if they are Baptist!), take long walks with God, or play with their pet dog? Will the pet dog be there?

You also have to look at the unfairness of heaven and hell. The key to a ticket to one or the other is the belief (or lack of) — so say the Christians — in Jesus Christ as the son of God and the resurrection that brings about salvation and heaven for all of us — who believe. And it makes no difference when you believe in this, provided that you do it in time, before your last breath runs out. After your last breath, you are too late and have missed the bus.

It is a fact that Charles Dobson, the evangelist, met with Ted Bundy a few days or hours before Bundy was executed. Bundy was the nice-looking lady's man credited — if you can use that word — with killing thirty-some young women. There is and was an unsubstantiated rumor that during Dobson's meeting with Bundy, Dobson "brought him to Christ" with Bundy accepting Jesus and thus going to heaven when he was executed. Is that fair?

Assuming the rumor to be correct, then Bundy, seconds after his death, was and still is with Jesus in heaven. By the same token, some of the 30 plus girls that he murdered (probably an assortment of believers, non-believers,

Jews, I-don't-carers, atheists, agnostics, Hindus, Buddhists), are burning in hell for eternity, according to the born-again Christian religion.

Guy Harrison in his book 50 REASONS PEOPLE GIVE FOR BELIEV-ING IN A GOD, notes that if Hitler — during his last few moments in his bunker before taking cyanide and shooting himself — had repented, given his life to Christ and become a true born-again Christian, he would have gone to heaven to be with God and Jesus. That's of course according to the Christian faith, of which Hitler was a firm believer as a Catholic youth and presumably throughout his life.

By the same token, Anne Frank, being Jewish and presumably never hav-ing converted to Christianity before dying in a Nazi concentration camp at the age of 15, would have gone to hell. No ifs, ands or buts about it. That's again according to the Christian religion and beliefs, which states unequivo-cally that only those with a belief in Jesus as their Savior will go to heaven. She, since March 1945, would be writhing in the agony and flames of hell, according to Christians.

Could it be that there is no heaven? In the scheme of evolution, accepted by virtually every scientist that deals with any of the dozens of forms of biol-ogy, geology or cosmology, when did the soul and the concept of heaven (or hell) enter the picture? When did the body evolve to have a soul also? If a soul did enter the picture, did it enter at a certain point in evolution or was it always around? If it was always around, does that mean that we will also see our pet dogs and cats in heaven, or will they go to a different dog and cat heaven? Or is there no heaven for dogs and cats? If they do go to a dog-only or cat-only heaven, since they are used to us as a part of their substitute pack, will they not miss us and thus will it not be heaven for them? Will we not miss them and thus have our heaven not truly heaven by the absence of our wonderful earthly four-footed family members?

If there is a heaven for all things, does this mean that there are separate or collective heavens for mosquitoes, scorpions, flu bacteria, great white sharks, lung flukes, hyenas, sloths, and turkey vultures?

And since the spotted, striped and brown hyenas eat things such as im-pala, would that not mean that the heaven for hyenas would include impalas on the lunch menu? Would that not make heaven for hyenas a hell for im-pala? Since it is heaven, could we have lobster to eat at least once a week? Would that not make it a hell for lobsters? Do plants have a soul and thus a heaven? Does anyone ever consider these ecclesiastical and existentialist possibilities?

Do chimps, orangutans, bonobos, and gorillas have a soul since they are so closely related to humans? If so, is it a complete soul or just a DNA 98.5 percent soul, or what?

The irony of all this is that for a non-believer (and some few believers in Christianity), this is all nonsense. For those believing in a soul and heaven, then the release of that soul and acceptance into heaven would be immediate upon death. With this, the soul has gone to heaven and what remains is an empty earthly body. It is like a shoe box without the shoes, a peanut shell without the peanut or a room without the furniture. But in our current scheme of funerals, Christians are mourning the bodily loss of their loved one, while at the same time celebrating the meaningless empty shell that remains. It is a conflict on many levels, and a disgrace to the idea of Christianity.

Another problem with the soul and heaven scenario is those many stories, newspaper items, magazine articles and books on "near-death" experiences. One such recent popular book is *90 Minutes In Heaven* by Texas Baptist minister Don Piper, about his experience of "dying" in a head-on auto crash in 1989. He claims that despite being initially declared "dead," he was found to be alive, revived and through a long and difficult hospital stay with many surgeries, finally restored to health. His book is an account of this. Ironically, only about six pages of this 206 page book are on his so-called "death experience" in heaven with his deceased relatives.

The bottom line of all this is simple. IT IS A FAKE! PIPER DID NOT DIE — HE DID NOT SPEND 90 MINUTES OR ONE MINUTE OR ONE SECOND IN HEAVEN! "NEAR DEATH EXPERIENCES" ARE CALLED "NEAR DEATH EXPERIENCES" FOR A REASON — THEY ARE NOT DEATH EXPERIENCES!

Dying is not the damage done to the rest of the body, it is the death of the brain. Suppose as a terrible, horrible experiment, researchers took a living human and completely removed all four limbs, internal and external genitals, one lung, one kidney, part of the liver, part of the stomach, a fair amount of the small and large intestine, blinded him/her, deafened both ears, cut off the nose, cut out the tongue and removed all the teeth, maybe all of the lower mandible. It is an awful, horrible mental and visual picture, but you still would have a biologically functioning, living human, who if cared for, kept clean and fed with a feeding tube, could and would live for many years. Take one massive crushing injury to the head or cut off the blood supply (oxygen) to the brain and you have death and flat-lining in minutes. Death is the death of the brain, not the supporting cast of dancing organs.

There is some early work on a natural or scientific cause of these so-called NDEs and the bright or white lights, the tunnels, the white figures, the darkness that precedes all this. Scientists have discovered that bright or white lights might be caused by a buildup of CO_2 in the blood or a deprivation of oxygen in the blood system. These of course are really two ends of the same stick, with a loss of oxygen increasing carbon dioxide, or increased carbon dioxide the result of lowered oxygen content in the blood. In either case, this can lead to feelings of peace and joy, spiritual thoughts and beliefs, light at the end of a tunnel, brightness or bright lights, light or bright figures or people. In all cases, those patients studied who have had the highest levels of carbon dioxide and lowest levels of oxygen have also had the most of vivid NDE's reported.

Other reports indicate that this CO_2 buildup or O_2 lack can affect the temporal lobe which in turn can lead to seizure-like activity in the cerebral cortex which in turn can lead to lights, tunnels, appearances of white clothed people, etc., all similar if not exactly the same as the effects of the NDEs that so many have experienced.

In addition, some doctors and anesthesiologists have suggested that patients are visually seeing things to cause these NDEs. In this, they found that oxygen deprivation can cause pupil dilation so that normal light in a room or average hospital setting can lead to a very bright view of the surroundings with this highly dilated eye. It can also lead to a beginning breakdown of the blood supply to the periphery of the retina so some vision surrounding the eye is eliminated or diminished, sort of like the look that macular degeneration patients have, or like looking through a tunnel. That same tunnel effect is frequently mentioned by patients with an NDE.

Michael Shermer, in his book *Why People Believe Weird Things,* mentions a variety of biochemical and neurophysiological reasons on why and how this can happen, including natural chemicals of the brain and body and also the use of various hallucinogenic drugs that can trigger feelings or visions of a tunnel, white lights, flying, and surroundings shrinking or expanding. He suggests, based on the research of others, that perhaps these near death experiences and similar out of body experiences can be triggered by the trauma of an accident, operation or perhaps with the body coming close to death without actually dying. It could also be from various synergistic effects of some medically prescribed drugs during a trauma.

Despite what is said in the Bible or how many times it is said, there is ample evidence that there is no heaven and there is no evidence that there is or ever was a heaven or a hell. Christians will point to the fact that heaven is mentioned over 600 times in the Bible. References to hell vary, with the mention of hell 14 times, Hades 9 times and Lake of Fire 4 times but the latter only in the book of Revelation.

Most Christians believe that neither exists for any animal or plant form other than man. However since we know by provable evidence that mankind evolved from a common primate form beginning millions of years ago, you would have to ask the question as to when did the soul — the part of us going to heaven, according to believers — enter the picture?

For this denial of science to ring true, you would also have to believe or accept that all of these separate scientists in separate and distinct scientific disciplines were and are conspiring, or that there was and is a giant conspiratorial effort mounted and taught in college science courses as to how to fool the Christians and others currently believing in creationism or the creation of man and woman fully formed as we read in Genesis in the Bible. That's a pretty long stretch of disbelief or non-acceptance of the sciences that we use every day. Realize that polls and studies have shown that some 700 scientists of all different stripes do not agree with the evolutionary theory as originated in the theorem by Charles Darwin. But some 480,000 scientists in the same polls and studies do accept evolution as continually changing and since proven through 150 years of constant research and evidence.

No one ever came back from heaven. Houdini did not come back, the séances in which he promised to reappear or leave a coded message to his wife came to no effect. Some magicians have continued these séances since Houdini's wife Bess discontinued them in 1936, ten years after Houdini's October 31, 1926, death. But there was no result, nothing to prove or even suggest that Houdini could come back or repeat the words and code on which his wife and he agreed before his death.

If Heaven was important, we should know a little more about it and how it works for us. We don't. Do our heavenly selves wear clothes? Can we get new clothes from Wal-Mart? Do we go to the bathroom? Do we eat? Do we sleep or get sick, or have accidents, or argue with each other? Can we talk to each other, even with those who on earth spoke different languages?

Check with the on-line encyclopedia Wikipedia and you find a 20-page single space brief description of heaven or heavens of different faiths, and the firm belief of those in each faith that they are right; all the others are wrong. The bottom line is that they are not right, but then neither are Christian heavenly beliefs. If so, prove it. That's just what I thought — you can't.

CHAPTER 15. PROPHECY

The Webster's Dictionary definition of prophecy is as follows. "1. Prediction of the future under the influence of divine guidance; act of practice of a prophet. 2. Any prediction. 3. Something prophesied or predicted; specifically, the divinely inspired utterance or utterances of a prophet. 4. A book of prophecies." In contrast to the noun above, prophesy — pronounced slightly differently — is a transitive verb indicating the act of prophecy or to speak and utter prophecies. Of course, don't forget the "divine" part of all that in the definitions listed above. It is always there and always addressing the involvement of a deity.

You can't wander through history without stumbling over secular and religious prophets, prophecy, those prophesying, predictions, and future events. These might be secular or religious, anything from the Oracle of Delphi of ancient Greece to Nostradamus (December 14, 1503–July 2, 1566).

Today, on almost any day in major network areas, you can find a religious channel such as Trinity Broadcasting Network that will sometime in a 24-hour period have one or more ministers preaching about prophecy as it relates to the Bible and to our lives today.

Jack Van Impe and his wife Rexella have their weekly prophecy show, as do those such as Grant R. Jeffrey. In addition, most of the TV evangelists sneak some prophecy into a sermon as often as they can to "prove" that they know what they are talking about and to "prove" that the Bible is right and does have relevance for us today by being an ancient predictor of current events and worldwide happenings.

Anybody can make predictions. Here, I will try my hand at prophecy. Let's see how I do. My predictions — or prophecies — as of early 2015 are as follows:

- There will be terrible wars before 2025.

- Major advances in medicine will occur before 2025.

- A world leader will be assassinated in the next ten years.

- Tsunamis and hurricanes will continue to terrify the world, starting this year.

- Disease will decimate worldwide food stocks.

- Aids will destroy much of the population of several African countries.

- A pandemic of disease will destroy much of the world population in the future.

All and any of these are no better or worse than the predictions of Nostradamus or other religious predictors and prophets. My predictions — just as with those of Nostradamus and his quatrains — are vague and ill-defined. Thus they cannot really be wrong. Usually, with a religious prophet, the prediction will be tied into some religious or Biblical event or prediction such as the Rapture, the second coming of Christ, Armageddon, the Tribulation, or some other sort of vague writings presumably from the Bible.

Let's look at my vague prophecies to see what we can determine.

- There will be terrible wars before 2025. This is a pretty safe bet. Mankind has been at war since before recorded history. Also, look at the adjective that I used — "terrible." All wars are terrible, so the use of that word is meaningless. Any war will fit this prophecy. Look for example at the 58,000 American lives lost in the Vietnam War. I could have just as easily used the adjectives "bloodthirsty, abominable, wasteful, useless, horrible" or other words to describe this or other conflicts. The point is that all wars are all of the above, regardless of the rightness or wrongness of one side vs. the other. I can't lose this one. Were it a true prophecy, I would list the exact date of the start of the conflict and the countries or groups involved or some similar details. Now, that would be a prophecy!

- Major advances in medicine will occur before 2025. That's another given. A major advance in medicine will be one that helps you or your family or friends or is a biggie and helps cure some forms of cancer, diabetes, heart disease, AIDs. Certainly major advances under this description are occurring all the time. Hardly a week goes by without the national nightly news reporting on some increase in medical knowledge, some advancement in the treatments of some diseases. You can't lose on this prophecy. Again, a detail as to specifically when this might occur and just what disease would be helped, alleviated or cured, would make this closer to a true prophecy rather than an obvious guess.

• A world leader will be assassinated in the next ten years. Another absolutely true prophecy. World leaders, from US presidents, to tin horn dictators in third world countries have been assassinated over the years. It is not too much of a prediction that one will be deliberately killed — murdered — in the next ten years. With approximately 195 countries in the world and hundreds of tribal or sub-set groups, it is almost a given that one or more leaders in these countries or groups will be killed. This one is still a good bet. A REAL prophecy would be to name the year and month of the assassination along with the name of the leader and his or her country. But no "prophet," including me, is going to do that.

• Tsunamis and hurricanes will continue to terrify the world. In December 2004, a tsunami in Indonesia killed an estimated 250,000 to 300,000 people. Note that in this "prophecy" I list no outside date and only stated that it could begin anytime. Thus, with this one I can't lose. The next tsunami that comes along — small or large, with few or massive numbers of deaths, I win. It is a sure bet that the undersea tectonic plates will continue to shift, that they will cause massive waves and that with the propensity of people to live near the oceans of the world some deaths will occur. But I do not even list deaths — only that these tsunamis "will continue to terrify the world." That is for sure a safe bet. Were I to list the date of such a tragedy, the country or place where it is to occur and the number of deaths, then I might have something like a true prophecy.

• Disease will decimate worldwide food stocks. Hey, that is going on right now, even though we do not hear much about it. Poor storage, rats and other pests, infected rat urine in food stocks (such as caused the Black Death or bubonic plague of 1348 to 1350), mold, mildew and various diseases such as rye mold, potato famine, citrus canker, rice blast, soybean cyst nematode, chestnut blight and others have at times decimated plant stocks. Mad cow disease, foot-and-mouth disease, avian influenza and others have similarly destroyed animal stocks, farm animals and food supplies. A specific true prophecy would be to name the disease, the place the disease started, when it began as to accurate date, how many people died, and the animal involved.

• Aids will destroy much of the population of several African countries. This is also well on its way to happening now, with African countries generally having the largest incidence of AIDS infected and diseased people. Again, I did not list a country, when this might happen with an accurate date or how this would affect the rest of the world. Also note that I said that AIDS will destroy "much" of an African country's population. I did not say a "little," because already there are massive AIDS epidemics in some African countries. I did not say "most" since that would suggest that it would kill a majority of a given population. It might end up being most of a population, but I am staying on the safe side in my predictions. That way, any continued devastation of a country through AIDS would keep my prediction safe, and allow me to be "right." These carefully couched words and phrases make this a safe estimate, but no more than that. The lack of this makes this no more than a nice but obviously educated guess, not a prophecy.

- The prediction of a worldwide pandemic is also safe, since all I say is that this will happen in the "near future." What is the near future? Is it a year? A few years? A decade? A century? Different people could argue over the definition. Scientists dealing with nasty bugs agree that such a pandemic is not a matter of "if" but only "when." When it happens is anyone's guess, but it is a sure bet that it will occur at some point in our future. It could be the Black Death — bubonic plague — again.

The obvious irony of all this prophecy talk is that whether secular or religious, no one predicted accurately and with certainty the assassination of President John F. Kennedy, November 22, 1963, the disaster of September 11, 2001, the December 26, 2004 tsunami in Indonesia, the date of Katrina and the 1800 lives lost, or a few years in advance the election of President Barrack Obama in 2008. No one predicted the assassination of Robert Kennedy during his run for the US presidency, nor the Watergate situation with President Nixon, nor the necessity of the US government bailing out banks in 2008 and 2009.

According to reports, the Christian evangelist Benny Hinn prophesied the date or time that the end of the world would occur along with the second coming of Jesus. This, according to reports about Hinn on these events, occurred several times in his ministry, along with other prophesies and predictions. Some of these, as reported in the press at the time and currently on respected sites on the Internet include:

- With fellow evangelists Paul and Jan Crouch on the stage with him, Hinn predicted during an April 2, 2000, Trinity Broadcast Network program that at some future event, Jesus would be going to the Muslim world. In a later prediction/prophecy, Hinn predicted that Jesus would/could appear in Nairobi, Kenya and that Hinn might come back from that crusade with video footage of Jesus on the stage with Hinn and Crouch.

• Reports are that Hinn made a prediction and prophecy about the homosexual community on December 31, 1989, during a sermon and talk at the Orlando Christian Center. He noted that in the mid 1990s, around 1994 or 1995, God would destroy the homosexual community of the US. This destruction, according to Hinn would be by fire, with some homosexuals converting and being "saved" but with many rebelling and being destroyed. Obviously, whether the correct date was 1994 or 1995, Hinn was wrong. At this writing, gay marriage was just made legal in all 50 states by a 5–4 Supreme Court decision. The effect of this on US society is yet to be determined.

• Another prophecy from Hinn during the December 31, 1989, Orlando Christian Center message concerned earthquakes on the east coast. The prediction was that during the 1990s, an earthquake — it had to be massive — would hit the east coast with much destruction. Not one place (presumably on the east coast) would be safe. Earthquakes are not unknown on the east coast or other parts of the country. The largest earthquake in this country occurred beginning December 16, 1812, in Northeast Arkansas, causing the Mississippi River to run backwards for a short time, sidewalks to crack in Washington DC and chimneys to topple in Maine. It was felt moderately over one million square miles. An earthquake also occurred on August 23, 2011, at 1:51 p.m. eastern time in Louisa County, VA. No deaths occurred and only minor injuries were reported. An equally large quake (estimated) occurred in western Virginia in 1897. But no massive east coast earthquake has occurred yet as a result of Benny Hinn's 1989 prophecy. I guess that we can rule that out, and as many have, list Benny Hinn as a false prophet.

True, there are specific prophecies and predictions. The most recent one at this writing was that Jesus would return to earth on May 21, 2011. This would be in advance of the death of the world as per the Mayan calendar on December 12, 2012, (which also did not happen) but still, it was a neat prediction. But it failed — nothing happened. This failed and the "prophet" of this — Harold Camping — then predicted that it would occur on October 21, 2011. This particular prediction, to the best of my knowledge did not get into the timing of Jesus' return in relation to the Rapture, pre- and post-millennialism, etc, but just that Jesus would return on that date. As with dozens of such predictions in the past from various preachers, ministers, apostles, bishops, pastors, priests, this one was a fake.

Even Jesus did not do so well in the prophecy department. Theoretically and theologically, and again according to the Christians, there are no mistakes in the Bible. There are no errors, no contradictions and certainly Jesus would not make a mistake in anything in his life or any of his utterances as found in the Gospels.

Quotes from Jesus are almost identical in three spots in the New Testament of the Bible, in Matthew, Mark and Luke. These sayings occur identically in Matthew 16:28, Mark 9:1 and Luke 9:27. They are easy to check in any Bible.

In these sections, Jesus is supposedly predicting his own death to his disciples and others (Mark). In Matthew 16:28 it reads: "I tell you the truth, some who are standing here will not taste death before they see the Son of Man coming in his kingdom."

This openly refers to the second coming of Christ after his crucifixion. It states that the youngest among the disciples to whom he was talking would experience the Kingdom of God and the second coming of Christ before they die. They will not "taste death" until after this second coming. They will experience his second coming before they physically die. That would mean that second coming of Christ would come no later than fifty–sixty years from his statement, perhaps sooner.

The same thing is said almost identically in Mark and Luke. These both state as a quote from Jesus: "I tell you the truth, some who are standing here will not taste death before they see the kingdom of God come with power." Luke leaves out the end part "come with power" and ends with "before they see the kingdom of God." In essence, all three of these verses in Matthew, Mark and Luke are the same and all are direct quotes from Jesus, if you believe that sort of thing. Jesus was wrong in his statement and prophecy. He was either stupid, faulty in his prediction or lying.

The fact that three of the four gospels state this mistake as factual from the very lips of Jesus, should make some people think about the truth of the Bible, the facts of the New Testament, and the veracity of their religion and the purported accuracy of predictions and prophecy, even by Jesus.

Shortly after this section in Matthew, there is also an indication that Jesus is not so good in the prophecy department. In a discussion (Matthew 24) of the end times, Armageddon, the second coming of Christ, etc, Matthew 24:26 states, "No one knows about that day or hour, not even the angels in heaven, nor the Son, but only the father." Admittedly, some translations do not include the phrase "nor the Son" (Jesus). That makes no difference since the meaning is the same. If only God knows about this end times, and if Jesus is making the statement as per the Bible translation, then the de facto result is that Jesus cannot predict or prophesy as to when he (Jesus) will return. This also creates a lot of questions as to the divinity of Jesus, the Trinity or the three gods-in-one (God, Jesus and the Holy Ghost), as was covered in Chapter 12. This is a particularly vexing problem for theologians.

But not so fast. You get into all the additional prophecy of the second coming. This includes getting into subjects such as amillennialism, postmillennialism, pre-millennialism, pre-wrath rapture, post tribulation rapture, pre-tribulation, mid-tribulation and post-tribulation. These in and of themselves would take a book or two to thoroughly discuss, dissect, dismember, and cover as to both pro and con thoughts.

This all basically revolves around the idea of "The Rapture" a concept from 1 Thessalonians 4:15-17 with some input from Matthew 24:30–31. Matthew states in this passage in a direct quote from Jesus that, "At that time the sign of the Son of Man will appear in the sky, and all the nations of the earth will mourn. They will see the Son of Man coming on the clouds of the sky, with power and great glory. And he will send his angels with a loud trumpet call, and they will gather his elect from the four winds, from one end of the heavens to the other."

In 1 Thessalonians 4:15–17 we find, "According to the Lord's own word, we tell you that we who are still alive, who are left till the coming of the Lord, will certainly not precede those who have fallen asleep. For the Lord himself will come down from heaven, with a loud command, with the voice of the archangel and with the trumpet call of God, and the dead in Christ will rise first. After that, we who are still alive and are left will be caught up together with them in the clouds to meet the Lord in the air."

Thus, much of this revolves around the thinking that at some point in the future, graves will burst open, the dead will float up into the air, followed by live believers rising up also to meet Jesus. It is like the *Walking Dead* or *Zombie* TV shows. Take your pick. These dead and live believers will suddenly disappear and rise into the air to meet Jesus with his second coming, or prior to his coming for those believing the pre-tribulation and mid-tribulation theories of this hocus pocus.

The obvious answer for our sake here is that these analyses of the Bible are all so much pixie dust and one more way in which Christians cherry pick around to select one small verse can be used, modified or justified into a Biblical concept that in turn is used to make up an entire philosophy and time frame for the various aspects of the end times. Realize also that much in these theories of Rapture and the associated beliefs that go with it are nothing more than the dreams, ideas and crackpot schemes of a single man, John Nelson Darby, who wrote about such in early writings in the 1830s. Naturally, it is a prophecy from which will come nothing but smoke and mirrors, more wishful thinking and hoping, and the belief of the believing faithful that this Rapture, in whatever form believed, crafted or created by man, will occur someday in the future..

For a true prophecy, you have to have some or a lot of the Who, What, When, Where, Why and How of journalism. Thus, whether devised by John Darby, Nostradamus, the Pope, Benny Hinn or the author, anything less is just a wild-ass guess and no better than the guess or guesses of anyone else.

To think anything else is to be captivated and beguiled by those who might as well tell you that you are going to win the lottery next week, or that your long lost uncle left you a lot of money, or that your son will cure all cancer and win the Nobel Prize or that someone on your street will grow up to be President of the United States. Prophecy of any type and hype — secular or Biblical — is a con, a sham, a shell game, a three-card Monte trick. It's a lie.

Chapter 16. Science and The Scientific Method

All vertebrate animals, including and especially man, are curious about the world in which they live. Primates, as shown with apes, exhibit almost daily curiosity about their world, their habitat, and their surroundings. In some cases you can find invertebrates with similar curiosity. An example is the octopus, which through various experiences has shown a relatively high degree of intelligence for its invertebrate brain, along with a constant curiosity about its world. An octopus will open a clear jar with a screw lid to find out what is inside of it. They will pick up and examine tools being used on the ocean bottom by SCUBA and hard-hat divers.

Curiosity is related to problem solving, so that early man solved the problem of constantly gathering food or hunting with the development of agricultural practices and hunting tools along with animal husbandry and raising cattle to eat and produce milk.

Without this human curiosity, we would not only be lacking trips to the moon, airplanes, computers, penicillin, automobiles, TV, skyscrapers, telephones and the like, but also be missing out on fire, clothing, spears, spear throwers (atlatl in north Europe or woomera in Australia), knives, cooking, pots, weaving, pottery, and sewing.

I have always considered religion as an early, very primitive and obviously erroneous way to try to explain the world and an example of part of our curiosity about it. It was not science but a precursor to science. It preceded science in the same way that astrology preceded astronomy and alchemy preceded chemistry. Science explores the bounds of knowledge logically, correctly and accurately while religion stumbles around with weak and false explanations about gods, demons and supernatural beings. That does not lessen its early importance of providing man with some sort of "explanation" — even if wrong — for the natural events of the world in an attempt to satisfy curiosity. Here we are not just talking about Christianity, but also early religions of Egyptians, Greeks and Romans with their many gods, along with other religions and gods that mankind and tribes invent and have invented along the way in their course through history.

These gods were the Big Brother, the daddy figure, the confessor, counselor, controller, big Poo Bah, Sky Guy or Sky God of life for humans, and thus served as a source to which people could go when things went wrong or were unexplainable in their primitive stone-age world. Today, we are a 21st Century people but living with and believing in 1st Century superstitions! Science replaced the obvious false and ridiculous myths of early religion that are still hanging around in churches, cathedrals, monasteries, convents, synagogues, temples, mosques and the like. If you think of it, the beliefs of Christians today as to their religious history, Jesus, God, the power of prayer, miracles, the truth of heaven and hell, religious prophesy, etc are no different and certainly no better than the religions that all Christians reject, such as the gods of early Rome and Greece.

Early curiosity led to answers such as the sun going around the world (as mankind thought up until the time of Copernicus and Galileo). Early religions had a giant chariot pulling the sun through the sky. Death occurred in Egypt by crossing the River Styx. If you were a pharaoh, you crossed the river with an assortment of necessities including stocks of food, clothing, crowns, chariots, weapons, sporting equipment, and housing implements. You would also have in your tomb killed and mummified pet dogs, horses, servants, maids, etc, all of them sacrificed to go with you in death and to serve you, comfort you and provide you with enjoyment when reaching the other side of the River Styx.

Religion was — and still tries to be — a way of explaining the world. It was an early attempt — obviously wrong and in error and failed today — at science and the study of things. Quite the contrary, religions became and are so divisive that it is a wonder that anyone believes anything in the religious arena, considering the often opposite views of their common religious base.

The most blatant failure of religion was the distinct goal of retaining the ideas of the old and to never, never, never allow anyone or anything to interfere with the doctrine and dogma of the past or the old writings and thoughts of priests, theologians, ministers, rabbis, gods and such in early religious documents and dogmas.

Science is exactly the opposite of religion in that any given fact, idea, theory, theorem, hypothesis, or experiment is subject to constant review — forever. Thus in any science at any time we can check or repeat an experiment. If errors are found or data different from what others have reported, he or she has an opportunity — an obligation really — to report those findings through scientific journals so that facts can be refined, fine tuned or even flat out rejected.

The use of the word fact here should be explained, perhaps as a fact as we now know it, or a fact up to this time in science and with the tools currently available. Recent reports disclose four types of breast cancer with several or more subtypes of cancer. In the past we knew only about "breast cancer." That does not mean that science and medicine were wrong but only that our knowledge up to that time was not able to separate out various types of breast cancer. This continues in all fields of science and medicine with advances constantly allowing for a refinement of information, description and in the case of disease, diagnosis.

In some things, we can never get to a final totally accurate "fact" as we might like to think of it. A prime example would the mathematical constant *pi*, used to determine the circumference of a circle from a measurement of the diameter of that circle. We know *pi* to be 3.1416. Thus, if a circle has a diameter of 10 somethings, then the circumference of that circle will be 31.416 somethings or ten times *pi*, or 3.1416. It makes no difference if the somethings for this measurement are millimeters, angstrom units, cubits, feet, yards, miles, leagues or fathoms, the constant is the constant. But the result is not completely and absolutely accurate, since *pi* is an irrational number that never ends. Thus *pi* can read as 3.14 or as 3.14159265358979932384626433. It has been calculated out by electronic computer to one trillion (10^{12}) digits. The point is that there can be no final truly ultimate accurate *pi* number, since it goes on forever as an irrational number.

Facts and information in science are constantly being revised and made more accurate. All this scientific methodology does not mean that we have to be a scientist or that we have to know how to do all the experiments noted. We do have to know that the scientific method is one in which experiments are set up under specific accurate guidelines with testing and controls that can be repeated by others, and that such experiments are best when they reduce or preferably eliminate all variables other than the one to be tested, and that the tests are reproducible by others for checking each result after being published in peer-reviewed scientific journals.

Another problem with science is the use of the word "theory." I do not like this, since I think that it creates confusion with non-scientists about the word. With many, the word theory is another way of making a guess.

A theory in a scientific sense is a given set of facts or knowledge with a proven conclusion, even if we do not know everything about it. For example, we know about germ theory through the works of early doctors and through increasing knowledge of sepsis, antibiotics, infection, and microbes. We know this through the work of Pasteur, Lister, Redi, Jenner and others. We know through microscopes and electron microscopes about cells, how they divide, their specific anatomy. We could fill massive libraries with the books, data, fossils and research papers that confirm the accuracy and validity of the unfortunately oft-contested "theory" of evolution and the often Christian-contested dating method of radiometric dating such as carbon 14 and such. We use the word theory when it comes to germ theory, the theory of gravity, big bang theory, cell theory, quantum theory, plate tectonic theory, heliocentric theory, cognitive dissonance theory, atomic theory and dozens more.

A word that I would prefer that the scientific community use is the word "theorem." It is a word left over from high school days and geometry. In the case of geometry and other fields of mathematics, it is a statement of fact which can then be proven by a series of simple statements or steps of obvious facts that in turn ultimately prove the original statement or theorem.

The use of the word "theorem" would be different from "theory" which many people consider a guess. A theorem would make any scientific work — once proven — into a statement of fact proven through various steps of experiment or facts of data. That does not mean that it cannot be refined — only that it is accurate within our given knowledge at a certain point in history.

Similarly, I never really liked the word "believe." It is a wussy word, a wimp in the dictionary, a cop out for real words that actually mean something. It often implies a choice of two things, either one can be right or wrong (if you don't believe it), depending upon a viewpoint. It suggests doubt in any answer or statement and does little to foster a positive attitude for those using it. Thus, I do not like the following:

"I believe in evolution." "I believe in creationism as the only way that God could have made people." "I believe that I'll get a beer." "I believe that I will complete all my course work and graduate from college this year." "I believe that I might get a promotion from my boss this year."

There is a weakness and questionable variability to such statements. I do not care if the terminally deluded Christians use it for their thoughts as to Genesis, but I do not like it when educated types opt for this word in discussing the scientific world.

It can also be used in all sorts of things that are weak and wobbly.

"I believe that sport fishing is the best participant sport in the world."

"I believe that golf is the best participant sport in the world."

Both statements suggest rather than emphatically state that a certain activity (fishing, golf) is the best possible activity in which to participate. In fact, there can't be a definitive statement about either of these statements, since they are subject to the whims of the believer, the practitioner of the sport, the eye of the beholder or the degree to which a person likes or does not like fishing or golf.

To suggest that you "believe" in evolution implies that you are not sure. You would never find someone saying that they believe in the theory of gravity, or atomic theory, or cell theory in biology or a heliocentric earth theory or a round earth theory as opposed to flat earth concepts.

All this and my disillusion with the words "theory" and "believe" does not mean that we have to know how to do scientific experiments or conduct the research or do the math, only that we have to accept the results after they have been proven by peer review and sufficient experimentation by other scientists in the field. It must also be printed in respected scientific journals for other scientists in that field to check and confirm or question.

For example, we (or at least I) do not know how to conduct the math for the calculation of the various numbers in the mathematical constant *pi*. I have to — and do — accept the results of qualified mathematicians in the field who work on this, the formula for calculating this and the computer or math calculations involved.

The story of the rapidly increasing improvements in science and the recalcitrance of religion to accept these developing truths and facts continues today. While not of Biblical basis, the story of the truth about spontaneous generation is likewise a measure of science in the battle with ignorance.

The idea of spontaneous generation was that animals — some animals and plants at least — would arise from dirt, or from the effects of the sun. Mice were thought to arise solely from dirt and filthy rags. Some if not all of this was based on the Bible, specifically sections like that of Genesis 1:20. This states, "And God said, 'Let the waters teem with living creatures, and let birds fly above the earth across the expanse of the sky.'" This continued, but the idea was that even if vaguely referenced, living things could originate, develop and grow without the benefit of biological parents.

This was put to the test by Italian scientist and physician Francesco Redi (b. February 18, 1626, d. March 1, 1697) with a test that was also perhaps the first successful attempt at a truly modern experiment. It was "known" that maggots would spontaneously develop from rotting meat. Redi did not think so. To test this, he arranged for six jars of three items in each of the two groups. In the first of each pair of jars he placed an unknown object. In the second two he placed fish and in the third pair chunks of veal. He left the jars open, but with the first group of three covered the opening with fine gauze so that air could enter but that insects could not. The result was that the completely open jars developed maggots on the fish and the meat, while those covered with gauze but otherwise equally open did not develop maggots. This was published in his 1668 work, "*Experiments on the Generation of Insects.*"

But the lid on this spontaneous generation idea was not sealed for another 191 years, until 1859, when French scientist Louis Pasteur boiled a meat broth in a glass flask and then with heat bent the thin neck of the flask in an S-shaped curve that would allow passage of air but would not allow passage of microbes. The meat broth did not become contaminated until, as a later part of the experiment, Pasteur tilted the flask to allow broth to enter the S-shaped curve containing microbes.

Superstition and fear, often spawned by the clergy, continued to infect populations throughout the world as dissection gained more respect as a method — the only method — of learning the parts of the body as a precursor and basis for learning about medicine and the treatment of disease and injuries. It continued into the 1800s with a fear and abhorrence of mankind dissecting human cadavers to learn how the body works.

This same fear exists today with the idea of "playing God" by toying with the end of life including physician assisted suicide or euthanasia. Should we "play God?" No, of course not, insist the religionists in these debates. We should not take over God's role in the life and death of humans. Do we participate in physician assisted suicide and euthanasia? Of course we do. Do we participate in "playing God" in other ways? Of course we do — and this continues all through the lives of each one of us.

CHAPTER 17. MORE SCIENCE, MEDICAL ADVANCES AND STUDIES

My father at close to the age of 92 fell in his apartment and broke his hip. He went to a hospital where a new artificial hip was implanted. Coming out of the anesthesia and resting in his room, he was given a bowl of broth to eat — but with no one to assist him. He got aspiration pneumonia, immediately went into a coma, and was sent to the Intensive Care Unit. After trying a large number and variety of drugs to cure the pneumonia, the doctors realized that they had done all they could. At my request they removed the intubation tube and eliminated the oxygen that helped him breathe. He was getting a little morphine, just in case of any pain.

After about two hours, a nurse turned to me with a question. "Do you think that we ought to give him a little more morphine to make him comfortable?" she asked.

"Yes," I answered, "I think that you should give him a lot more morphine to make him comfortable."

As any doctor or nurse can tell you, morphine works to relieve pain, but it also slows respiration. Two hours later, my father died. The morphine did not do this, but possibly it slowed his respiration and hastened the inevitable — his death.

Do I feel guilty? Not in the least. Did the addition of morphine kill my father? Not in the least. He was dying anyway. The morphine may have slightly changed the timing of that death. Was I, in concert with the hospital, doctors and nurses, "playing God?" Maybe — just barely — but in a beneficial way to stop his potential suffering and to aid only in bringing about the ultimate result of his inevitable and imminent death.

But if you want to follow the "playing God" scenario a tad, consider the following. "Playing God" would have been replacing his hip in the first place. Maybe

151

God wanted it broken. Maybe God wanted him in a wheel chair the rest of his life. Maybe even having wheel chairs to help people is also "playing God." "Playing God" would also involve the anesthesia used in his operation, the use of the ICU bed and care, the IVs, the skill of the hip surgeon. Maybe God wanted him to be in pain.

Let's ask a few questions.

1. Did you get your kids vaccinated against diseases such as mumps, measles, rubella, small pox, polio, diphtheria? You were playing God.

2. Did those of you who are female go to the hospital and get an epidural and a doctor's assistance when giving birth? You were playing God.

3. Did those of you who are female and pregnant get prenatal care? You were playing God.

4. Did you and your family members get a flu shot this year or last year? You were playing God.

5. Did you at the appropriate time get a pneumonia shot? You are playing God.

6. Do you get a tetanus shot if injured with a rusty object or stepping on a rusty nail? You were playing God.

7. Do you apply sunscreen when going on the beach? Yep, you were playing God.

8. Do you see the dentist regularly to protect your mouth and teeth? You are playing God.

9. Do you wear glasses and see the optometrist regularly to check your eyes? You are playing God.

10. Have you or has anyone in your family had an operation? Or been given anesthesia? Or been given pain medication? Or been prescribed for antibiotics?

Hey, you are playing God, and God does not like that, according to the Christianists. Perhaps God wanted your child to die from a childhood disease which would have been prevented by vaccination. Maybe God wanted you to be in pain during childbirth (check Genesis 3:16).

After all, when dentist William Morton invented or discovered anesthesia in 1847 by using ether (nitrous oxide had been used previously, but with poor results), the clergy at the time thundered from their pulpits against women getting anesthesia in any form during childbirth. After all, the religious rights cited, all you had to do was to look at the Bible, at Genesis, for proof that God was against anesthesia for women giving birth.

If everybody were really religious today and following the Bible, women would never have gotten to vote, be allowed to enter public service, be permitted to own or run businesses, to join the military, to own property.

Maybe God thinks that you and your family should have gotten the flu, even if there was a possibility of death. When you get old, God might want you to die of pneumonia, as did my father. Maybe you should have gotten skin cancer from spending too much time in the sun. Maybe you should have been born black to prevent that skin cancer. Maybe God wanted you to get rotten teeth and a tooth abscess that would go to your brain and kill you early in life.

Also, if God had wanted you to see better and longer in life, he would have arranged for better eyes for those of us made in his image. Hawks, falcons and eagles have far better eyesight than we do. Better, longer lasting eyes would have been possible for a species made in God's image. Yep, you can play the "playing God" game forever and with anything in life regarding life and death, health and care, medicine and operations.

Another way of playing God is in the genetic testing of in vitro embryos to determine their sex. That is being done right now to allow couples to choose the sex of their baby. While this testing for non-medical reasons is banned in many countries, it is at the present legal and unregulated in the US. The method of testing for sex is the same used to genetically test for diseases which can be everything from Tay-Sachs disease to sickle cell anemia and cystic fibrosis to those that are possibilities later in life such as colon cancer and breast cancer. It is a technique called PGD or pre-implantation genetic diagnosis.

The technique is to allow for in vitro fertilization, mixing the eggs of the mother and the sperm of the father into a Petri dish, even though the couple does not have a problem with pregnancy. After a few days, during the blastocyst stage (about 150 cells), a few cells are removed and tested using a check against the human genome. If the gender of the embryo is the one desired by the parents, then the developing embryo is implanted into the wall of the uterus. If not, the developing embryo is discarded — scrapped, thrown out with the trash — and another embryo from the many created is tested, and so on until the right gender is found. Thus, at this early stage and for a fee of just under $20,000, you can have a designer baby of your dreams and of the "right" sex. Then you can start buying the correct — pink or blue — clothes, crib and accessories.

In an example used on the 60 Minutes TV show, a couple with no pregnancy problems had three boys but always wanted girls. Thus, they went to the guaranteed in vitro testing (99.9 percent sure) to get the two girls that they wanted to "complete" their family.

However, for those thinking that every little bun in the oven is a precious and inviolate gift from God, this might be "playing God" — picking what you want like shopping for red peppers instead of green peppers at the grocery store. Of course, if you also have a genetic disease pattern in family history of mother or father, you can use this test for strictly medical purposes (approved in other countries — but again "playing God") to weed out any of a number of diseases, some relatively well known and others (about 100) extremely rare.

Of course, for the faithful, this might also be "playing God." After all, maybe God in his infinite, ultimate wisdom wants you to have a child with Tay-Sachs, sickle cell anemia, cystic fibrosis or the possibility later in life breast or colon cancer. Perhaps that is part of God's plan. It may be part of his ultimate wisdom, if there is a God. And of course, all the other little fertilized embryos of the wrong sex or with a bad disease are tossed out, the same way those from couples using fertility clinics and with pregnancy problems are tossed out.

By doing a medical testing, never mind whether in time your offspring will be buying footballs or fancy dresses, you can play God. Want to play God anyone? Want to be your own Supreme Being with ultimate power? Hey, we do it all the time.

The question of abortion is one in which science, morals, ethics, politics, government and religion intersect (collide might a better word) with seemingly irreconcilable differences. Certainly, science and medicine have figured out several ways in which an abortion can be accomplished at various times in a pregnancy. The fact that it can be done does not answer the question of whether or not it should be done. Can you do it? Is it moral? Is it ethical? Does it fit in with God's law? Should it be done in any case at all at any time during the pregnancy and for any reason? Should it never be done, even in those cases of rape and incest? Should it be done only to save the life of the mother?

This latter question comes into effect with a sad 2010 case from Brazil in which a nine-year-old girl became pregnant from a boyfriend of her mother, the pregnancy resulting in twins. The frail young nine-year-old was unable to carry the two fetuses and would have been unable to carry even one fetus, given her age, malnutrition and slight frame at the age of nine. Had she tried to carry the two fetuses to term, she would have died before the birth of the children. The two fetuses would have died also. The two fetuses were aborted, but not without the condemnation of the local Catholic Church who would not condone any exception to the Church rule against abortions. Of course in the United States we go the other way and are obviously not consistent enough with sex education and birth control for our kids. The lack of good and thorough sex education you can blame on the Religionists also, since in their small minds teaching sex education is tantamount to encouraging the little darlings to have sex as often as possible. Thus, up to 200,000 teenage girls have abortions annually in the US. The state with the most teenage pregnancies is Texas, which also ranks very high with the poorest possible sex education in the country. Could there be a connection here?

The question of abortion goes back far into history, even before abortion was thought of as a possible option (scientific and medical if not moral and ethical) in the days prior to the mid-1800s and the development of anesthesia. And part of this thinking involves the concept of a soul, since without a soul, a fetus is just a bit of viable tissue developing in the uterus of a mature woman. St. Augustine thought of the conceived child receiving a soul at 40 days if a male, 90 days if a female. On that basis, presumably, aborting a fetus prior to those deadlines would not be in conflict with God's law, since these are merely stages of a blastocyst and not a living, conceived, soul-bearing human being. If there is no soul for 40 days or 90 days, how can there be a murder of an unborn soul-bearing child?

It is also interesting that at the time of St. Augustine, males received souls at 40 days and that females gained a soul 50 days later. It is also interesting that in St. Augustine's time, there would be no way to determine the gender of a fetus in that stage. How would a mother know which sex she had in her uterus or how many days old that fetus was?

As atheist Sam Harris notes, the early human blastocyst is about 150 cells, with no brain, no neural tissue, and is about 1/1000 the size of the brain of a fly, which is a little more than 150,000 cells. Also, you really don't have a viable fetus until a few days after fertilization when the fertilized cell lands on and implants into the wall of the uterus. If it does not implant, it dies — God's method, if you will, of abortion.

At this writing, abortion remains legal through federal law, although rightly or wrongly, there are constant attacks on it. The rightness or wrongness of this depends upon your view — religious, moral, ethical, biological, women's rights, or otherwise — on abortion.

The interesting thing is that abortion is not listed or mentioned at all in the Bible. Why then are the religionists so upset about all this? Is it because of the admonition against killing, the sixth commandment of the Big Ten in the Old Testament? Is it just in general that Christians want to have their own way for themselves and thus dictate to the world how everyone should live and the rules they should follow?

While there are no definitive answers to the above that will satisfy all, there can be definitive answers to the question of stem cell research, the morality of such, laws on the books, the past, present and future concerning this, the politics such as that of former president George Bush (43), and the possible research value of such embryonic stem cells.

Stem cells are embryonic basic cells that can and do form into specific cells of organs, each with a specific purpose for that organ. The controversy over them arises from the fact that they are gathered from living human embryos, usually embryos frozen for possible or potential use in so-called fertility clinics. When George W. Bush took office in 2001, he stopped federal funding of stem cell research and limited the current stem cells for research to the 70 lines that were in use at that time. Unfortunately some of these lines were contaminated, thus further limiting pure research. This ban was lifted by President Obama early in his office so that more stem cells and stem cell research can take place. This ban at this writing is again in question, due enactment of an earlier law — never repealed — that stopped the stem cell use as per George Bush.

The ban by Bush resulted in a delay of pure science, putting us behind the rest of the world in this vital research that has the potential to save lives, cure diseases (such as Parkinson's Disease) and possibly even correct, reverse or alleviate spinal injuries. Conservatively, about 400,000 fertilized frozen embryos stem cells are produced each year, presumably to aid those women and couples who want to have a family, but are unable to do it the natural way. (Want to talk about "playing God"? Perhaps if a couple can't have a child, God is telling them to not have children or to adopt one of the many children available from orphanages. Otherwise, you are "playing God" by artificially creating something to satisfy your selfish wishes — instead of listening to God.)

And since these are from fertility clinics, you also have to wonder how many of these are from "good" Christian families who used one or two of these collected and frozen embryos to produce the child that they wanted and now have no use for the other excess frozen but viable embryos sitting in tanks of liquid nitrogen. No use for them? Might as well toss 'em.

Of these 400,000 created frozen, fertile embryos, about 125,000 are used annually to implant into woman for fertility efforts. The remaining 275,000 are left bottled up in liquid nitrogen for months or years, ultimately thrown out (some by those "good" Christians who used the fertility clinic). These cells are going down the drain — into the sewage, poured out with the pooh, tossed with the trash — where they would have and could have been (barring Bush) going into stem cell lines that could have potentially benefited people through science and medicine.

Realize that this would be an additional 275,000 people added to the US and planet each year, and even if this were viable, possible and cost effective, less than 100 such babies are produced and placed in surrogate mothers each year — nowhere near the 275,000 that would be needed to balance out the frozen embryo books and the baby fetus glut. The fact remains that the excess frozen embryos, now tossed into the trash when not used and excessive of the necessary embryos to be implanted into the woman, would be an exciting medical and biological resource for future medical advances.

What can we say about evolution? Since Charles Darwin's definitive work published November 24, 1859, there have been incessant religious and Christian attacks against it.

When in college in the late 1950s I read (really skimmed) Darwin's two books, *The Origin of Species* and *The Descent of Man*. I also checked out the college library for those books, often by ministers and others of a different moral, ethical and truth persuasions, written to disprove Darwin. Sadly, those books at that time were pathetic, simplistic, wrong and childish in the extreme. I do not remember any titles or authors, but only remember the paucity of their reasoning in their texts, particularly in relation to the voluminous, thorough, well researched and definitive work of Darwin. I also remember the gratuitously emotional writing, the false pleas to a god or God, the lack of anything that would be any sort of scientific approach or the use of the scientific method as we understand it. The books were sad and embarrassing.

Today, the books condemning Darwin have gotten larger, but no better. They still skirt the edges of what the authors really want to prove — the truth of the Genesis Bible story, the truth of God, the truth of creation and creationism. The more Christians try the more they lose, often without even realizing it. The more they do, the more they put the United States behind the rest of the world in terms of scientific and particularly biological knowledge and development. The Religionists thinking has shifted through creationism, to intelligent design and constant loses in state and federal courts and in the court of public opinion of thinking people.

Unfortunately, the lack of ability of people to think, to understand science, to accept the various facets that prove and refine evolutionary concepts has condemned the United States to a third world state in science, particularly in biological sciences. In comparisons with 30 countries of the rest of the developed world, currently the US ranks 25th in mathematics, 17th in general science and 14th in reading skills. In other surveys of the same top 30 countries in the world, the United States ranks next to last — just above Turkey — in general acceptance of biology, particularly evolution.

The point that always escapes the Christian is that Genesis is not journalism. Scripture is not science. The lame flaws in their arguments are many. One argument of the fundamentalist Christians is that man did not — could not have — come from a monkey. Of course not. No evolutionary textbook ever said so. No scientists teaching or working in the field ever said so. First of all monkeys have tails, while apes (which the Christianists really mean) such as chimps, bonobos, orangutans, gorillas, do not. What evolution has said and proven through fossil and other evidence is that monkeys and mankind both originated from a common primate, dividing off about seven million years ago. And that chimps, bonobos, orangutans and gorillas have about 98.5 percent of the same DNA that we have.

Second, the uneducated keep pointing out that you can't ever find a monkey (or anything else) changing or evolving. Of course not. The evolution from a basic past primate or ape to either a chimp or a human took seven million years. It is not something that you will see or notice at all in the puny 60 year lifespan of a human or even the several thousand years of recorded history. That 70 year human life span is about 1/100,000 of the time frame needed for basic primates such as apes and us to make the small change involved between chimps and humans of today.

Another concept of the creationists is that the theory (theorem) of evolution is a vast conspiracy of the scientists, educators, secular humanists, atheists, agnostics and disbelievers, who are out there to "get" religion, to prove that it is not true. Well, the so-called "truths" of religion are not true, but the idea of a vast conspiracy boggles the mind. Proofs of evolution can fill dozens of libraries with the books, research papers, evidence, fossils, photos, data and such that little by little stack up to an incontrovertible stock of evidence as to the basic correctness of Darwin's Theory. To discount this would be ignoring, countering or disproving all the various studies of cosmology, geology and biology. It would have to reduce to nothing or foolishness all the "-ologies" and sciences such as microscopic anatomy, comparative anatomy, human anatomy, zoology, botany, paleobotany, paleolozoology, histology, geology, archeology, anthropology, ornithology, entomology, embryology, herpetology, ichthyology, invertebrate zoology, and mammalogy. It would rule out all the genome projects accomplished and being done in the world today, the forensics of medicine, the cures and research into deadly diseases, the forensics of criminology, genetics of farm animals and food crops.

The basic flaw in creationism and it's poorly renamed intelligent design is that they are all false. They keep trying to prove that they are equivalent or an alternative study to evolution. In reality, creationist beliefs are only a fable or fairy tale of the past striving futilely against the truths of science, and drowning in the process.

Those espousing the ideas of creationism or intelligent design (creationism in a new but cheap suit), are harming the US and the world. Their backward thinking and inability to look forward with the increasing knowledge of science stymies the advances of the world and harms all of us. Admittedly, they sometimes point to the 700 scientists who agree with the ideas of Christianity and creationism. They often neglect that from the same polls of scientists, some 480,000 active scientists agree with the theory/theorem affirming evolution.

CHAPTER 18. RELIGIOUS HEALING AND FAITH HEALING

On a recent Pat Robertson 700 Club TV show, Pat's son and co-host Gordon Robertson and another preacher were praying reverently and fervently for a caller and for the healing of the scourge of his pancreatic cancer. They were sure that God had driven the cancer out that day, at that hour, in that moment. Presumably, everybody seemingly believed that this healing had happened. Me? I think that I will wait for the 700 Club to report on the six-month check-up by a real, card-carrying, AMA member, board-certified doctor specializing in pancreatic oncology. That should tell the tale or spill the beans. Of course, that will never happen because the Robertson crew would not like the answer.

Lest you think that this is a mischaracterization of the 700 Club TV show, consider the following taped on August 22, 2012, with Pat Roberson and his sidekick Kristi Watts. This was their divine realization of ills and woes of those in TV land and their response to their problems. Or could all of these patients been made up?

Pat Roberson: "If two of you on earth agree, there are people in this audience who have crippling arthritis. They have been crippled, they have not been able to move properly. Their backs are twisted, their arms are twisted, their hands are twisted. In the name of Jesus, that arthritis is going away, your limbs are going to be normal, you will be able to extend your arms and your back will be straight and you will be able to stand up straight in the name of Jesus. Kristi?"

Kristi Watts: "There is a person out there and you have a lingering case of bronchitis. What should have been healed months ago, it has continued. The Lord is healing you right now. There is another person who has a tickling in the back of your throat. No matter what you do, it does not go away. Today you are going to feel a healing, that is rolling down your throat and that is healed right now."

PR: "You have swelling in your knee and I believe that you have an ice pack on it right now. If you will just touch that knee, in the name of Jesus, that swelling is going down, the inflammation is going down, and your bones are being healed and anything arthritic is going away, in the name of Jesus."

KW: "There is a person who made a quick move and you hurt your hip and it seems like a bag in that area. Put your hands on that area and as you do that, you are going to feel the warmth of the Holy Spirit and you are healed. If you could not do this before, do it now."

It went on a little more, with Pat Roberson commenting on an individual (possibly made up) who is (or is it now was?) constantly afraid and injured or diseased and through the power of Pat and Jesus, that illness or disease is now gone. That gets into the psychiatric or psychosomatic area of medicine rather than physical healing. One of the questions of all this, even if you believe this malarkey, is how do the Big Three of the Trinity divide up who is going to do what? How are the various medical healings divided between God, Jesus and the Holy Spirit? It would be like medical specialties, where one physician might concentrate on infectious disease, another on joint replacements and a third on genetic medical problems.

Naturally, the same dog-and-pony show can be found from many other such TV shows with practicing larcenous charlatans. Lacking any sort of authentic medical follow up with any of this nonsense, Pat Robertson, his son Gordon and their sidekicks along with others should all be charged in Federal Court with practicing medicine without a license and duly put on trial. That won't happen either.

It also won't happen with the healings by Benny Hinn, Peter Popoff, Paul Crouch, John Hagee, Ernest Angley or any of the other characters, charlatans, thieves, con men and bunko artists on TV or elsewhere who are swindling the innocent and gullible while trying to separate the faithful from their money through any means possible. This of course, includes the fake curing of medical diseases, elimination of physical problems, healing of injuries, and sickness. In this, we would not only have to have a medical proof of healing of an individual, but also a continued, established proof of other healings along with the presumably negative results in a control group with the same problems and who were not "healed" by anyone of any religious stripe. True, some of these individuals might be "healed" but that only proves one of several things — none of these religious or God-like.

The individual in question might say that he or she has some disease or medical problem, without ever really having anything wrong with them. They might believe that they have a particular illness or specific disease.

Without true medical tests and appropriate examination prior to any "cures," anybody can say that they have anything wrong with them, without really being sick or injured. In my early life, I had an aunt who to get attention from others, was always "dying" of something. She would switch back and forth between cancer, gout, diabetes, migraine headaches, glaucoma, indigestion, back problems, pneumonia, kidney problems, respiration problems, fluttering heart, a bad liver, lung disease, circulation problems, tape worms, and heart problems. Naturally, she ultimately died, but only after about 30 years of other so-called assorted ills, the main one of which was always "cancer" of some form or another. To have "healed" her during these 30 years when she really had nothing wrong with her other than a perceived lack of attention by her son and husband (I wonder why?) would only have "healed" her of nothing and proven nothing.

The placebo effect is known by all doctors in which giving some placebo or similar false cure to a patient will result in an often almost immediate "cure" by the patient — at least for a short while. In a reported 1967 case in Philadelphia, evangelist Kathryn Kuhlman "cured" a woman of spinal cancer, had her throw away her brace and run across the stage to demonstrate that she was cured. The next day her spine collapsed and she died four months later. Temporarily feeling that you are cured does not mean that you are cured.

Outright fakes are and have been practiced by some religious charlatans such as Peter Popoff, as reported by the writings of faith-healing exposer James Randi. Popoff's crew would seat so-called injured and diseased people in the front rows of his evangelist meetings, often in wheel chairs — which they did not need — supplied by Popoff's workers as the faithful entered for the meeting. During the service, he would call out specific people, name them and describe their ills as told to him by God — all before supposedly curing them. As Randi discovered, it was not God telling Popoff about these people, but a tiny receiver in his ear with information as to the specifics of the person (carefully placed in a prearranged seat) and their disease transmitted from his off-stage wife. The information that she passed along was from detailed health and personal information cards filled out by the faithful as they entered the auditorium.

Doctors are not gods. They do make mistakes, as much as we and they hope that they never do. Misdiagnoses do occur. A basic misdiagnosis might be one of cancer when in reality the patient only has a skin or organ cyst that is and will remain benign. By misdiagnosing a simple non-threatening problem into a major disease and then having the patient "cured" through religious or other quack cures only serves to reinforce the faith healing which is really not a cure. Sadly it is bad on two levels. It gives the gullible patient a mistrust of doctors and qualified medicine. It also reinforces in them a faith or belief in some sort of nostrum, placebo or other quack cure or instant faith and a religious/God cure.

Spontaneous remissions do occur in virtually all diseases. The fact that it occurs occasionally in one person proves nothing other than we do not yet know enough about all people, genetics, DNA, science and medicine to know completely and absolutely what is happening. We are all mongrels; we all re-act differently to different ills and various cures. That's why any pill or cure always lists a series of common to rare side effects that may or may not affect any one individual. We mongrels cannot predict who will or will not have any of the simple or serious side effects listed. There might be a cause that we discover in time or we might never find a cause. But to jump to the fanciful conclusion that Pat Robertson or Benny Hinn or someone else through God has "healed" that person — or talked Jesus into healing that person — only adds injury and insults the intelligence of any thinking person.

Even without the fake or presumed healing of the TV evangelists or the tent preachers or fundamentalist church ministers who promote the belief in the absurd, there are religions that do not allow their faithful members to use real medicine to cure a disease. When I was young, our Christian Scientist neighbor had an attack of appendicitis. She prayed, her husband prayed, her Christian Science church both in their home and in their church prayed. All to no avail. She survived, but just narrowly when at the end of their prayer rope (or prayer chain, as the religionists like to think of it) and with a burst appendix, she was taken to the hospital and then got some real although last ditch medical treatment and antibiotics that saved her life. So much for faith healing with quack religions.

The main visible proponents of healing through God, prayer, religion, preachers as God's emissaries and the Bible are those charlatans who on TV have the supposedly sick or injured on their stage and with stage presence and staged procedures, perform a little rite and ritual that is so common and canned that it is laughable. Usually the "anointed one" (the preacher) calls on God or Jesus to heal this person, uses a demonstrable and authoritative voice in asking for this and then places hands upon the forehead of the in-dividual. At the same time, or after a little shaking of the hands on the fore-head, the ill parishioner falls back into the waiting arms of the ministerial cohorts. He or she is then placed on the floor of the stage for a time, seem-ingly shocked or unconscious. Usually they then weakly get up and are es-corted off of the stage. A variation of this is to have the parishioner, after be-ing struck on the forehead by the minister and "slain in the Word" (or "slain in the Spirit" — another variation), they stagger back and then are coached by the minister to run around the stage, get up out of their wheelchair, throw away their crutches or perform some similar act to "prove" that God or Jesus healed them and that they are now cured with the blood of Jesus. Often the wheelchairs are provided by the church for those walking into the service, to supposedly make it easier for them to sit and also to wheel them to an upfront spot for their convenience and also for the minister to be able to call on them and "heal" them.

The sad thing about all this is the loss for the ill or injured individual participating in this charade of chicanery. Often people like this, firmly believing in the power of prayer, God, Jesus and the charlatan-turned-minister and in turn completely gullible about God and the con men at the front of the church and masquerading as ministers, will shun their medical doctors. They will also stop taking proven medicine that has been prescribed for them, stop seeing their regular or specialist MD and thus eliminate their best chance of recovery. They can and usually do get sicker, have more problems and if truly sick hasten their date with death.

In addition, many people conned by these scams have spent a lot of money to go to "shows" (there is no other or better word for this) to be "treated," with their money going to travel, lodging while there, food, and similar expenses. In addition, many feel compelled or encouraged to give money through cash, checks or property to the minister and his crew for the "treatment" that they are receiving or expect to receive. Many of them are also totally depressed with a feeling that perhaps they are not good enough or worthy enough for God or Jesus to heal them. Or so they think.

A particularly sad example of this appeared on TV recently. It started with a man, perhaps in his late 30s, who had a speech problem as a result of an early accident. A later accident paralyzed him from the waist down. He was shown sitting in his wheelchair in the hallway of a faith healing venue, waiting for the third of the three days of healing, talking with difficulty to TV interviewer Lisa Ling.

This was part of one of the saddest TV shows I have seen in a long time, a one-hour documentary on faith healing. The show concentrated on Todd Bentley, a faith healing minister with a questionable past and a turned-around life.

His South Carolina "school" taught faith healing and the three-day event featured day-long prayer sessions and workshops. The badly crippled man and a family who brought their cancer-ridden Mom to the three-day healing event were among those attending.

God had talked to him, so the crippled man said with difficulty, and God told him that his time of ultimate healing was to occur during the last hour of the last day of this healing workshop. He was positive of this. God had talked to him. He would then talk normally again and walk freely for the rest of his life.

The woman brought by her family had no more money or insurance coverage for the chemotherapy treatments for her pelvic cancer. She and her family were expecting a "miracle," knowing that God would completely heal this devout and believing woman.

The program build-up contained interviews of young and old about the positive and miraculous effects of faith healing of those whose bodies were damaged — seemingly ruined. It showed aspiring 20-year-old faith healers attempting to heal those they met while walking the streets of Charlotte, SC. It showed the faith-healing Todd Bentley trying to work his magic and relaxing at home while discussing his work and the miracle of Jesus.

The show covering the last day of the healing was particularly telling. Two strong men struggled to get the paralyzed man out of his wheel chair and into the healing line for Minister Bentley to do his magic. The cancer-plagued woman's family struggled to get her a place at the front for her healing.

The minister did his thing. As expected for those who have seen such shows and church services on TV, the minister placed his hands on each believer, saying his "bam" or "bang" almost like chef Emeril Lagasse does when using spices to kick up the flavor of a chicken cacciatore dish.

It was for naught. The last minutes of the last hour of the last day came and went. The crippled, speech-impaired man was back in his wheelchair, still crippled and still speech-impaired. The Mom was still deathly ill, ready to go back to her Georgia home to die. The documentary, failing to answer any questions, did not follow up on her illness.

It was all for naught and any reasonable person could have and would have expected the non-results. The disappointment and misery was almost palpable through the TV screen.

For the crippled man, his expectations now shifted. Instead of the absolute knowledge of God's healing from his talk with God, he now explained about his plans. He knew — God told him — that his time on earth was nothing compared to his time in eternity when all believers will have new bodies in heaven. In other words, he was buying into the carrot of the carrot-and-stick theory of heaven and hell, and he had assured himself that his time here was nothing compared to his time in heaven with his beautiful new healthy body. How sad. How evil of those who promote this trickery, this falseness, this con, this prayerful Ponzi scheme payable only upon death.

While adults can do what they want with their time, money and thoughts, this type of faith healing is particularly egregious when it comes to children. Early in 2010, the Oregon courts heard the case of Jeff and Marci Beagley being tried for the death of their son Neil. Neil, 16 years old when he died, was not taken to a doctor or to a hospital as he should have been. Neil had a treatable bladder infection for much of his life, but his parents were members of the Followers of Christ Church which, according to news reports, believes in faith healing and does not believe in or rely on standard medical treatment, medicine or doctors. As reported in the news, the death rate of children in this church is twenty times the national average.

Sadly, much of the testimony — at the time on an "In Session" TV show — involved the parents on trial stating that Neil did not want to go to the doctor. Instead, he wanted to rely on God, praying and laying on of hands for healing. That was apparently the delusion that he had been taught his entire short life.

He had been brainwashed and undoubtedly wanted to please his parents, his family, his church, his community and perhaps to show how Godly he could be by believing in faith healing through prayer. Instead, he died.

His parents honored his objection to getting medical help and thus did nothing medically to help him. The parents were sentenced to 16 months in prison and three years of post-prison supervision after being found guilty of criminally negligent homicide.

Eleven-year-old Madeline Neumann died in March 2008 of an undiagnosed but treatable form of diabetes. Her parents, Dale and Leilani Neumann, were reported to have ignored obvious medical symptoms such as weakness, resulting in her inability to speak, eat, drink or walk. The parents relied on prayer for healing, with the girl dying on the floor of their Weston, Wisconsin, home as her parents and others of her church surrounded her and prayed.

The sad thing about this is that parents are morally and legally responsible for children under the age of 18. You do not have to buy your children a cell phone, but you do have to provide them with nourishing food. You do not have to buy children Nike shoes, but you do have to buy them shoes and necessary clothing, and provide a bed, housing, nourishing food, and an education. And you do have to provide them with medical care.

Constant statements in the TV broadcast on the Neil Beagley case referred to the parents allowing him at 16 to decide whether or not he wanted medical treatment.

The problem with this type of deluded thinking is that Neil at 16 was not an adult and should not have been allowed or considered able to make decisions about his life. You allow kids to make decisions as to whether they want to eat a hamburger or hot dog. If you are an orthodox Jew, you do not allow your child to eat a shrimp cocktail or a pork chop. You allow children to make decisions as to which acceptable TV show to watch, perhaps which pants to wear to school, whether he/she wants a thick or thin pillow for sleeping, whether or not he wants to play basketball or football in school or she wants to become a cheerleader.

You do not allow minors to decide whether or not to get medical help, to get vaccinated, to go to school, to do their homework, to ride their bike on the Interstate, to jump off the roof, to eat dog poo or get involved in other concerns of health or childhood protection.

The problem does not go away, and requires uniform legal penalties for those — including parents — who engage in medical neglect that harms or kills their children. In 1977 Rita and Doug Swam lost their only son as a result of relying on Christian Science practitioners. As a result of this they in 1983 formed the organization Children's Healthcare is a Legal Duty, Inc. (CHILD). They continue to try to work for those children whose parents are involved in faith healing or medical neglect. They documented that for the years 1975 through 1995 there were 172 instances of children in the U.S. dying from illnesses that could have been treated by standard medical procedures. The parents of these children rejected any medical treatment.

Rita Swam, according to reports, also notes a 1972 outbreak of polio at a Connecticut Christian Science boarding school. As a result of lack of standard medical treatment, 11 children became paralyzed.

As this is written in early 2015, there are increasing trends for personal or religious exemptions for childhood vaccinations, vaccinations that would save children's lives. These failures to vaccinate end up costing society millions of dollars. According to a report in the Canadian magazine *Macleans*, during two decades when USA has had thousands of cases of measles and Canada had 2,000, one country had none. That's because they have universally required vaccinations. Also, health and medical care including the importance of vaccinations is covered in school and everyone can talk intelligently about preventable diseases and the importance of vaccinations. That country is Cuba, where they have twice as many doctors per population units as in Canada and the US.

Jehovah's Witnesses also have rules that involve medical neglect, although they are not heavily involved with faith healing in areas of prayer, laying on of hands, anointing with oil. They do not believe in or practice blood transfusions, even though this medical life saving method is proven and has been around since early experiments in 1492

Why give God the praise for a medical healing, positive surgical result or cure of disease? Should we close down the Mayo Clinic, Johns Hopkins, Sloan Kettering? Should we just let Benny Hinn have at it? Why could not Benny Hinn just walk into a hospital and cure and heal all the patients? (He reportedly tried this once and no one was healed!)

Why do Christianists constantly and consistently make exceptions to everything? Christians can point out a disease, financial crisis, medical emergency or family disaster when it happens to a "bad person" who in their eyes displeases God ("God is bringing him down to his knees"), but excuse same when it happens to a "good Christian person." That's totally illogical, ridiculous, and insane. It seems, in their minds, that God and nature are two different things, separate and completely divorced from each other, with God getting credit for all the good stuff that happens while "nature" or "man" gets all the blame for any bad stuff. It would be funny it were not so strange and sad.

The blame for this sad charade of justifying good and bad by Christians belongs in three places — State and Federal legislatures, the medical profession and the AMA, and the collective "standard" or "normal" Christian churches, both Protestant and Catholic. The US Federal Government, through the Constitution and added Amendments, has the power to charge faith healers with practicing medicine without a license or training, since the entire Constitution, and especially Article I Section 8, covers various contingencies that deal with citizens and the protection thereof through various government offices.

Part of Article I Section 8 starts out, "To promote the Progress of Science and useful Arts. . ." We are certainly not doing this, if we allow unscrupulous scoundrels of the religious ministry to make unwarranted and unproven claims about religion and healing. Science, as mentioned in the Constitution, does not deal with the hocus pocus of religion or claims there of as to cures, healing and such.

If we truly have a country that has a separation of church and state, as designed by Thomas Jefferson and the Founding Fathers, then a separation of the powers and roles of government and the fables of religion is a must. If we have a government with the power of sustaining an army to protect us from without, then that same government also has a duty to protect us from those citizens within the country who would rob us of the proven cures of medicine and replace these with the unproven claims of religion and faith healing.

TV minister Ernest Angley was on TV recently with a woman with a defective ear drum that had a hole in it. He held her head and noted that Jesus was healing her defective ear drum as he spoke and told her that she could feel the healing of her ear drum. Naturally, she agreed. What else could she do? Would she disagree with Angley and state that she could not at all feel any healing "power"? Would she argue with this revered man of God? Would she disavow Jesus for something that Jesus was supposedly doing for her in healing a ruptured ear drum?

Next, he was introduced to a woman who had a self-described brain tumor. Again through the power of Jesus, Angley immediately healed this "brain tumor." Of course, with all of this and more by Angley and others, there are two things lacking that are requirements in medicine.

First, there is never any requirement of proven medical records in terms of examinations, X-rays, MRI scans, CAT scans, written reports from qualified professionals, other medical tests and procedures, etc, to state with a medical certainty the medical condition of the named patient to be "healed" and any suggested treatments.

Second, after the supposed healing by religious quacks, there is never any truly qualified medical follow up to prove that the condition, previously affirmed through medical records in advance of the religious "healing," has been cured or aided through the miracle power of Jesus. Personally, were I Jesus or God, I would very upset about a minister or anyone using my name and claiming things that were and are impossible.

Chapter 19. Show Me the Money!

All churches and ministers want money. Certainly this is true of modern churches who have completely abandoned the "church" of the Bible and Jesus who suggested meeting in homes and in small groups. Meet in a small group in a home or mutual meeting place and take turns preaching or in Bible study and you do not need money. That's what the Amish do. They have no physical church structure. In this practice, each of the small group could share in various tasks of preaching, brainwashing the children, doing good works (how about Habitat for Humanity or any local conservation project?), sharing meals, helping church members and/or neighbors, volunteering at local charitable projects or hospitals. That of course is not the story today other than perhaps small store-front churches in very poor neighborhoods.

Today, all religions are Ponzi schemes, except that they do not even promise anything and certainly nothing tangible. They take and take, with the only promise being some vague "heaven" after you die, and that only if you have been a good boy or girl. Sorry, I would like a return on my investment here, on this earth, today, while I am still alive to use it and enjoy it. Churches do demand — or strongly suggest that to be a good Christian — the money of tithing to pay the many bills incurred.

But often they are not satisfied with a normal income from the tithing parishioners to maintain a normal balance of income and outgo of expenses. Near where I live there is what I call a mini-mega church. Currently it has about 4,000 or so members, all attending church in the most recently constructed building that most closely resembles a large auditorium perhaps more suitable for a rock concert or a dog show. Take out some pews and chairs in the center and you could feature basketball games. This particular church has many church buildings, on a large property, each built for different purposes and in different styles of architecture. It has even spawned "daughter" churches, as they like to say in religious circles. These are small churches, often in the same general area as the main church, but spread out through a county or state to further spread the Word of God, as they see the Word of God. It also has and supports missionaries going to other parts of the country or mostly to different countries to spread the delusion of their particular brand of Christianity to people who would be far better off without these additional lies in their lives.

This particular church now has a just-announced two-year project fund-raising drive to get the faithful to contribute a total of $14,200.000. The money will go to creating new churches, salaries for staffing said churches, printing Bibles, and other efforts to sell Jesus. Naturally, they look upon this as working for the world by continuing to promote the pie-in-the-sky Jesus-loves-you salvation folly — the Ponzi scheme of a promise that never has to be delivered — at least in this lifetime.

This new $14,200,000 church promotion is designed as contributing — according to them — both the regular tithe of at least ten percent that they want (or expect) from their members with extra funding on top of that. The commitment card to be signed, sealed and delivered by a certain date clearly states that. According to the slick sales pitch, in short order, they supply a pew membership card outlined for members to fill in the regular annual tithing for the next two years along with the extra that you are going to pledge to this special $14,200,000 effort.

Naturally, the rest of us are also paying for this through the added burden of no taxes for churches and religious efforts. In this the faithful as well as the faithless will be indirectly paying for churches and charities by shouldering the burden of those same churches and charities not paying and that the rest of us pay. This church — or any church — could have requested money for something that would truly impact lives and help children. While there are lots of problems in the world, and lots of notable worthwhile charities, I am thinking right now of Operation Smile (888-677-6453 — www.operationsmile.org) and SmileTrain (800-932-9541 — www.smiletrain.org). With both of these organizations, it is easy to compute the direct help to individual children and also to calculate the money necessary for this help. For a grand sum of $250.00 and the volunteer aid of doctors going to help these children, one child can have a cleft lip and/or palate corrected. There are many other worthwhile charities, but these serve well as an example that is also easy to compute with the math involved with the results gained. It is easy — a contribution or combined contribution of $1,000 will correct the cleft lips and palates of four children. A total of $10,000 will help 40 children. A sum of $100,000 will help 400 children.

These organizations train local or send volunteer doctors to countries to correct cleft palates and lips of kids whose poor parents or impoverished village cannot in any way pay for these operations. The operations are simple, not costly by our western standards, but out of reach of most if not all in Third World Counties of principally southeast Asia. The result of these operations impacts the lives of these children forever, giving them a medical, economic and social chance in life that otherwise would be impossible.

With volunteer doctors contributing time to go to these countries, the bare-bones cost of each cleft palate operation is $240/$250. That means that this church with their $14,200,000 solicitations could forget their edifice complex and pay for an additional 56,800 operations to truly help 56,800 children cursed through no fault of their own with a cleft lip or palate.

So let's see now. With $14,200,000 this church can pay for material things such as monuments to themselves. That same $14,200,000 could truly, literally change the lives of 56,800 children. (Interestingly, a TV minister does the same thing with his ministry, but the cost is $500.00 per child and operation. I wonder where the extra $250.00 goes compared to the Smile Train/Operation Smile costs?)

Which one would God want, if there is or was a God or a God who really cared? Of course, if God (if there is a God or god) really cared, he could wave a little finger and do it him/her/itself to helps these kids. This sort of thing keeps me both skeptical and bitter about religion, Christianity, Christian love, Christ-like care and the absolute total lack of Godly concern by Christians for their fellow man. These people and this church are certainly not interested in any way in helping their fellow man. They are only interested in building monuments — literal and figurative — to themselves. And oh yes. They have also just announced a plan for 100 members to go as missionaries to Kenya during the summer. The cost for each church member will be $3,000. That's a total of $300,000 for these self-aggrandizing trips by members who can only totally screw up the thinking of native Kenyans presumably happy with their own religion. Let's see — that same $300,000 or $3,000 per person could be used for cleft lip and palate operations for another 1,200 children, waiting for their chance to get this life-altering operation.

The other question that comes up in all of this goes back to Chapters 10 and 11 on prayer, Chapter 6 on miracles, and Chapter 17 on religious healing. Thus, if God is omnipotent and all powerful, why can't he take care of this small problem so that no more children in any part of the world get cleft lips or palates, or get cures automatically, all God-ordered and God-enacted, cured after one week of life, or in the womb, or something similar, all courtesy of God?

The most egregious examples of pure unadulterated greed are those of mega-churches and those on TV who are constantly pleading for money. Ironically, one of the more stable and traditional big churches came under fire for financial shenanigans. Robert H. Schuller, who started the huge glass Crystal Cathedral filed for bankruptcy on October 18, 2010, with financial records becoming available in early December 2010. Basically, his operation with the Hour of Power TV show each week has been considered one of the saner and more stable of the various TV religious programs. But the documents released show otherwise. According to these news reports, the income for the Crystal Cathedral was $54.6 million in 2008, but dropped to $41.2 million in 2009 and for 2010 as of October 18, income was at $22.3 million. As a result of this drop of more than half in income, vendors and some employees were not paid. During the year leading to the October 18 bankruptcy, some $1.8 million was paid out to 23 family members and insiders. This included $832,490 in tax-free housing allowances to eight people and payments to all five of Schuller's children and their spouses.

Since religious institutions, churches and ministers do not have to disclose financial records, this was all private until the public disclosure of bankruptcy. For example, Crystal Cathedral Chief Financial Officer Fred Southard received a $132,000 housing allowance that he claims he is entitled to as minister. Guess who ordained him? You've got it — the Crystal Cathedral ministry.

According to reports, Schuller's son-in-law Paul Dunn, Schuller's daughter Carol Milner and his son Robert A. Schuller — all involved with the church presently or in the immediate past — received housing allowances of more than $100,000 each. Founder Schuller received a housing allowance, along with son-in-law Jim Coleman, son-in-law James Penner and Southard's son-in-law William Gaultiere. In addition, questions have come up about the minimal work done or redundant duties of some of the above and others for the Crystal Cathedral.

Dunn, the pageant director for the Easter and Christmas programs, received a tax free housing allowance of over $300,000. Expensive homes that seem out of line with normal or typical allowed expenses were enjoyed by all five of Schuller's children, including $1 million homes in California and Boulder, CO (Milner and husband Timothy), Dunn (two homes in Hawaii) and the $1 million Laguna Beach home of founder Robert Schuller.

There are many of the so-called "prosperity gospel" preachers around today, with the most visible of them on TV in their various programs, or purchasing time from the Trinity Broadcasting Network. The founder of this method and theology of preaching is considered to be Kenneth Copeland, who along with his preaching wife Gloria, has TV shows through his Fort

Worth, Texas Word of Faith movement. Early in life he was a recording artist, with one Billboard hit, and was later the pilot and chauffeur for TV evangelist Oral Roberts.

His pitch is that God wants you (and me and all of us) to be financially successful and that all we have to do is to "plant our seed." The whole idea of this ministry of him and so many others is that "if you plant your seed, you shall receive a harvest far greater than the seed that you planted." In one ministry sermon, there was a reference of a planting of corn, stating that if you plant one kernel of corn you will get (optimally) one corn stalk. If you plant more than one, you will get proportionally more and more corn.

In one show, the reference was made to receiving what you plant. Plant corn and you get corn, plant soybeans and you get soybeans, plant money as your seed (to their ministry of course) and you get money. The inference is obvious. You have to give money to these televangelists to get money. God will bless you with more money. One report on the Kenneth Copeland ministries notes that the giving envelope states that "I am sowing $_____ and believing for a hundredfold return." While a tad short of a guarantee, the idea of a hundredfold return on your money is far beyond an implication or simple possibility.

This is also the big push with many TV ministers today, with Mike Murdock being one of the main offenders — uh, participants. Turn on his channel on the TV and he will not go more than about a half dozen sentences without suggesting or insisting on a "gift" from you, the TV viewer, for his ministry in terms of "sowing your seed." To further push this along, many of these ministers will run a scroll along the bottom of the screen with the names of those viewers who have just given money to the cause. These may be real or just names propped up there to encourage the giving by others. Naturally, if it is fake, no one will know it anyway. If it is real, no one will know other than the person who just gave by donating funds through a credit card number to the person on the end of the constantly manned ministry telephone number.

And this also provides some wiggle room and an out for this or any other similar claiming ministry such as those by Benny Hinn, Peter Popoff, Creflo Dollar, Marilyn and Sarah Hickey, Joyce Meyer, Andrew Wommack, Jack and Rexella Van Impe, Gregory Dickow, and others. Don't get your monetary return or the amount of return that you expected? Probably you were not believing strongly enough. Don't get what you think that you deserve as one of God's followers? Maybe you did not have enough faith. Your seed money puts you into debt instead of making you money as a solid investment? Maybe you are still sinning. Maybe your thoughts and actions are evil. Perhaps you held back on your pledge and did not give enough. Maybe your seed money was insufficient to please God.

All this for Kenneth and Gloria Copeland has made them a lot of money. A LOT of money. Published reports note that they own a large estate near Fort Worth Texas. This includes an 18,000 — yes 18,000 — square foot home

Their holdings also include a private airport and air strip (Copeland early on was a pilot) with four Copeland or Copeland ministry planes, including a $20 million Cessna Citation X along with a Cessna Bravo 550 ($3.6 million) and two others. In addition, the ministry or Copeland (one or both) own profit ventures in cattle, horses, aviation, gas, oil wells and real estate development. Not bad for a good 'ole country boy from Lubbock, Texas who wants you to plant your seed to make God and the baby Jesus happy.

In addition to the shouting pleas for money, a crawler runs along the bottom of the screen with Bible verses that "prove" the truth and necessity of seed planting. Often they will separate verses that otherwise would run together, such as this following passage from 2 Corinthians 9:6–12. Specifically, 2 Corinthians 9:6–12 says: "(6) Remember this: Whoever sows sparingly will also reap sparingly, and whoever sows generously will also reap generously. (7) Each man should give what he has decided in his heart to give, not reluctantly or under compulsion, for God loves a cheerful giver. (8) And God is able to make all grace abound to you, so that in all things at all times, having all that you need, you will abound in every good work. (9) As it is written, 'He has scattered abroad his gifts to the poor; his righteousness endures forever.' (10) Now he who supplies seed to the sower and bread for food will also supply and increase your store of seed and will enlarge the harvest of your righteousness. (11) You will be made rich in every way so that you can be generous on every occasion, and through us your generosity will result in thanksgiving to God. (12) This service that you perform is not only supplying the needs of God's people but is overflowing in many expressions of thanks to God."

It seems as if many TV evangelists have picked up on this con of trying to get people to believe part of the Bible to give to their particularly "ministry" or religious endeavor. On Trinity Broadcast Network, you can find constant references to Bible verses to prove that you should give and "plant your seed." Some of these are: 2 Corinthians 9:10, Mark 10:29, 2 Corinthians 9:11, Malachi 3:10, Matthew 26:8–10, Proverbs 19:17, Proverbs 21:13, Proverbs 22:9, Proverbs 28:27, Nehemiah 5:19, Psalms 54:6–7, 2 Corinthians 9:6, Psalms 96:8, Psalms 112:1, 3, Psalms 112:9, 1 Corinthians, Isaiah 58:10, Luke 21:1, Matthew 19:21, 1 Corinthians 29:13, 1 Corinthians 29:14, 2 Corinthians 9:11, Acts, 10:4, 2 Corinthians 8:2, 2 Corinthians 8:3, 2 Corinthians 8:7, 2 Corinthians 8:9, Exodus 34:26, Psalms 41:1.

You get the idea. Many talk about sharing with the poor money, harvests or livestock. Others describe providing the "first fruits" or the "first born" of livestock to the Lord, thus playing directly into the hands of the charlatans who are trying to extract anything and everything possible from the gullible and believing. Give them the first checks and money you get, and don't worry about how to pay the mortgage, car payment, rent, gas bill, food bill, phone bill or medical expenses.

Some of these ministers regularly appear on TV with a large low coffee table — often like a very low card table in square format — this table filled with stacks of so-called prayers and prayer requests, often perhaps a dozen reams high, all covering the table surface. A ream of paper is 500 sheets. Ironically, all of these prayer requests are on seemingly identical paper. None seem to come in from notebooks, torn out of spiral bound pages, on memo pads, scraps of paper, or back of envelopes. They all look as if they are 8-1/2 X 11 inch sheets of paper, torn open from packaging right after being delivered from an Office Depot store. Then all involved — the host and any visiting firemen — oops, ministers — bow down, kneel, sit on their chairs or stand around (if the table and stacks of paper are high enough) and "lay hands" on the stacks of so-called paper prayer requests as if this was important, bow heads and pray over these requests. Such nonsense!

Another trick to deceive the terminally and willfully ignorant parishioners and those out in TV land is to "anoint" the prayer requests. Yep, literally anoint them with oil out of a small vial. At least, it looks like oil. They never make it clear what kind of oil it is. It could be 30 weight motor oil, 10W-40 weight, or various kitchen oils such as corn oil, canola oil, olive oil. A nice touch here on which they could probably capitalize would be to use olive oil, extra virgin, which would tie in neatly with the birth of Jesus and virgin birth. I have never heard of this and am not sure that any of the TV proselytizers have ever made this connection or mentioned it on TV. In this magic trick, they are careful to anoint or pour oil on all the top sheets of the stacks of prayer requests, although the oil does not soak in very far through the top sheets of paper. I guess that they are considering osmosis — or religious figurative anointing — to get the special anointing (it is always special, just received from God) through the various stacks to "anoint" all the prayers in all the stacks.

All the money collected of course is to help the station and the individual ministers program or ministry to stay on the air, to convert all the rest of the world, to send the word about Jesus throughout the globe, to spread Bible teachings and the Christian faith who were in all likelihood doing just fine in the religion department until the Christian missionaries showed up. Remember the little tale of the missionary and the heathen Eskimo (or pick any heathen you wish).

Eskimo — "Since you taught me about Jesus and God, this means that if I believe I will go to heaven and if I don't I will go to hell?"

Missionary: "That's right, my son. Now that you know about Jesus, you must believe in him to go to heaven."

Eskimo: "And if I did not learn from you about Jesus and God, would I then go to hell if I do not believe?"

Missionary: "No son, if you did not know about Jesus and God, you would not know about the saving power of his salvation and by not knowing about it, you would certainly not go to hell."

Eskimo: "Then why did you tell me?"

And usually when the missionaries of the past showed up at the front door of the Eskimos (Inuit) or other peoples, they brought with them sickness and pestilence, illness and communicable diseases of which native populations were not immune nor protected against.

Chapter 20. The Disconnect of Faith from Reality

"God can do anything that he wants to." That's the constant refrain of Christians when faced with a "why," "how" or "what-if" question. "God can do anything he wants, any time he wants, in any way he wants. God is in control, now and always. God is a just God. God is a loving God." The religionists usually follow this with a smug: "And he doesn't have to do anything just to prove it to you!" So there! Now you know! Of course, by doing this, they completely rule out the possibility of any proof, science, knowledge, facts, logic, scientific method or truth that would definitely prove that their religion is real and beneficial to mankind.

Prove it. Prove that God can do something, anything, by God doing something good. Admittedly, according to the religionists, God's timing and God's ways are different from our ways. But why not have God do something, anything? Did not God supposedly do something good now and again throughout the Old Testament and New Testament to prove that he was worthy of being called God, or conversely, display his wrath to show what would happen to those who did not follow his rules?

OK. Find something in the past that through empirical methods can be shown to be from God, or God-caused, or truly supernatural, or a real "miracle." Prove something that will show that God is in control, that God is loving, that God is good, that God is caring of mankind and this world. Just prove that God is around, for pities sake! Prove something, for pities sake! Prove this from past history or past experience. But just make sure that it is provable and that it can be shown without doubt that God did this thing that you are going to prove to me. That's what I thought. You can't do it. There is nothing there. There is no history, no event, nothing that is provable by current standards that there is a God and that this God has ever done anything.

God as the Christians call him or her or it, is no different than Zeus, Apollo, Odin, Ra, Isis, Nut, Minerva, Diana, Thor, Mars, Achilles, or any of the other gods of the ancient periods of Greece, Rome, Egypt, Norse country, or anywhere else. The only difference between you and me is that I believe in one less god than you do.

Christians point to their magic book — their Bible — as "proof" that God is and was around, that God can do things, that God can cause miracles Use the Bible to prove to me that the earth is only 6,000 years old, that dinosaurs and man lived together, that the earth was flat, that the sun goes around the earth, and that evolution as described by Charles Darwin never occurred.

Let's look at a few things where perhaps God (any God — pick one!) could have made a difference, had he wanted to, or if there really is or was a God.

- On June 28, 1914, a disgruntled 19-year-old student and Bosnian-Serbian nationalist, Gavrilo Princip, fired a shot that killed Archduke Franz Ferdinand of Austria who was in a parade through Sarajevo streets. Because of alliances then that had built up over recent years between the political powers and major and minor countries in Europe, countries began to line up and support those countries with which they had agreements. The result was disastrous. World War I, or the Great War as it also became to be known, started on August 4, 1914. The end came at 11 a.m. on November 11, 1918, with 17 million dead and 20 million wounded on both sides.

Had God wanted to — if we believe the "all powerful" part — he no doubt could have had Princip miss his shot, been too late to his vantage point to get in an accurate shot, overslept, missed the whole parade where the Archduke was killed, been distracted by a friend, had a relationship with a girl that involved him past the killing time, had a faulty pistol, had faulty ammunition, etc., etc., etc.

Of course, we can't know the outcome of the world had God changed or done any one of these little history-altering things, and we can't know how nations and peoples would have acted or reacted had this beginning of a domino effect not occurred. It is unlikely that any result would have been as bad as, or worse than, the worldwide conflict that did not end satisfactorily at the treaty table and that ultimately led to World War I, Part II, sometimes called World War II, that began 20 years later in 1939.

- World War II began September 1, 1939, when Hitler ordered the German army to invade Poland. It was twenty years after the end of WWI, the loss of German territory and the massive economic reparations required of Germany by the Allied powers. Hitler had gained control of Germany in 1933 after losing a bid to power in 1923. Would WWII have happened had Hitler not been alive or if someone else or some other party gained control of Germany during these decisive years? If Hitler had been killed instead of shot and wounded in WWI, would another leader as bad, or worse or perhaps better have taken his place in post-WWI Germany? We do know that by any account, Hitler was a truly bad guy. We also know that he was a minor hero in WWI when as a private he stepped in front of a German officer to take a bullet and performed well and perhaps even heroically during four other events in various battles. Wouldn't, couldn't God, flicking some little switch somewhere, perhaps have changed this outcome, all this misery, and prevented all or most of the many deaths and maimings?

• During late summer of 2005, weather began to build up in the Gulf Coast, culminating with Hurricane Katrina. The storm had started in the Bahamas on August 23rd, crossed southern Florida, then lost strength before gaining strength again on August 29th in southeast Louisiana. It was listed as the most destructive natural disaster in the history of the US, with 1,836 lives lost, 705 missing, $81.2 billion cost ($89.6 billion in 2009 dollars) and affecting the Bahamas, south Florida, Cuba, Louisiana, Mississippi, Alabama, Florida panhandle and parts of eastern North America. The most severe damage in dollars and loss of life was to New Orleans. The question is why did not God modify this a little to dissipate the hurricane, have it spin off into the Atlantic before making initial landfall, or cause it to hit some relatively desolate part of Mexico or Central America where it would do little material damage and cause little or less loss of life? No one among the Christian community wants to hear this or juggle with this type of question or possibility. And of course, for many religionists and Christians, God is in charge of the weather!

• A shift of some underwater tectonic plates caused a tsunami on December 26, 2004, that killed an estimated 250,000 innocent people and children (recent figures are up to a possible 300,000) in the eleven nations of the Sumatra area including Asia, Sri Lanka, India, Thailand, Myanmar, and the Maldives. People were killed up to 2,000 kilometers away from the epicenter. Could not God have kept the tectonic plates intact, or allowed them to move just a teeny-tiny bit at a time so as to avoid the 45-foot high wall of water surging ashore in this tsunami? Would it not have been possible for God to have caused a giant wind to push the tsunami wave back offshore? Should not God have "talked" to people to convince them to stay home and away from the beach that day? Shoulda, woulda, coulda! Didn't happen. And again, God is in charge of the weather, according to many.

You can postulate about thousands of similar examples, small and large, old and new, natural and man-made, involving one person or thousands of people where God should, would or could put his finger in the dike or on the switch to change the outcome. But God obviously did not do this and does not do this. Perhaps God is fictitious.

Of course, you can suggest that God did do a lot of things that we don't know about. Maybe there were other world wars that were stayed by the hand of God. Perhaps there were other huge hurricanes of the past, about which we know nothing, and which God caused to go out to sea instead of making landfall and striking us. Maybe tectonic plates often do gently shift and do not cause problems, and all by the hand of God.

But that is just conjecture into a magical world of nonsense, about which nothing can be said, nothing proven. You can guess all your want, but guessing on lottery ticket numbers never proved anything either. It is fanciful speculation. Let's, just for giggles, accept for the moment that such things did really occur and that God stayed these other unproven, unnamed and unknown destructive events. Let's assume that other wars were stopped, massive tsunamis stayed, devastating hurricanes diverted. If that is the case, then it only makes God as fickle as a 17-year-old picking a date for her first prom night. If a god or God stayed these other things about which we conjecture now why did God not stay the events and facts mentioned above? How come some people and countries would be worth saving in our imaginary postulations, yet others were not worth saving during the devastation of wars, tsunamis, hurricanes, religious crusades of the past, the Inquisition, the burning of "witches" at the stake as per Martin Luther and others, and so much more? All this does not make God a god of reason, goodness and fairness. It makes God a god of fickle, childish and quixotic behavior. Why did God have it out for some and yet be kind and benevolent to others?

Magic of the stage only involves magic and tricks. We are thrilled with the magician who turns a tiger in a cage into an attractive, scantily clad girl. We are amazed with the girl (again often scantily clad) being cut in half with the huge lumber-size buzz saw. We are thrilled with the 37 pigeons (or doves, parrots, finches, rabbits or anything else in any numbers) coming out of the magicians top hat that would obviously not hold all these creatures. But we know that it is trickery, fakery and magic. We just do not know how it is done, and this leads to our amazement, amusement and wonder. But real life goes by real tests, real events, real experiments, real facts, and demonstrable happenings.

The sad thing about all this is that the religionists are more likely — far more likely — to attribute anything and everything good from their prayers, supplications, and entreaties to God rather than just to circumstance and coincidence, facts and evidence. These Christianists applaud and are grateful for the three lives saved from the crash of a commercial airplane with all other 113 passengers killed during the fiery disaster. Saving those three people was God's will and a result of God's goodness, they will solemnly tell you. Naturally, they attribute these three saved lives to the love, care, grace, goodness and beneficence of God as a glorious example of his love and concern for all of us. All of us? How about the 113 people who died? Were they all bad? Were they all atheists? Even if God had wanted to kill all us atheists, certainly there would have been among the killed passengers some few — or more — young and old avid and devout believers in God and his heaven and works.

Certainly these people — at least some of them — would have been worth God's love and thus worth saving. The fact that he did not save them brings up two questions. Is there really a God or is life just a crap shoot in which getting on the wrong plane at the wrong time, and sitting in the wrong seat, and perhaps even leaning over the wrong way at the moment of disaster would lead to death — or perhaps to life? It's obvious — there is no God or god or gods.

If God cares about those who live, should he not also be blamed for those to die tragically in plane crashes and in other ways for which God is also getting a piece of the applause for saving some, or at least not creating a worse disaster?

Reasons why religion fools people into thinking that it works fall into three distinct areas. First, religious belief is promoted by authority figures when we are young, convincing us of the truth and value of religion, never mind that there is just the same amount of truth in it or value to it that we find in most children's stories. The facts from verifiable history sources and archeology just do not match what is found in the Bible.

Religiosity can also be thought of as a combination of mass hysteria and cognitive dissonance, even mental illness. Religion is not found in the normal lexicon of mental illness, but if we consider the evidence that, in extreme cases, religious fervor can and does affect normal everyday life, then it fits one meaning of mental illness. For mass hysteria, evidence can be found in claims of visions such as the sightings of Mary and the sun dancing around, as claimed by tens of thousands of pilgrims to Fatima, Portugal, on October 13, 1917, following earlier apparitions reported by the shepherd girl Lucia Santos and her two cousins. Similar claims have been made by visitors to Lourdes, France, and in Medjugorje, Bosnia and Herzegovina, among others.

Let's admit that few people go so far as to see the saints. More often, people get themselves profoundly mired in cognitive dissonance, a term outlined in the 1950s by psychologist Dr. Leon Festinger. This is the ability to convince ourselves to maintain two divergent views at the same time. In the case of Judeo-Christian beliefs it is the ability to believe (there is that word again that I do not like) — in the religious statements that Jesus can walk on water, raise the dead, cure leprosy, and that floating ax heads, sticks becoming snakes, snakes becoming sticks, talking snakes and donkeys, people turned into a pillar of salt, women made from a man's rib, virgin birth, pushing back the Red Sea and other discordant beliefs are true, when we all know that based on the laws of physics, chemistry and biology, they are all patently false.

It is the same concept by which children state that a special favorite toy is really not interesting or fun to play with when they are denied access to the toy. They discount or reduce the value to them. By the same token, someone who is ardently concerned with animal care and who is opposed to circuses and zoos is also an avid hunter, knowing full well that not every shot can be a kill shot and that some animals do suffer from his or her hunting.

In Aesop's *The Fox and the Grapes*, we see that when people want something that they can't, they may try to reduce the mental conflict by trying to convince themselves they do not want it after all. In this fable, the fox spies some grapes hanging from a high vine and wants some to quench his thirst. He cannot reach them and, after trying many times, decides that the grapes are either sour or not ripe and thus are of no value. It is cognitive dissonance in that he convinces himself that he does not want the grapes that he really desired very much.

Belief and faith have nothing to back them up. There is no proof of a God, no proof of anything that would, could, should or will back up and define faith, belief and prayer. Science, knowledge and facts are factual and known because our senses know that they are real, that they are provable and have been tested and proven by experts in a particular field of study. Facts, knowledge and constant testing are proof over and over again that science works. Science moves forward — religion retreats. Religion fails; religion proves nothing. Even beyond our senses we are proving things through the technology that mankind has developed over the years.

Copernicus and Galileo proved things about the cosmos through their development and use of telescopes. Microscopes proved the existence of microbes described by Leuwenhoek while electron microscopes of today prove even more in the microscopic and unseen world of bacteria, microbes, viruses and such. As a society, we know these things.

The sad thing is that people play hop scotch with religion, God and the Bible to conjure up all sorts of ideas and ideals as to why religion works, how God works, how God answers our prayers. Think of this critically and you realize that this is all an act, a fiction, a misuse of intelligence and a misunderstanding of facts, science and knowledge.

With science, we can figure out the facts of something and make it work for our world today. That does not mean that we have a definitive answer for everything. For example, we can't know a final answer for the mathematical constant of *pi*. The simple 3.14159, etc., is close enough to enable us to figure out the circumference of a circle when we know the diameter. It is an irrational number — one that has no end. Thus, while it has by computer been taken out to two trillion decimal points, there is still no end. Similarly, we do not know all the answers to string theory, the cosmos, black holes, or even light.

By the same token, people conjure up religious reasons as to why their prayers are answered, as to why their wishes are fulfilled, why good things and religious things happen. But this is merely conjecture, and no different from the concepts of early man. Nick Harding in his book *How to Be a Good Atheist*, points this out with the example of a primitive hunter. The primitive hunter, he postulates, throws a stone in a pool of water and a deer shows up on the bank which can be shot with his bow to provide food for his family and tribe. He concludes it must be because of the thrown stone, and thus a stone must be thrown into the water each time when starting to hunt.

All sorts of myths like this abound in primitive cultures. We know and man always knew that sometimes the sun was shining and sometimes it rained. And primitive man probably figured out fairly rapidly that the rain caused more growth in plants, with some of those plants good to eat and thus able to sustain people. Lacking rain for a certain period of time, perhaps some members of a tribe danced in an effort to please the rain gods and to cause those rain gods to release the needed rain. Of course, with rain occurring naturally anyway, at some point in time it would rain again. This time table could be hours, days or sometimes weeks, but it would rain. But in the mind of primitive peoples, it became necessary to dance to cause rain to grow crops and plants to have food to eat. Certainly, this was religion.

Primitive man knew that he needed the sun for warmth, and also to make crops grow. Thus, it was necessary to keep the sun and the sun gods happy. Since the sun was pulled across the sky from morning to evening by sun gods and a chariot (different stories along this line have emerged) it was necessary to worship the sun god and to keep him or her happy. At some point in time a solar eclipse would occur, blackening the sun for a short time and scaring the beJesus out of the assembled society and reinstituting the practice

(whatever it was) of honoring and worshiping the sun god. Maybe that practice would be throwing a virgin into a volcano, doing a sun dance, sacrificing
a newborn child as a burnt offering, killing a goat, or reading the entrails
of a sacrificial lamb. This was of course during a geocentric period when
people "knew" that the sun traveled across the sky (long before Copernicus
and Galileo) and thus that gods were involved and had to be kept happy.

Somebody prays to god or God or Jesus because a relative is sick or injured or diseased, and in time the relative gets well, or better. "Praise be to
God! God did it! God is wonderful! God is merciful. God is good!" Forget
about any help or praise to any medical staff involved.

Of course, if the patient dies, then there is another answer that conveniently gets God completely off the hook. "God needed him/her more than
we did." "God has a special place for him/her in heaven." "Now she/he is in
a better place." "She/he is with God (Jesus, the Lord) today and held in the
comfort of his arms." "Fortunately, God has stopped his/her suffering and
taken him/her into his loving arms." "He/she has no more suffering — he/she
is with the Lord."

This is a great deal for God. God gets all the "attaboys" if the patient lives
or does well. God does not get the "bad dog" scolding if the patient dies or
the operation goes south. He still gets the 'attaboys'. You can't beat a deal
like that.

The oddity of all this is that Christians living in a modern world insist
on the FDA to test food and drugs, a good UL laboratory to check the table
lamps that we buy, an experienced DOT to check for rules of the road and
safety in trains, busses and automobile traffic, an effective FAA to check air
travel and airport safety, a CDC to check on diseases and their prevention
and possible stoppage of pandemics. We all want and Christians also insist
on those factors in modern life that protect us, save us from ourselves, guard
us from the unscrupulous practices of others and in short make life not just
bearable, but really livable, safe and hopefully comfortable in the world in
which we find ourselves.

And yet, were I to seriously describe to a close friend walking on water, picking a floating axe head off the surface of the water, watching some
friends (Shadrach, Meshach and Abednego) walk out of a fiery furnace, see
a woman turned into a pillar of salt, describe turning a snake into a stick or
any or a few dozen more fanciful tales of nonsense, my friends would undoubtedly arrange with my wife to have me immediately committed to the
nearest mental hospital.

Evangelical preacher John W. Loftus, in his book *Why I Became an Atheist*
(written after he switched teams, naturally), describes in detail the obvious
conflict of believing in fanciful tales, miracles and impossibilities from the

Bible while still maintaining a sense of common sense and living in a modern world in everyday life.

If Christians want anybody to truly believe or accept anything, they are going to have to do better. By better, I mean that they are going to have to do something. Something is better than nothing. There is no proof for the historicity of the Bible in the modern facts and evidence of archeology or through any written evidence outside of the Bible. Using only the base book of anything as a "proof," I can "prove" that there really is a stuffed bear that talks as per Winnie the Pooh, talking cats and dancing teapots as per Alice in Wonderland, a Wicked Witch of the West and a cowardly lion as per the Wizard of Oz, a Santa sliding down chimneys to leave gifts, a talking rabbit in the briar patch as per the Uncle Remus. Oh, you say, that is just fiction, a fanciful tale for children. That's fine for children. But we adults, thinking as adults, know that these stories do not hold up in real life. We should also know that the puffery, pixie dust and magic of the Bible do not hold up to the slightest scrutiny. Think seriously, solidly and critically, and you have to know that the so called facts, miracles, stories, reports and chronology of the Bible just can't be true and are not true.

We know that prayer — a mainstay of almost all religions and especially Christianity — DOES NOT WORK. The fact that Christians do not demand scientific tests of prayer is in essence a de facto acceptance by them that they cannot prove the value or efficacy of prayer in any way, shape or form. There are no miracles. A miracle by definition has to have occurred by some other-worldly event, from a deity, through a god or something that is a result outside of normal possible causes. We know that all the miracles ascribed by laymen, ministers, priests, the media and the like are nothing more than improbable marvels or coincidences. They are not miracles.

If the goal of Christianity is to worship God, it fails miserably. There is no proof of a God, god or gods any more than there is proof of dragons, unicorns, leprechauns, fairies, trolls, elves, or gremlins. You obviously can't prove the reality of any of these made-up creatures and you can't prove the existence of the equally fictional God or god or gods.

CHAPTER 21. A CURE FOR CHRISTIANITY — CONCLUSION

So — is there a cure for Christianity? Well, there is, but how you view this depends. You might already have your answer to this, with either a total rejection of everything written in the previous pages or by a total understanding of the questions posed and answers (non-answers) stated or suggested. You might have a little of each — rejection of some things in this book and acceptance of others. For example, you might accept the idea that there are contradictions in the Bible that are troublesome, that some physical acts are impossible, but still think that faith and prayer kindda, sortta almost work, sometimes, or now and again.

If you have started with a clean slate by which to think, analyze, consider and compare, you have a head start on most people. You have the mechanism of critical thinking by which to study religion, specifically Christianity. If you did not start with a clean slate, then in the text and chapters above you may find obstacles everywhere, conflicts with what you have been taught and how you have been brainwashed. You might also have problems in believing what is in this book or in not believing what revered priests, ministers, rabbis, pastors and parents have told you. After all, if you find the truth in what has been written here, you might not go to heaven. But then again, there might not a heaven or a hell. You have to believe, so you might think, in the fiction of the faith and the codes of the Church if you want eternal life. Despite strong evidence to the contrary, you may still affirm and believe the myths of the past as taught in Sunday School. If so, go back and read this book again. And this time, start with an open mind, willing to accept evidence, facts and nothing else. Read other books, as suggested in the bibliography for more information and details on these subjects.

If your views are negative to the book contents, you may be just like the views of the priests of the Vatican during the early to mid-1600s at the time of Galileo.

Galileo saw things that no one else had ever seen before such as the craters and mountains on the moon and later the movement of the several moons around Jupiter. It was the movement of these moons that caused Galileo to realize that the universe was not a static stationary place as perceived and stated by the Catholic Church, but a place in which planets and other cosmological bodies moved. This led to Galileo's ultimate proof that our solar system was not geocentric (earth centered) — as insisted upon by the Pope and Church — but heliocentered (our sun as a center around which planets, including the earth, moves).

Galileo showed this proof to cardinals of the Vatican when he was charged with heresy and blasphemy, allowing them to look through his telescope and to view the moving moons and to check his calculations as to the moon movements. The cardinals, so brainwashed with Biblical dogma of the church, could physically see what Galileo was describing (they could not avoid it), but they would not and could not mentally or psychologically accept this, and thus denied Galileo's proof. They were in a state of complete denial or cognitive dissonance, just as Christians today are also in these states when it comes to any proof or evidence against the concepts of the Bible or the Judeo-Christian religions.

Those who do not use critical thinking are subject to mental house arrest of their faculties. There can be no cure for Christianity if you do not allow yourself to look at true facts and to accept truth and evidence — however it falls — as facts and science dictate. There can be no clarity of thought without rejecting thoughts of fictional tales such as those of Santa Claus, Peter Rabbit, Winnie-the-Pooh, and yes, the Bible.

Listen to reason, facts, science, testing, experimental results, logic and common sense. If those work for anything you are considering and studying, you are on the right tract. If it ends up differently because a minister or the Pope say it or C. S. Lewis wrote about it, or Benny Hinn on TV announced it or that it is in the Bible, watch out. You are probably on your way to being scammed and conned; sold a bill of goods, a bunch of bull or a bottle of snake oil.

Realize that this book covers just the tiniest tip of the biggest iceberg in terms of religion and Judeo-Christian studies. The brief bibliography includes some additional books to help you continue religious studies.

Is there a cure for Christianity? You bet. Let's see what we have from previous pages. We know the basics of Christianity. These are both simple and complex. These are simple, since it boils down to the comments of John 3:16, often seen on signs at baseball and football games by the religiously faithful in trying to sell their message that Christ is the answer to the world's problems. All are trying to sell you Jesus. John 3:16 reads, "For God so loved the world that he gave his one and only son, that whoever believes in him shall not perish but have eternal life."

This, according to Christian scripture, is the basis of all Christian religion. Naturally, Christians are perfectly willing to adjust, modify, delete, explain, add and subtract to other verses as they cherry pick their way through the Bible to choose those verses that tend to prove their point or attempt to disprove the facts of skeptics. Naturally they also ignore or change those verses or comments that do not prove their point. But remember — you can have your own opinion, but you can't have your own facts.

In many cases — most cases really — religion gets very complex, as per the many sects, cults, divisions and diversions among basic Christian denominations. Thus, you can find many varying beliefs of Baptist, Methodist, Presbyterian, Lutheran, Episcopalian, Eastern Orthodox, and Catholic. You can also find multiple variations among lesser Christian religions such as Mormon, Scientology, Amish, Jehovah's Witnesses, Seventh Day Adventists, Christian Scientists, Pentacostals, and others.

In some cases, there are different views of the Bible. With many Catholics and Catholic priests, the Old Testament is marginalized with most of the emphasis being on the aspects of Christ and Christ's life as outlined and covered in the New Testament. At the opposite extreme, many fundamentalist, evangelical and TV churches consider the entire Bible as written and translated to be the absolute factual inerrant word of God, to be read and accepted exactly — literally — as written.

To read this Bible literally is why — sadly — many people in this country including political and educational leaders are so far behind in science. To read the Bible exactly as God's writing and Word, you have to "believe" in the creationist nonsense, an earth-centered (geocentric) universe, an earth no older than 6,000 years, man and dinosaurs living side by side and the principles of the Flat Earth Society. To accept as truth the beliefs of the Stone Age is patently ridiculous.

If we look at the background of Biblical texts and books, we find that the belief that they were written by God is a circular argument with God stating that he wrote the Bible and the Bible stating that God is God. We also find that even without the problems of translations and the various changes in meanings of words, punctuation, spacing, paragraphs, and the like we do not have any originals of the important Matthew, Mark, Luke and John New Testament gospels. We also find that these writings, even with scraps and copies, are not always the first inviolate words of civilization, but often only plagiarized documents from early writings of other peoples such as found in the Epic of Gilgamesh that earlier records the flood story of Genesis. The Code of Hammurabi has just under 300 laws, covering the Ten Commandments, and much that is outlined in Leviticus. For a real comparison with your Bible and for your critical thinking, download from the Internet the Epic of Gilgamesh and the Code of Hammurabi.

We also have to consider that a Bible is a religious book and as such should be one to promote peace, harmony, humanity, tolerance, and all the other good societal traits along with the worship of the particular God of that religion. In Christianity you do not find this, or you only find bits and pieces of this along with large sections of intolerance, evil, hatred, killing, immorality, violence, death, torture, and Draconian rules, laws and punishments. Reading about Passover leads many to think of the wonder of God in convincing the Pharaoh to release the Israelites from their bondage. But you must also think of the first born of Egypt — all innocents — who are killed by God (Exodus 12:29) and who had no part in the Pharaoh's acts. If you use the generally accepted figure of an Egyptian population of 3.5 million, and a family of five offspring, then perhaps 20 percent of these — or 700,000 innocent Egyptians would be first born and killed by God's directive to free the Israelites.

Read the book of Joshua and you can marvel at God finally giving the Israelites the land which was promised to Moses with Joshua and later Joseph leading the Jews into this land of Canaan. Of course this was not vacant land, but land that had been occupied perhaps for hundreds if not thousands of years by the Canaanites and other tribes including Israelites. But you must also recoil in horror at God through orders to Joshua insisting that all of the citizens of the 31 named cities in this chapter being put to the sword and killed. This included every single person, young and old, male and female being killed so that the Israelites can steal Canaanite land.

There is also the problem of how this religion of Christianity fits into the world around us, and how it deals with and compares with others in this world. For example, the concept of a three-in-one God, a Trinity of God, Jesus (son) and Holy Ghost (spirit) does not fit well into any thinking and is not easily if ever explained or understood by any seriously thinking individual. That, combined with angels which as per the Bible were often described as "gods" (Exodus 23:20) makes this early Israelite religion henotheistic, not monotheistic. Monotheism is not mentioned in the Bible until Isaiah.

Christianity in society and how it fits into the morals, ethics, mores and folkways of our society also leaves huge gaping holes and questions. In studies done and polls taken, those states that are part of the Bible belt or smack in the middle of religious conviction and Christian fervor are always those states (often south or mid-west) that have the highest and worst results on child abuse, spousal abuse, murder, robbery, theft, animal abuse, illiteracy, gambling addiction, alcoholism, divorce, adultery, petty crime, school drop-out rates, teenage pregnancy, out-of-wedlock pregnancy, health problems, and drug use.

Those states with more liberal views, more accepting of homosexuality, more tolerant of abortion rights, less adherence to religion, lower church attendance, have the higher standards of societal tolerance, acceptance, morality and ethics than religious states. The people in these states are less religious but better people than Christians.

Look at the United Nations figures on standards of literacy, health, life span, schooling, income, pregnancy, divorce, domestic abuse, women's rights, and tolerance of others, and you find the religious countries at the bottom of the list with the most crime and abuse. The less religious, less believing, non-believing or more atheistic countries such as Canada, Norway, Australia, Sweden, Netherlands and other northern European countries are at or near the top of the list for human rights, women's rights, reduced crime statistics, better education, and greater tolerance for all, individual rights and higher incomes.

Look also at how Christianity and other religions also have held back mankind in so many ways. The idea of the Jews as a "chosen people" of the Old Testament only promotes hostility. Any such "chosen people" concept is obviously biased, prejudicial and wrong. The concept of Christianity and even specific cults and sects of Christianity being "the only true religion" also promotes the seeds of hostility ending with the tens of thousands of women burned at the stake as witches during the Dark and Middle Ages and tens of thousands of apostates tortured under the auspices of the Catholic Church and the early Protestant religions after Reformation of 1517 and Martin Luther.

"Witches are the whores of the Devil, which is why they must all be killed," was one famous but little known statement of Luther. His works, particularly his writings *On the Jews and their Lies* was used as a blueprint for the genocidal action by the Nazi Third Reich some 400 years later in their treatment and killing of Jews and others. Perhaps partly because of Luther, Hitler in his speeches and writings (*Mein Kampf*) was sure that he was doing God's work in killing Jews.

Do you really want to be aligned with the Christian religion with its feeble attempt at a three-in-one god, lack of morals and ethics, blanket condemnation of others as per Martin Luther and similar "reformers," with all of this trying to force Christianity down the throats of those who do not want it? Do you really want to be associated with a religion with the "convert or die" philosophy of Constantine?

Do you really want to be associated with Christianity which has tried to steal morals and ethics from society in general (both were here with primitive man long before any religion), while erroneously painting itself as the bastion of goodness, moral standards and societal improvement?

When we consider the Christian religion, we also find that the Bible is man-made. This starts with the concept of church as a plotted out, patterned rite that must contain certain elements, including of course, the tithing to church pastors preying on the praying parishioners, all of which keeps the Ponzi scheme of religion going. And yes, it is a Ponzi scheme.

A church is the best Ponzi scheme, since it gets money from believers for buildings, preachers, priests, missionary work (more sales pitches to innocents to further the Ponzi scheme), salaries, homes, boats, luxury cars and lavish life styles. The return to the original faithful only has to be the constant appearance and charade of care, love and the promise through belief of a wonderful afterlife — forever. You don't have to deliver anything — just promise. The afterlife is the carrot of the carrot-and-stick deal of heaven and hell. Promise and you are home free! You never — never — have to deliver anything! How much better could it be?

This continues with the rites, liturgy, church documentation, various creeds of belief (all man-made, man thought-out and man-written) such as the Nicene Creed, Westminster Confession, Catholic Catechism, and others, all made up and written long after the death of Jesus. The Westminster Creed for example was written in 1647 CE. The Nicene Creed was cobbled together in 325 CE. It was then also that the idea of the Trinity was crafted and only then approved. Parts of the Bible which are taken on faith include ideas such as "original sin." This "original sin" was not and is not mentioned anywhere in the Bible. It was considered by some including Augustine and was only totally accepted at the Second Council of Orange in 529 CE.

The ideas of grace, justification, redemption, conviction, mercy etc, are human and man-made concepts applied and redefined by men for the use of men believing and accepting these man-made concepts and conscriptions in life.

The Catholic Church rite of the Eucharist that the host or the bread or cracker and the juice or wine actually becomes the real, honest-to-God (no pun intended) true biological body and blood of Christ is obviously a man-made concept, and a disgusting one at that. It hints of cannibalism. No wonder Jehovah's Witnesses get upset with the idea of blood transfusions.

Why people believe in what they believe is somewhat of a mystery. It is that religion is embedded into culture, that we learn it at a susceptible age when it is taught to us by our parents, whom we trust. We tend to put beliefs into a totally separate category than our skepticism and acceptance — if that — of other aspects of life.

Parents have a lot of influence in all of this and have a lot of explaining to do. Did you as a little boy or girl, consider yourself a Republican or Democrat? Most likely, you were — or thought that you were — whatever your parents proclaimed for their political party.

Did you when small or under age look forward to the time when you could legally at least, go to a bar and enjoy a beer, or were you appalled by the recreational use of alcohol in any form? Regardless of your choice, it was probably a result of the beliefs and habits of your parents. Perhaps your parents were Baptists, Mormons, or another religious group deliberately avoiding and perhaps condemning alcohol.

You can go on and on with choices that are not so much choices as a result of home, family, community and parental likes and dislikes. If you had been born in Pakistan or Afghanistan would you likely have the Christian religion in which you profess absolute belief? Of course not — you would most likely be a Muslim and quite faithful in your religion. If you were born in India, you would most likely be a Hindu, as were your parents.

Miracles are another mainstay of religion. Of course if you want to state that your dog finding its way home after being out all night is a miracle, then you don't understand the meaning of the word. A miracle, according to dictionary definitions, is something that cannot be explained by normal or natural means, and which can only be attributed to the act of some deity.

The problem is that Christians never consider the possibility of coincidences and improbabilities meeting and intersecting at the same time and place. Just as bad things can happen in life, so can good things. But they are all coincidences, not a deliberate act by God or a god. Does this blatant hopscotch of things randomly happening now and again really prove a religion or Christianity? Does it prove God or Jesus?

In addition to the impossibility of miracles happening, we looked also at the various physical impossibilities of the Bible. The earth starting some 6,000 years ago (October 23, 4004 BCE) as counted backwards by Bishop Ussher (born 1581 died 1656) and printed in the Bible does not jive with the facts of geology and cosmology. Science though geology and cosmology has shown us that the earth is about 4.5 billion years old, with life starting at about 3.4 billion years ago, give or take a few hundred million years.

The idea of a worldwide flood that covered all the mountains over a 40 day period would mean that rain or springs would be raising water at a rate of 30 feet three inches per hour, 24 hours a day for 40 days. It would mean that to load two of each species (assuming the animals were lined up, tamed and ready to be loaded) would take about 4 years, assuming a bare minimum of two million land-living species on earth. And that is assuming loading pairs of animals at a rate of one pair per minute, around the clock.

Couple that with the size of the ark and the fact that there would be ¾ of a cubic foot for each pair of animals. That's maybe OK for bees and fruit flies, but quite a problem for elephants, wolves, polar bears and elk. And how did all those worldwide creatures get to the mid-east anyway, to get loaded onto the ark? How did North American elk get across the Atlantic and to the Mid-East? How did a South American sloth, zipping speedily along at a mile a month, get to the Mid-East in time for the ark sailing date?

Do you really want a religion and a belief that paints marvelous happenings of faith when they are totally unproven and outside of the physical possibilities of our life in the realm of mathematics, physics, chemistry and biology?

Even without the impossibilities of the Bible, there are the immoralities and the outright evil of God in wantonly, whimsically, and constantly killing innocents. There is no tolerance — no love, no care, no concern for fellow mankind — which perhaps is why civilizations were faced hundreds of years later with the Inquisition in which individuals were burned at the stake those for blasphemy or heresy, of burning 50,000 or more women thought to be witches. And all of this can be directed squarely at God or man's belief in his God. It is all sick and a vivid example of the evil of God, the Christian God and Jesus, and the sickness of Christianity and of Christians in accepting this evil as from a deity.

Do you really want to believe in an evil God? Can you even accept, like or approve of the evilness of this Christian God? Do you really want to worship a God who kills innocents — men, women, children, babies, pregnant women, old men and widows?

Contradictions in any document or article should leave one with a lot of questions about the authenticity and accuracy of any such work. That being the case, it should make the Bible highly questionable for any thinking person. In any field, you can't say one thing or prove one thing and then immediately or later say the exact opposite.

The Internet if full of sites that outline the many contradictions and errors of and in the Bible. Writers have written detailed books that point out the errors of the Bible and the sheer awfulness of Christianity. Naturally, with Christians playing hop-scotch around the Bible, readers and the faithful conjure up (there is no other word that fits so well) explanations, different meanings of words and faulty translations to explain the unexplainable. In many cases you get from the Christian apologists the simple explanation along the lines of "that is really not the way that it (a given section) is supposed to be read" or "that's not what the gospel writer meant," or "you can't look at it from our standpoint — you have to look at it from God's standpoint — and we can't determine his ultimate goals and God's goodness."

Sure, and if I had two wheels, I would be a bicycle. All these things are a way of trying to explain away what something means to make it sound better when it is impossible to do so. No one among Christians wants to touch a word of John 3:16 which points to God giving the world Jesus and that salvation and heaven only come from believing in Jesus. However, everyone wants to change Luke 14:26 in which Jesus says (in a direct quote, if we can believe direct quotes) that you to follow Jesus, you must hate your parents, your wife or husband, your brothers and sisters and your children. Want to hate anybody or everybody, especially your blood relatives? Want to hate in this childish religion of supposed love and kindness? Want to explain how something said in the Bible does not mean what it says when compared to another verse?

Prayer has always been important in both Judaism and Christianity, but falls short of fulfilling the stated reasons for prayer. In valid tests that have been done on prayer, prayer always fails. Prayer is not provable. When positive, prayer results are no more than chance. One would think that noting the importance of prayer in churches, life, prayer meetings (that's why they call them prayer meetings) that Christians would be clamoring to have prayer tested, to prove to the world and the scores of unbelievers that prayer does work, that prayer to God is answered, that God works wonders through honest and persistent prayer. But no, Christians do not insist on this, various denominations and delusions do not insist on a scientific study of prayer and believers do not run control groups

The Ten Commandments are also a biggie for Christians, even though they appear in the Old Testament, in Exodus. But to look at these critically, you have to realize that only three of the big ten are applicable to law and modern society rules. These are the ones on killing, stealing and lying or serving as a false witness. This latter of course only applies to courts (it should apply to everything as per perjury and appearing before a judge). The first four about God are only examples of an obviously weak, man-made insecure God with serious self-esteem issues wanting to make sure that he is the best god, and on top in the God or god contest.

Do you really want a series of absolute, carved in stone (literally, some would say), definitive rules that leave out some big violations of societal rule, with 40 percent of these on protecting an imaginary insecure God who has serious self-esteem issues?

Eternity with the heaven and hell the carrot and stick are the unknown and unproven reward and the impossible punishment of Christian religion. These are the candy and the bludgeon by which to brainwash and frighten small children and to allow the priesthood to continue to prey on the adult prayers (the persons) to filch these payers of earnings under the guise of religion and tithing, and the impossible thought that all the money is going to God. And what would God, if he/she got it, do with all this wealth?

There is no proof of heaven; there is no proof of hell; there is not one tiny scrap of evidence that either one exists. If so, when did they and when did the soul required for this nonsense evolve into developing primates that over seven million years ultimately became man? Why are Near Death Experiences nothing more than a fanciful myth and wishful thinking?

Prophecy is another biggie in the Christian religion, with this particularly evident now with the TV charlatans who are prophesying about the end times that are almost upon us. Or so they say. They point to the terrible times of today that are supposedly mentioned in the Bible in Revelation, not realizing or talking about terrible times with the Huns and Visigoths invading Europe, Hannibal crossing the Alps in conquest of Rome, the Inquisition, witch trials, the Christian Crusades against the Muslims, the Black Death plague, wars that raged through and ravaged Europe, the dicey-until-the-end American Revolution, the American Civil War, World War I, World War II, Korea, the 1850–1864 Tai Ping Rebellion based on Christianity in which 20 million Chinese were killed, Cambodia and Pol Pot, Stalin and the 20 million killed by him in Russia; Vietnam, Alexander the Great against Persia's Darius. OK, you can take out the few before the 1st century CE since Jesus was not around then to save us. But Jesus and his possible(?) return have been postulated since then, and no one has done much serious prophesying until now when we have TV and credit cards and the ability to extort money from the gullible and those terminally believing in Biblical nonsense.

Do you want a TV religion that can tell you nothing other than where to send your money, or how to call with your credit card information to give to the preacher — oh sorry — to God?

That religion has held back science through the ages — or tried valiantly to hold back science — is without question. Whether that science was early or late, correct, slightly off-key, religion and Christians have tried to excoriate it and to demand through punishments that include burning at the stake the "rightness" of religion and the evil, heresy and blasphemy of science in denying that religion. Those believing the Bible literally are the worst of this batch of thieves for stealing the future from the rest of us and mankind, and trying to hold on with all their might and stake-burning zeal to the superstitions of the past.

After the potato of the South American Andes was introduced to Europe in the late 1500s, the clergy rejected it. The religious argument, especially in France, declared that since the potato was not mentioned in the Bible, it could only be the handiwork of the devil. Because of the odd shape of early wild potatoes, it was compared to a leper's hand and was suspected of causing leprosy. In France, some clergy preached that it was a sin to eat a potato. Do you really want to believe in a religion that once held such beliefs and was so attuned to the literal interpretation of the Bible that they would reject anything else, despite the fact that the Incas had developed many potato varieties and had eaten it since at least 5000 BCE?

Currently, we have since 1859 and Charles Darwin's work *The Origin of Species*, continued embattlements and retrenching by religion into the nonsense of Genesis instead of the proven facts of evolution and science. The battle goes on today with Christians wanting creationism and it's modern cousin Intelligent Design to be taught as science in schools, despite the fact that is all fable and folly, lacking even a shred of science. In addition, the Christian religion wants to stop and condemn all possibility of stem cell research despite the fact that these left over embryos are from fertilization clinics (often endorsed and applauded by the Christianists). These Christians want to create fertilized embryos for their own use and selfish purposes. If you can't have kids, did you ever think that maybe, just maybe, your God was telling you to not have kids? Naturally, the excess fertilized embryos are thrown away and thus going into the sewer instead of a science lab where they might help doctors and scientists possibly develop cures and aids for many diseases.

Do you want to be associated with a religion or statement of beliefs that applauds and works for the disposal and tossing in the trash heap biological tissue that could benefit mankind? Do you want to be part of a backward-thinking, superstitious crowd that insists that they are right — without evidence — and that science is wrong?

Among the more disgusting elements of the Christian religion is the idea of faith healing. This is the ridiculous idea that laying on of hands, using anointing oils, prayer, prayer chains, baths, and fasting, with prayers and supplications to God or Jesus or the Holy Spirit will cure a designated party of a particular disease or affliction. It just is not true. Certainly there is no question that a patient's mental attitude can play a big role in their recovery. This applies to both a good mental attitude and a bad mental attitude to the religious and non-religious alike. Caribbean believers in voo-doo with a "hex" on them often strongly believe that they are going to die. Some have been taken to top medical institutions in the US, examined thoroughly, found to have no debilitating illness, but they die anyway. Such is the power of the mind. The same can have a positive effect whether praying to God or a spark plug or a McDonald's Happy Meal, provided that the prayer is honest and sincere. Most likely, those prayers to God or a god will be more sincere than those to a spark plug or Happy Meal. The positive effect of any positive feeling and buoyed mental attitude can be an aid in healing, but it will not cure a disease. You can't pray or do anything in the superstition field to get rid of cancer, diabetes, glaucoma, kidney disease, Alzheimer's, gangrene, cirrhotic liver, gout, gall stones, gingivitis, strokes, heart attacks, irritable bowel syndrome, blood clots, muscular dystrophy, multiple sclerosis, Parkinson's disease or any of the thousands of additional diseases and illnesses. And as atheist Sam Harris once said, you can have a billion Christians pray that a specific given named amputee grow a new limb. It will not happen. Yet salamanders can regrow a limb and do so without the benefit of prayer.

This praying and faith healing by a preacher or a church or a family is particularly egregious when it comes to juveniles. Families and their churches (almost always fundamentalist churches) will pray and lay hands or do something else equally ridiculous to save a child from a terrible disease. In many or most cases, these are diseases that could be alleviated or cured by standard medicine and medical science, but which cause death or crippling results to the child with the superstition of religion and Christianity. In some cases, the child, brainwashed by the parents and the church, wants this faith healing in place of standard medical treatment. However, no child has rights to refuse treatment if the parent wants it. Unfortunately, in some states and jurisdictions, religionists are given a pass on this if they can state or prove that faith healing or prayer is a tenant, doctrine or dogma of their religious belief. That's sad, since prosecutors should prosecute parents and pastors practicing faith healing as medicine. Laws should be written to jail them for this act of violence against children.

Do you really want to buy into a religion or idea in which the ridiculous act of some faith will cure somebody of something? Do you really want to throw out the centuries and decades of medical research, study, experiments, practice and such with proven results and instead substitute a primitive superstition?

Larcenous Christianity comes with preachers and pastors anywhere — but mostly on TV — extorting money from the poor, gullible and superstitious. These con artists misuse verses from the Bible to prove the validity of their extortion scheme. They reference verses that talk about "planting your seed" "sowing what you will later reap," "the multiple returns of your seed planting from God," "planting what you want to reap." This last is particularly egregious since they make the point that you only reap what you sow. Sow money and you get — wait for it — money! Some have even gone to the extent of pointing out that you have to sow a lot. Plant one kernel of corn and you get one corn plant — if you are lucky and the corn kernel does not die from too much or little sun or water. This is the so-called relatively recent "prosperity religion" "prosperity Christianity" and "God really, really wants you to get rich" religion.

This is sick, evil and those extorting and conning money from the poor and gullible are often buying the most expensive clothes and shoes, living in one (or more) huge expensive mansions, driving the most expensive cars, traveling in privately owned or leased jets, and often with their family or friends on the payroll with huge salaries also. Naturally, these charlatans do not "own" any of these riches — their ministry does, so that they are "poor" also and so that the ministry does not have to pay taxes on their ill-gotten gains and riches. That means of course, that the rest of us — non-believers, atheists, agnostics and the like — are by default supporting those with whom we have no interest or belief.

Do you really want to send money to those who are taking advantage of people in the same way that a Carney working a game in a circus side show takes your money? Do you really want to affiliate yourself with those who are doing this to others, even if you are not buying this three-card Monte trick? Do you really think that you will get a magical huge return from God for the money that you send to these thieves?

But let's summarize:

• The Bible is weak in all proven historical ways and devoid of most provable historical facts.

• The Biblical archeological record of major events of the Israelites is weak, non-existent or disproves Biblical claims.

• The Bible record and external record of the acts of Jesus or events surrounding him is virtually non-existent, even among those meticulous record keepers, the Romans.

• Any Bible records and external records of the movements and migrations of early Israelites are completely lacking.

• During Jesus time, the mid-East was filled with magicians, seers, miracle workers, of which Jesus was only one. Some 400 "messiahs" were killed — crucified — in one year in the Jerusalem area.

• There are no miracles in the dictionary meaning of an event caused by a God and outside of normal natural causes. Those with your hands up and wanting to offer up as example the parting of the Red Sea, the Egyptian plagues, the deaths of first born Egyptians, Daniel in the fiery furnace, a talking donkey and snake, a floating iron axe head, Jesus walking on water, the virgin birth of Jesus or more, remember that you have to have proof. There were no past Biblical miracles, since those were only "proven" by those of primitive societies and of tribal nomads just out of the Stone Age who were susceptible to magical explanations.

• Prayer does not work. Double blind scientific tests have shown this. Ironically, considering the importance of prayer, Christians always back away from and never insist on scientific proofs of prayer.

• Faith healing does not work. This has been proven over and over again, sadly often through the court system where parents are tried and often jailed for killing their children by not getting them standard medical treatment and instead relying on the myth of faith healing

• "Prosperity gospel" whereby parishioners "give to God" (really a TV charlatan) with the idea of reaping in money to a ten-fold or hundred-fold benefit does not work. Scientific tests could be easily done on this, but have not been tried to date.

• There is no Biblical heaven. There is no proof, there are no facts about it, there is no evidence, and the Near Death Experiences of some are complete fakes or of a phenomenon not yet understood by science.

• There is no Biblical hell. As with heaven, there is no proof. References to hell in the Bible are far fewer even than the references and non-evidence of heaven.

• Biblical prophecy is not a fact and is in fact a sham and often a scam. There is no accurate detailed evidence of anything in the past prophesied that has come to pass, and there is nothing that is detailed about the future that can be checked. The hundreds of prophecies by preachers of the second coming of Jesus, the end of the world, the Rapture, Tribulation, have all completely failed. The world did not end, Jesus did not return, we are all still here.

• Biblical religion holds us back constantly in competing in the fields of science. It constantly tries to hold on to past religious thought and edicts while rejecting the facts, truth and exploration of science into the future.

• Biblical texts are questionable at best, since they are only copies of copies of copies. No originals are available that would provide any proof of any Christian of Judaic religion. But even if we want or do believe in them as written and translated, hard core Christians twist them to their own purposes. One time I was in a Sunday school class studying Genesis. We were at the section on Lot and Sodom and Gomorrah (Genesis 19:1-38). The Bible clearly describes two angels visiting Lot when a crowd gathered outside of Lot's home to demand that he turn the two over to the crowd so they could have their way with them. The Bible says this about the situation. "They [the men in the crowd] called out to Lot, 'Where are the men (the angels) who came to you tonight? Bring them out to us so that we can have sex with them.'" "Lot went outside to meet them and shut the door behind him and said, 'No, my friends. Don't do this wicked thing. Look, I have two daughters who have never slept with a man. Let me bring them out to you, and you can do what you want with them. But don't do anything to these men, for they have come under the protection of my roof.'" The end result was that this offer of solicitation did not happen and that the angels, according to the Bible, turned the crowd blind so that they could not find Lot's home and break in.

The leader and Christians in this Sunday School class all excused this, claiming that since nothing happened, it made no difference and that Lot was still righteous in God's eyes. That is nonsense. The very fact of solicitation for illegal activity is in itself a crime against society's laws and any basic morality, regardless of the faulty thinking — or non-thinking — of Christians. Solicitation of prostitution or other illegal sexual activity, including adults or children is illegal. So is solicitation to commit murder, arson, robbery, mugging, extortion, bank robbery, home invasion, car theft, or any other major or minor crime. And that is true regardless of whether or not the crime is or was committed. The fact that Christians justify their thinking this way makes one wonder about their true thinking, their ability to think and to truly rationally consider options, and to lead moral lives. If they can justify Lot's perversion of offering his virgin daughters to strange men for their sexual pleasure in exchange for leaving him alone, what would Christians think of the options for punishments to the rest of us non-believers?

The direct quotes of Jesus in the New Testament are from writings begun some 20 to 90 years after the death of Jesus. The total number of Jesus quotes from Matthew, Mark, Luke and John respectively are 654, 277, 575 and 411. This alone makes them at the very least highly questionable as to accuracy and authenticity.

Most of the agreed-upon aspects of Christianity are man-made, and include nothing about religions, but only about man-made definitions, written creeds, confessions, edicts, dogma, discipline, doctrines, along with the rites and conditions of religious acts and services. Included are the special clothing and buildings ascribed to these acts and services. And yes, I am a Creationist. I do believe — no, I am sure — that man invented God.

* * *

Let's face it, with all the promises of Christianity, there is not one promise that has been fulfilled or can be proven to be fulfilled. There is not one prayer that has been or can be honestly answered. There is not one shred of evidence that prayer works. There is no provable evidence that there are or were miracles as defined by the dictionary (with a deity). There is only con-fusion and no proof of a heaven or a hell. There is no suggestion or any proof that "God is in control" of this earth and of us.

Are we talking about the right God here? Is this the God who could have saved twelve million lives — half of them — six million — God's "chosen people, the Jews"? Is this the same God who chose to do nothing about the Holocaust and the twelve million deaths that resulted from this crime to humanity?

Oh sure, you can get the pie-in-the-sky promise of a wonderful heaven or the awful punishment of hell, or God in control, but no one has ever proved that. It has never been proven that a belief in a fictional return to life and res-urrection of a wandering mooching shepherd/carpenter from the first cen-tury will somehow give you an automatic ticket into heaven. Examine life and religion and Christianity critically, and you will find that Christianity is a bag full of nothing, a list of empty promises, a stretch of the imagination, a box of bogus ideas, vacuum of anything and everything real. Stick with the reality of life for an honest, happy life — the one that we all have here and now. It is the only one that we have or can ever have. It is up to us to make the most of it.

AUTHOR'S BACKGROUND

This is a book based on an average person's common sense, thinking, and reading the literal messages of religion, the Bible and Christianity. The truth is that there is no truth, facts or logic to religion, Christianity, the Bible, or various beliefs of the various denominations. It is built on myths, primitive superstitions, and early beliefs often stolen from other pagan religions.

Christianity is just one more religion in a long list, then and now, of religions throughout history. Religion continues to have a hold on people through the carrot-and-stick promises and threats of the afterlife of heaven and/or hell. The irony, in this technological age in which we live, is that the absence of proof is considered an affirmation of faith in religion, while an absence of proof is considered an acknowledgement of failure in science. Do you want to sort of guess or do you really want to know?

I look upon religion as pixie dust involving the Tooth Fairy and superstition, a belief system that has cast a pall and dark shadow over the world for several thousand years and which continues to do so today. In my mind it is a combination of mental illness, mass hysteria and cognitive dissonance. I see, talk to, and associate with people who firmly believe in their religion, God, Jesus and Christianity — especially those of the fundamentalist and evangelical faiths. Often they are those truly deluded into the faith from a childhood brainwashing by their parents.

I strongly think that anyone over the age of seven who believes in an invisible friend needs some serious therapy, heavy medication or both.

I see religion as slowing the progress of mankind, of science, of fact finding, of useful discourse, of invention, and of honest evaluation of the world around us. I see Christianity as a 1st Century primitive superstition in a 21st Century technological world.

My continuing journey has taken me from a basic Baptist religion into which I was born to my current position as a severe and hard core atheist. Richard Dawkins in his book, *The God Delusion*, rates the religious and atheistic on a scale of 1 to 7. The rating of 1 would be a highly religious person, while a rating of 7 would be extremely atheistic. He rates himself in his book as a 6. I would rate myself as a 6-1/2 or 7. To avoid too much scorn, I often tell people that I am a born-again skeptic and evangelical cynic in and of all things religious.

The ride down religion lane started with my earliest introduction through my parents into a local Baptist church in Baltimore, MD, and has reached the level now of fulminating against the hypocrisy and delusion of religion of all forms, beliefs and sects. My earliest religious recollections were in Sunday school of the Baptist Church with simple lessons about the church, Christian belief, Jesus, the love of Jesus, the sacrifice of Jesus for us and forgiveness of our sins.

I did not realize then as a small child that the first indoctrination was through little nursery school songs of the type, "Jesus loves me, yes I know, for the Bible tells me so." I did not realize then that this was and is a circular argument. Where do we read about Jesus? In the Bible. What does the Bible say? It says that Jesus, the son of God, loves us. Thus, Jesus loves us. It says that Jesus and God gave us the Bible as a guide for our lives. And that guide says that God is God. You can't get more circular than that.

So say Christians: Are (or is it "is?") God and Jesus the same? Yes, they say pointing to the Trinity that includes the Holy Ghost or Holy Spirit. Does the Bible tell us that God and Jesus love us? Yes, they say. How do we know that there is a God? Because it is in the Bible, silly! Who wrote the Bible? Why God of course! It is all a circular argument of the Christians, pointing to their obvious answers, while obviously proving nothing.

I also remember my earliest religious experience, at least of a formal nature, in a Sunday School class. This occurred when I was about seven or eight. I remember it as clearly today as if it had happened yesterday. I was in the basement of the church where the Sunday School classes were held. I remember the face of the teacher, the faces of my half-dozen class mates, the general appearance of the classroom. I call it the chicken story.

"There was once a farmyard," the young male Sunday School teacher began, speaking softly in the classroom-like area. "And In this farmyard there was a chicken coop — a chicken house — (we were little — we might not have known what a coop was), where there were lots of chickens and their cute little baby chicks. 'Peep, peep, peep!' The little chicks were all saying.

They crowded around their Momma hen that was protecting them. They were all happy. Very happy. The momma hen was happy; the chicks were happy with their Momma protecting them. The hen was happy with her little chicks; the chicks were happy with their Mom. And then one day the chicken house caught on fire. It was a terrible, horrible fierce fire and this fire burned down the chicken house. It burned it completely to the ground.

"In this terrible fire, all the chickens were engulfed by flames and horribly burned and all were killed. And after the fire was out there was one chicken, seared and blackened by the flames, burned to death by the horrible fire. But with the fire extinguished, there was some movement of the burned wings of this horribly burned dead chicken. Out from under the stiff burned wings of this dead, blackened chicken came all of this chicken's — this hen's — little chicks. These little baby chicks were protected by the hen — their Momma — so that they would not burn up. They were safe.

"They survived — they were all OK. They were protected by their Mom. She protected them under her wings, even while she was being horribly burned up and killed. She gathered them under her wings so that even though she would be burned up and die, her little chicks would be saved. The hen chicken died in that horrible fire, but all those little chicks survived and were OK. They lived and their Momma saved them,

"See boys and girls — that is how Jesus Christ protects us. He died for our sins. He died on the cross to give us salvation and life. He gave up his life and was crucified 2,000 years ago so that he would save us through his gift of his blood and through our Salvation by our believing in him as our Savior. Because of his death, we will all go to heaven when we die if only we believe in him. We must believe in Jesus and that he is our savior, our Salvation to take us to heaven. He died for all our sins. Jesus Christ is just like that chicken in saving her little chicks. Jesus Christ has saved us — just like that momma hen saved those baby chickens — if we only believe. We have to believe in Jesus Christ and his saving grace to gain Salvation and go to heaven."

Say what? I was terribly upset. Terribly. It turned out that the simple little fable backfired on me. Even when I was little, I liked animals — barnyard animals, wild animals, pets, dogs, cats, raccoons, birds, fish, lions, ants, butterflies, fireflies, goats and yes, chickens. I liked all kinds of animals. I did not give a simple hoot about Jesus Christ dying on a cross, but I was terribly upset about that burned-up chicken. I still remember that day. And I am still upset about the chicken story, even though it was an obvious false fable to prove a fictional point about a fabled Jesus.

In a very real way my care and concern for the chicken and disinterest in Jesus made sense. It made sense then and makes sense now. That chicken — fictional or not — put itself on the line — put its life on the line — to protect its offspring — the baby chicks. In this fable, those baby chicks lived as a result of the direct and immediate action taken by the chicken. Or maybe it was just instinctual that the chicks ran under the wings of their mother hen.

The story about Jesus did not make any sense. Jesus did not do anything direct and immediate to save me, as the Sunday School teacher tried to insist. Jesus did not pull me from a burning building, losing his life in the process. He did not throw me out of the middle of the road with an oncoming bus during which he was crushed under the wheels. He did not dive into the water to give me his life preserver so that I could live, with him drowning in the process.

Sunday school lessons continued and with my increasing age they became more detailed, more complex, and included more stories and fables about and from the Old and New Testaments. These were and are the typical stories involving Moses, Abraham, Lot, Joseph, Joshua, Isaac, Noah, Adam, Eve, Cain, Abel, the Pharaoh and others. Naturally, I tried to believe, since I loved my parents and that is what my parents wanted for me. You try to follow the dictates and wishes of those who love and care for you.

And, as is traditional among Baptists, we reached a point of Sunday School study when we were being brainwashed, and educated about accepting Jesus Christ as our Savior and undergoing the Baptist (and some other religions) rite of immersion in water; Baptism. There was a special class for this, based on our age of about eleven or twelve at the time, and judged by the powers that be in the Baptist church as being an age at which children can logically, sincerely and carefully accept Jesus Christ as the Savior — their Savior — and thus guarantee entrance into heaven. We went through this course of several weeks or more, all leading up to the question of whether we would accept Christ right now or perhaps (certainly not encouraged) did not feel ready at the current time and wanted to wait.

The class of about a half dozen gleefully accepted Christ as their Savior and plans were made for an evening Baptism a Sunday or two hence. I think that they looked upon it as party time. These Baptisms were always held in the Baptismal font (a large bathtub type tank) in back of the pastor's lectern and at the rear of the podium of the church.

All of the class gleefully accepted except one. I declined, saying that I was "not ready." "Not ready" was accepted then as one who is still learning, not quite baked through and thus not ready for the import of this very serious moment that was to change my life forever.

"Don't want to — don't believe, now or ever" was not accepted and in fact was never in word, deed or intimation even suggested as a possible answer.

Those words are what I thought, but not at all what I would dare say. I wimped out. You WERE going to be a Baptist, a Believer, come hell or high water. It was just a question of WHEN you were going to come to your senses and decide that you MUST believe in Jesus Christ and ACCEPT this wonderful gift of Salvation and thus be absolutely GUARANTEED a place in heaven. There were NO exceptions. With the hard core cadre of adults all around expecting acceptance, along with my parents making all the appropriate excuses for me, it was even hard to say "not ready" but I did anyway. It seldom happened in this or any Baptist Church and I expect seldom happened in any church — Catholic, Episcopal, Lutheran, etc, in which a youthful (about age 11, 12 or 13) rite of passage and religious confirmation and conformation is standard fodder and expected fare. No exceptions.

The baptism in my particular church went as expected with the others of my class, all in their clean white clothes, getting dunked one at a time and then able to take their place with the adults of the church, partake of communion each month, and enjoy other intangible benefits. What benefits, I wondered? It was just like going from second class status to first class in the Boy Scouts. You got an attaboy, but not much else.

What happened next of course was a complete abandonment of my standards, ethics and principles under the parental pressure of the time. Casual questions from my Mom during the weeks following and around the dinner table were about not "if" but "when" I was going to join the church. There were offers of help, offers to answer any questions I might have had, even offers of involving the pastor to help answer my questions or help me make up my mind, reading suggestions (usually from the Bible). I had no questions. I perhaps should have had questions (I would today) but none occurred to me. I just did not give a lick about Jesus, heaven, hell, salvation, resurrection, redemption, God or anything else of the Christian faith.

Each Sunday in church, the service ended with the pastor inviting any and all who accepted "Christ as their Savior" to come forward, be accepted by the church body and later undergo the scheduled dunking required of this particular sect of Christianity. During each and every service at this appointed time, my mother, beside me in our pew, would look down expectantly and questioningly. It was sort of a downward look an emperor penguin would give its chick. Sometimes softly worded (my Mom, not the penguin), sometimes silently mouthed and sometimes just strongly suggested by body language was the question, "Are you ready to accept Christ today?" Nope, I wasn't. But little by little, I was being browbeaten into submission.

After about six months, I caved in. I caved in like a coal mine shaft with no roof supports. One Sunday, I wiggled my way past my Mom to the end of the pew, went down the center church aisle thinking that "This is ridiculous." I might have even been thinking, "This is baloney!" Externally if not internally, I accepted Jesus as my Savior, if you want to think of my head shaking "yes" while my mind was screaming "no." This sudden move down the aisle to the preacher was without any forethought or planning or real change of attitude on my part, or change of my ethics, principles and standards and without giving a hoot about my "I don't care" internal concern. Later, the baptism went as planned, my parents, especially my mom, beaming delightedly from their pew.

Of course, Mom told one and all that her son — her very special son — was just more intellectual, smarter, more studied, more cautious, more intelligent, more careful than others and thus, more a serious student of Christianity and obviously, a better Christian in the making. That, according to her, was the reason for my protracted time table before finally accepting Jesus.

Nah, I just didn't care. I just finally gave up putting off the inevitable and my principles caved. I guess that you could think of me as having no principles then but later in life having gained some principles and ethics to state to others my true thinking on religious matters. In cruder language, I grew a pair.

But at the same time, a strange thing happened. The embers of discontent and disbelief that perhaps started with the burned-chicken fable began to grow with more exposure to the religious society and church around me. I began to care more about the fact that I did not care at all about Jesus or about this or any other church. This did not land as an epiphany or great intellectual explosion in my life. It was just a gnawing constant and increasing awareness that in my mind, Christianity required a whole lot of suspension of belief, suspension of common sense, suspension of reality, suspension of the laws of physics, suspension of time and space, suspension of history, and suspension of the reality, truth, and facts of science. It was sort of a mental indigestion, a brain-spawned urge to vomit the fables of faith and the disbelief that I felt and knew.

When we are little, we rely upon our parents to guide us, protect us and teach us about life and the world. I just did not count on Mom and Dad inculcating me with a belief or "knowledge" system for which then or now there is no proof, no facts, no science. It is a sham, a superstition, a myth that has not yet died; it is pixie dust. As Christopher Hitchens said much later: "What can be asserted without evidence may also be dismissed without evidence."

And don't give me that circular argument again. I began to realize that the extreme strictures and "don'ts" of Baptists didn't work, at least for me. The rites, rituals, history, clothes, robes, beanies, post-hole-digger hats and transubstantiation of the Host Eucharist cracker of the Catholic Church did not work for me either. Nor did anything between these two extremes. The bias and prejudice and the cowardice of all Christians to face life full on and honestly and without a fanciful back-up plan of miracles, fables or a later eternal heavenly bail out from God was for me a cop out. It was an include-me-out, not a count-me-in. I wanted no part of it.

More happened as I was growing up that continued to erode any religious feelings that I might have had remaining. We still had "blue laws" that as a result of earlier Puritan and other religious beliefs caused most stores to be closed on Sunday. Realize that this occurred in the 1930s through the 1950s with some still continuing to the 1960s and even beyond. Today in my area at least, car dealers are not usually open on Sunday. It was then also considered immoral and sacrilegious for stores (most stores) to be open on Sunday. It was also against the law. We had a de facto theocracy then (and we also seemed to be heading that way in the early part of this century under George W. Bush), with the religious right (as it became to be called decades later) having enough power or persuasion to control the laws and governance of this country. This was to the extent of dictating morality, ethics, mores, folkways, memes and laws to all of us — believers and non-believers alike. The religious right is all for freedom of speech (and thought), freedom of the press and freedom of religion, as guaranteed in the Constitution, as long as it is their speech, their thought, their press and their religion. Anyone who does not think, read, write or worship as the religious right does probably should be thrown out of the country anyway, according to their thinking. That's what religious TV evangelist John Hagee thinks and says anyway — that all atheists should be thrown out of the country. Then again, George H. W. Bush (number 41) was quoted as saying that he would not consider atheists as patriots. Nice guys. Nice religion. Nice tolerance of others. Nice example of Christian love, from Mr. Hagee and ex-President George Bush.

Thus, no one went anywhere on Sunday when I was a youth, since there was no place to go and no shops open for buying anything anyway. Malls were not yet invented or developed, and while the occasional religious back-slider might go to the movies, it was frowned upon by most in the staunch fundamentalist don't-ever-ever-ever-have-fun, be-sure-to-look-sour-all-the-time, the-Devil-is-always-after-you, Satan-is-the-prince-of-this-world, sin-is-a-constant-temptation, your-immortal-soul-is-always-in-danger, and be-sure-to-have-a-miserable-time-living-and-going-through-life religions that seemed to be endemic at the time. They still are endemic to some parts of society, or trying to be.

Heck, or hell, if you like, reading the comics was considered amusement, and certainly not approved by the Old Testament, the New Testament, the Ten Commandments, Jesus, Moses, Abraham, David, Matthew, Mark, Luke, John or any then-current parson worth his fire, brimstone, hellfire-preaching and damnation-condemning rant from the Sunday pulpit. Billy Sunday, the evangelist of the early part of the 1900s was sure — absolutely sure — that reading the Sunday paper funny pages was a substantial cause of the degradation of morality of the country.

Sin just had to be stamped out. And stamped out now, regardless of what it took to do it. Closing the stores on Sunday would help. It wasn't so much that shopping or buying things was bad, but it was bad on Sunday, when one of the Ten Commandments forbad anything on that day other than worship of God. And it damn well better be the right god. Comstock Laws and the Movie censorship Hayes Office either led the charge or followed up with battalions of reinforcements.

The other problem was that if you were buying something, going to the store, playing sandlot baseball, fishing, going to a movie, reading something frivolous such as a novel, watching TV (for those wealthy enough to own a nine-inch black-and-white) or anything else, you might have some fun or degree of satisfaction in doing it. And that goes back to the basic fundamentalist concept of having a miserable time through life, looking and acting always as if you had just posed for that famous Grant Wood American Gothic painting, holding a hayfork with a sour lemon in your mouth. Or perhaps he had eaten a pickle.

After all, the Puritans were against all forms of blood sport such as dog fighting, bear baiting, bull baiting, and cock fighting, not in the least because it might cause distress, extreme pain, cruelty, maiming and ultimate death to the animal, but because humans might have too much fun watching the animal writhe in anguish and its incipient death. Puritans might also enjoy their constant betting (another sin) on the outcome of two dogs tearing each other apart, never mind how the dogs felt about it. And the enjoyment and pleasure of watching two dogs tear each other apart or betting on the outcome, was out of the question in those times — at least on Sunday, the Lord's day.

Even without the evil betting, just having fun by watching the torture was bad also. The torture of the animals through bear baiting, cock fighting, turkey dancing (putting turkeys on a red-hot metal plate to "enjoy" watching them "dance") wasn't the bad part — having fun and enjoyment through this "sport" was the bad part and obviously the fun that was damaging to your immortal soul, never mind what it might be doing to your immoral being. After all, you were supposed to be reading your Bible and not having fun by watching dogs tear up a bear or vice-versa or watching turkeys get their feet burned off as they "danced" around for your pleasure and enjoyment.

The irony of closing stores on Sunday was that the small confection, variety, news and similar stores — sort of the early Mom and Pop owned equivalent of 7-11 stores today — could sell newspapers, cigarettes, cigars, pipe tobacco, chewing tobacco, candy, snuff, gum, shoe laces and various other sundries. It seemed that the legislators who designed the laws did not want to go too far in preventing the masses from getting their "sinful" cigarettes, cigars, pipes, pipe tobacco, snuff and chewing tobacco, along with candy and sodas.

The result — as I evidenced early on during a summer vacation trip to Ocean City, New Jersey with my parents — was an unfortunate Blue Law experience that forbad stores from being open on Sunday, unless they were selling these specific items. Thus, sundry, convenience and similar stores could be open to sell the smokes, pipes, cigars, cigarettes, snuff, papers, candy and gum, but not to sell any of their other products so conveniently located on shelves and available the other six days a week.

At that time, my parents and I were browsing in a small boardwalk shop that sold the smokes and such (although my parents did not smoke) when a woman pushing a baby carriage came into the store wanting to buy a small cap or hat for her child. It was Sunday.

The child was obviously distressed by the high-in-the sky bright summer, bake-your-brains-out sun, and the carriage did not have the buggy top as do many today. The store owner, with a rack or two of different style and color baby caps, could not sell the Mom a cap, since such sales were prohibited by the Sunday blue laws. God only knows, the mother might have had fun immorally buying a hat for her child! The Mom could buy smokes, chewing tobacco, pipes, pipe tobacco, sun tan lotion, candy, chewing gum, cigarette lighters, cigarette papers, lighter fluid, newspapers, snuff, snacks and such, but nothing to prevent a baby from extreme sun distress, perhaps even sun burn, sun stroke or heat exhaustion. After all, we had to have our priorities straight and stamp out sin, regardless of the cost.

A kid in the Emergency Room with sun blisters was no problem compared with the more important priority of being able to smoke, chew, or enjoy a Baby Ruth candy bar. Apparently, the sinning but sinless-seeking fundamentalists had their way with their pleasures of smoking and chewing. Both chewing and smoking were officially forbidden of course by "Christians" as patently immoral, this decided by the staunch conservatives of the fundamentalist movement then, but who could not see their way clear with legislatures to allow an exemption for those seeking sun — or other — relief.

The store owner sympathized but would not and could not sell a baby cap, since such a sale could and would subject her to fines and possibly a loss of her retail license. After all, the Mom and baby could be a set-up by the Sin Police to ferret out such terrible illegal and obviously evil behavior as selling a small cap for a baby on a hot blistering Sunday, the Lord's Day. Perhaps the Sin Police were just outside, licking their mortal and moral lips as to the possible and potential arrest of a sting that would capture and jail an immoral, hardened baby-hat-selling criminal.

Heaven forbid — figuratively and literally. The Mom was only there for the day, and had forgotten to bring a cap from home. But sin — in the form of the sales of baby hats for sun shade — had to be stamped out. Otherwise we might all go to Hell, collectively, individually or maybe in a hand cart.

After all, it had only been a little over twenty years since the biology teacher John Scopes lost his case in a Dayton, Tennessee court despite the efforts of Clarence Darrow, and the strong — even back then — evidence of and for evolution. Darwin's *The Origin of Species*, was for a few minutes of history at least, firmly established as the work and words of Satan. Still is today, in fact, with the right wing, Christian conservatives determined to stamp out the facts and logic of evolutionary theory and replace seriousness of science with the fables of faith.

My eroding belief in Christianity and anything religious continued through my teen years, and eventually led to my desire to leave the church. This obviously upset my mother, seemingly less so my father, but both of whom still harbored a belief in their faith and a hope for their son. It was at first misunderstood, my parents thinking that I disliked the Baptist Church to which we belonged and merely wanted to switch membership to another Baptist church. I didn't. I wanted out. I called the church and talked to the pastor (the same pastor who baptized me) to ask him to take care of this. He insisted that I come in to talk about it. Reluctantly, I did. I told him of my lack of belief, and that the whole charade of Christianity meant nothing to me, that I did not associate at all with the church and that I just wanted him to take my name off the church roll. It turned out that it was and is not that simple and is more akin to somehow getting out of the Mafia than out of a Christian house of belief, goodness, kindness, mercy, love and worship.

"There are only three ways that you can leave the Baptist Church," he explained as I sat, sunk in a stuffed chair in his comfortable and cozy office. I guess that they neglected to tell us that before in our Bible/Baptism preparation classes. Soft light bounced off of the paneled walls and the large bookcase was filled with liturgical, historical and religious books.

"You can die." That did not appeal to me either then or now.

"You can transfer to another Baptist Church. Do you have another Baptist church to which you would like to transfer membership?" he asked hopefully, leaning forward expectantly in his chair. He was very hopeful. "Nope, I just want out," I explained.

"Well." He was now squirming around in his comfortable stuffed chair that seemed at the time to be decidedly uncomfortable to him. He was like a small boy being held down in the barber's chair for his first haircut. "Well," he started again, "the only other choice is 'erasure'. For that," he continued, "we have to have a formal church meeting and the full church membership has to vote on your request and then if voting 'yes', grant you removal from the rolls."

OK, I remember thinking, but not saying — and what if they vote 'no'? Is it like the Mafia where you get whacked? Is it two .22 or .25 shots in the back of the head or just cement overshoes and a one-way boat trip on the Chesapeake Bay? This did not sound that tolerant, Christian or Christ-like to me.

I did not go to the full church membership meeting, although I was told that I could if I desired. The end result was that they voted me out, "allowing" me to remove my name from the rolls of the church. Nice of them. After the meeting, I called the pastor for the news. "In the almost fifty year history of this church you are the first person to want to leave the church and to leave by erasure," he said resignedly and disappointedly. I was sorry to disappoint him — he was a nice person — but you have to remain true to your principles.

Christianity then and now just was not and is not logical, scientific, truthful or sensible. It is a sham. The concept of a Jesus born of a virgin, walking on water, raising the dead, dying and arising from the dead and then later flying to heaven is as preposterous as the idea of the god Minerva arising from the brain of Jupiter, of Alexander the Great being born from his mother's impregnation by a snake or Muhammad going to heaven on the back of his winged horse Buraq. Those things are not real, are they? Then why should the idea of Jesus flying around or walking on water be real?

By attending Gettysburg College after high school, I had to agree to attend Chapel twice a week and also to take mandatory first year courses, which included a first year course on Christianity. After all, Gettysburg was Lutheran when founded, and the originators of the college wanted to indoctrinate students into religion, specifically Lutheranism, if at all possible. The first semester was on the Old Testament; the second on the New Testament. Basically, the professor treated both as historical, skirting the "miracles" to some degree and looking at the history of the early Israelites in the Old Testament and the similarities, differences and lapses of the New Testament, specifically Matthew, Mark, Luke and John. It was an interesting basic course, but did nothing to sway my thinking one way or the other about religion.

Thus, in this first year of college, I pretty much read the entire Bible as a requirement for the course work. In some cases skimming or scanning would be a better verb to use. I read the Bible again, skimming again, just for fun during my sophomore year of college. No classes required this — I just did it. In four years, I graduated as a biology major with a split physics/chemistry minor. In the process and through classes such as comparative anatomy, embryology, botany, histology and others, I became pretty well versed in basic evolutionary concepts as they were understood and often poorly taught then in the late 50s. Sadly, it was not found to be as important then as it has become in successive decades and with successive research, particularly into DNA which continues to reinforce basic evolutionary concepts.

I read Darwin's *The Origin of Species* and *Descent of Man*. To look at the other side of this question, I also examined the many skinny and abysmally poor texts by religionists of the time from 1859 when Origin of Species was published to the late 1950s when I was reading these tomes. All of these counterpoints to evolution were so poor as to be laughable and were pathetic. So much for logic, truth, facts and science among religionists.

I continued through the next forty years with mostly an "I don't care" but atheistic attitude towards religion. Let people think and believe what they wanted, let them go to church if they want, let them engage in the rites and rituals they wish, no matter how ridiculous and delusional they might seem to the rest of us or those of us who were not or are not believers. I just did not care.

This continued through my first marriage. I did not go to church, although my wife (since deceased) did go to her Methodist church frequently. I opted out of all events, including the decidedly important (for religionists) Christmas and Easter stuff. I regret that now. I could have been kinder to my late wife, put in an appearance at these highly important Christian events, and shut my mouth about my thinking. It would have made my late wife happier.

During the early part of this time I was working and studying for a PhD in human anatomy at the Anatomy Department, University of Maryland School of Medicine. I was one of several instructors in the anatomy lab for first year medical students. I also had my own class of third year physical therapy students to whom I taught human anatomy, histology and neuroanatomy.

In my spare time, I had also started free lance magazine writing about sport fishing. I had some success, selling to major magazines of the time such as Sports Afield, Outdoor Life and Field & Stream. My main thrust was teaching anatomy and taking courses to advance in the PhD program.

During this time, and right before his retirement, an interesting thing happened with the head of the Anatomy Department. Dr. Eduard Uhlenhuth, originally Austrian, and with the autocratic disciplines of the middle of the 20th century, was strict in his approach to students and to teaching human anatomy. When Dr. Uhlenhuth asked a question, each student was required to stand, give his name and then answer. After one question, a student stood up, gave his name and then a little unsure of his answer, began as follows: "Dr. Uhlenhuth, I believe. . ." Dr. Uhlenhuth stopped him with a raised hand. "Just a minute, just a minute," he said. "We believe in Jesus Christ." He paused. "But in anatomy, we KNOW."

After some few years of this, I realized that I liked writing better than the teaching of human anatomy. In time, I left the university and started writing for the *Baltimore Sunday Sun*, then *The Washington Post*, and then after about eight years went into freelance writing full time.

During part of this time, I thought that I was perhaps an agnostic, but at some point realized that I am not. I am — and was — more of an atheist. I realized that I was an "agnostic" about religion, Christianity, and God in the same way that I was and am an "agnostic" about unicorns, dragons and leprechauns. Unless these things — and a host of others — are in a parallel world, fourth dimension or only visible in a wave length of light beyond our visual capabilities, then they are not around. But even if we can't see them and they are still there, I think that we would inadvertently bump into a few now and again. I think that we can trust logic and science on this one — leprechauns, unicorns and dragons don't exist.

I did not change religiously after my wife died of cancer, but I was introduced to some new concepts a few years later when I met Brenda, happily now my wife. She is of a basic Presbyterian evangelical fundamentalist background. At her request, I agreed to meet with her minister. It had been forty-plus years since I had examined religion closely, and perhaps, I thought, someone or something could give me new insights on the subject.

Thus, I started again with an almost open view, not involving much more than my I-don't-care attitude at the time. Brenda's minister had me start by reading John from the New Testament. We had some interesting exchanges, with him espousing religious views and my questioning and suggesting to him admittedly contrary ideas for sermons. My sermon or dialog suggestions to him and to other ministers since have gone along the lines of:

• Teresa the Terrible — On the horrors of Mother Teresa, and her death-wish Christianity, based on the writings of Christopher Hitchens and his book *The Missionary Position.*

• The immorality of Bush (43rd) and the Bush Administration in denying $34 million annually to the United Nations population fund to help undeveloped countries with needed family planning (reversed early — the first day — in President Obama's Administration.)

• Studies on the efficacy (or inefficiency) of prayer in controlled studies of intercessory prayer with cardiac patients.

- Throwing out the trash — discarding stem cells rather than making use of them as per stem cell research — and discarding them as per the horridly flawed pro-life policy of the theocratic Bush 43.

- The fallacy of inviting and endorsing abstinence-only church-based pregnancy centers ($2,000,000,000 in taxpayer funds) when over 40 studies have shown that abstinence-only programs do not — absolutely do not — work.

- Why Christians continue to call their religion monotheistic when it is obviously henotheistic or polytheistic?

- God as a bigot, since he through Israel and early Israelites had and has "chosen" people — an obvious bias and bigotry and a violation of the current Equal Rights Amendment

- The immorality and extreme (murder and killing of innocent Egyptian children) bigotry of Passover.

- The incest of Genesis — Adam, Eve, Cain, Abel, Seth and their wives. Were the boys having sex with their mother or sisters or both?

- How can Adam and Eve be the first humans on earth when there are cities mentioned in the Bible at the same time? That does not mesh! Studies of early human populations and migrations go back 195,000 years — not just a few thousand years.

- Why were Gnostic texts eliminated from the Bible? Who decided this, why, how, for what reasons and who gave authority for these early and different Christian texts to be destroyed?

- How come plan A, B, C, and D did not work for the salvation of mankind and it was necessary to go with plan E — crucifixion of Christ? (Adam and Eve plan A, Noah's flood plan B, Tower of Babel plan C, and birth of Jesus as plan D.)

- How can you separate fiction and symbolism from facts and truth in the Bible? Are there any facts or truths? How can we tell the difference?

- The conflict of the facts and proofs of evolution vs. the fables and fiction of Noah's ark and the number of animals on board.

- The accuracy — or lack thereof — of the Bible when it is based on oral tradition, recitation and weak history. It would be like writing a history of WWI today with only tales from others and no media, TV, Internet, movies, documents, books, magazines or newspapers to reference.

- How to explain the immorality of God in asking Abraham to kill Isaac?

Not surprisingly, most ministers do not care much for my ideas of sermons, nor do they want to touch any of my questions framed within my ideas, or my ideas framed within my questions.

I did gradually begin to realize the possibility of a historical Jesus, that there is some evidence of him through history and documentation and also oral history. There is of course also evidence that there is or was no Jesus or that the Jesus of the Bible was a conflation of many miracle men and magicians popular during that period of Israelite history. My view was at best that Jesus was a man, not a deity, the Christ, God or Supreme Being.

An interesting thing happened during this time when I was slowly creeping towards Christianity and a new belief system after decades of non-belief. At Christmas time, Brenda — not yet my fiancée or wife — took me to an informal church party at the home of one of the church members. During this time of food, celebration and companionship, they also played a game which required each couple to bring a small gift item of some sort. These items could be nice little gifts, or often by common agreement strange, weird or unwanted by the giver. Mostly, they were the odd and unusual. There was no theme, so these items included garden tools, kitchen items, knick-knacks, small items of new clothing, food, wall hangings and pictures, car accessories, and children's toys. The game was "Yankee Trader" which perhaps goes by other names in other parts of the country. I had never heard of it before.

The idea of the game was for everyone to put their gift item into a common cache, and when their name was called through a drawing system, to pick from this pile an item that they wanted. A picked person could also take without penalty or protest the gift chosen by another who had chosen a present earlier. It soon became obvious from comments of one and all that the purpose of the game was not to get something that you might like as a simple swap, but to select something that would keep someone else who had a gift or whose name had not yet been picked from getting what they really wanted. This went through several rounds so that there was no certainty what you would end up with at the end of the game. The point was to rob someone else — supposedly a friend — of what he or she truly wanted. It was not a pleasant game. It was vicious and mean-spirited.

It was evident that among this group of Christians there was a lot of glee and joy in keeping a friend from getting an item that they wanted. I refused to play. Had my turn come up and I knew that a friend really wanted a particular item, I would have picked it and then immediately given it to him. Among my friends of atheists, agnostics, I-don't-carers, Catholics, lapsed Catholics, retired Catholics, Jews, semi-Jews and a wide ranging assortment of devout to totally uncaring Protestants, all would have done the same for me or any of our other friends.

I quickly realized that these Christians might be head-bobbing syco-phants of the faith and the Bible, but they certainly did not live the life. They might have been talking the talk, but they certainly were not walking the walk of the supposed creed of Christianity. Action speaks louder than words. I realized that I could not play this Yankee Trader game the way that they wanted, since I did not have the necessary greed, avarice and larceny in me to play properly. In short, I had a higher sense of self, of ethics, of morality, of principles for my fellow man — as would any and all of my friends — than this crowd of preening, pompous, pretentious and pretending Christians.

My friends and I were — still are — all nicer, better people with a much higher sense of fairness, ethics and morals. I did not realize until much later that while wandering my way through the Bible to revisit Christianity, this game of greed, this adventure in avarice, this lesson in larceny in which I re-fused to participate spread the first sprinkling of religious skepticism in me. Later, that skepticism would snowball.

I continued going to Brenda's minister for individual instruction and counseling in Christianity. I did not always agree with the ideas of this min-ister, nor follow the logic (or non-logic) that he proposed to prove his points. I also told him that if I had to throw the "off" switch in my brain or leave my brain on the curb when going to church, I was out of there. He agreed with me, although perhaps not expecting the results that occurred a few years after marrying Brenda.

I did not throw the "off" switch, I never left my brain on the curb when attending church, and never put my thinking and analysis on hold. Instead, I continued to read, think, compare texts and information. I continued to look for facts to back up my thoughts and to confront my fears, to search for truth, and try to use basic logic in my thinking.

I am now out of there mentally. I occasionally attend church with Brenda. Going to church makes her happy. Unfortunately, I cannot find people to talk with, since the clergy and parishioners in the several churches Brenda attends are afraid of me, afraid of my questions, afraid of my thinking, afraid of my ideas, afraid of anything that might counter their carefully cherry-picked, error-strewn ideas and ideals. One pastor ignored me or gave me an-swers that are flat-out lies when I asked questions in private or public.

After marriage to Brenda I continued to read the Bible and to question philosophies, "facts," beliefs, opinions of various religious types, including those of Brenda's family and friends, those of ministers and religious writ-ers. This began in earnest in 2002 or 2003, about a year or two after our 2001 marriage.

I continued going to church and especially Sunday School with Brenda. She went for the religion, I went for the ammunition for a column — "Religious Skepticism Examiner" (you can Google it) — that started on the Examiner website in 2009. It covers the foibles and fictions of religion and especially Christianity, and the shallow thinking of those admitting their Christianity and advocating it as the best — or only — of all possible religious choices.

In this, and in going to various Sunday School classes, I discovered that the teachers often knew less than I did. For example, the teacher of the several-week course on the Ten Commandments seemed to know little or nothing about the Code of Hammurabi and its 282 rules — see section in Chapter 12 and 13). He knew nothing about the code of Ur-Nammu, both of which could have been texts from which the Ten Commandments were plagiarized. This does not mean that the Big Ten were copied, but only that they might have been, or that the Ur-Nammu and Hammurabi texts might have been used as a basis for rewriting in the Bible early moral and social codes of conduct. Further on, this teacher did not know about the 1631 edition of the King James Bible in which the word "not" was left out of one commandment, "Thou shalt (not) commit adultery." This is only indicative of the lack of total knowledge, the tunnel vision and shallow thinking of those of Christians.

Before concluding this book, I also heard and came to a realization about lies and truth. I do not know to whom to credit it, but someone said, "A lie is as good as the truth if you can find someone to believe it." Sadly that is true with Christianity. Christians have been listening to, believing and promulgating lies to others throughout the long 2,000 year history of this sham religion and the almost 2,000 years of Judaism prior to that. The lies are being told and sold as the truth and being believed by so many, many brainwashed since childhood. It is child abuse.

While wanting to "believe" to make and keep Brenda happy, I had to stand up for my principles and my beliefs. I became increasing skeptical in recent years, non-believing and instead seeing that religion — and indeed Christianity — is nothing more than pixie dust. It is a bag full of nothing, a box full of bogus dreams, a package of puff, a carton of contradictions, a hamper of vacant hope.

There is no proof of a God, there are no established real miracles, there is proof that prayer does not work. There is no proof of a resurrection or of walking on water or of raising the dead, and there is no proof of a heaven or hell or afterlife. Christianity remains pixie dust and horse feathers, with this book a culmination of those thoughts, conclusions and some of the reasoning behind them.

Boyd Pfeiffer

Bibliography

In addition to the works listed here, and perhaps far easier to find, are references to these subjects on the Internet, with the most comprehensive being Wikipedia. While care must be used in sourcing anything in writing or on the Internet, good sources are easily available that enable readers to check on the statements made in this book, and to continue the process of uncovering the problems, flaws and errors of religions.

Aronson, Ronald. *Living Without God, New Directions for Atheists, Agnostics, Secularists, and the Undecided*, CA, Berkley, Counterpoint Press, 2008

Baggini, Julian. *Atheism, A Brief Insight*, Oxford, NY, Oxford University Press, 2003

Baigent, Michael. *Racing Toward Armageddon*, NY, HarperOne, 2009

Barker, Dan. *The Good Atheist, Living a Purpose-Filled Life Without God*, CA, Berkley, 2011

———. *Godless*, CA, Berkeley, CA, Ulysses Press, 2008

Bivins, Jason C. *Religion of Fear*. NY, Oxford University Press, 2008

Brogaard, Betty. *The Homemade Atheist, A Former Evangelical Woman's Freethought Journey to Happiness*, CA, Berkley, Ulysses Press, 2010

Bock, Darrell. *The Missing Gospels*, TN, Nashville, Thomas Nelson Publishers, 2006

Cresswell, Peter. *The Invention of Jesus*, London, Watkins Publishing, 2013

Charles, R. H. *The Book of Enoch*, Dover Publications, 2007

Crisswell, Jonathan C. compiler, *The Wit and Blasphemy of Atheists*, Berkley, CA, Ulysses Press, 2011

D'Antonio, Michael. *Mortal Sins: Sex, Crime, and the Era of Catholic Scandal*, New York, Thomas Dunne Books, St. Martin's Press, 2013

De Waal, Frans. *Primates and Philosophers, How Morality Evolved*, NJ, Princeton, Princeton University Press, 2006

Dawkins, Richard. *The God Delusion*, New York, Houghton Mifflin Company, 2006

Douthat, Ross. *Bad Religion*, NY, Free Press, 2012

Durschmied, Erik. *Whores Of The Devil*, Sutton Publishing, 2005

Ehrman, Bart D. *Forged*, NY, HarperOne, 2011

_____. *Misquoting Jesus*, NY, HarperOne, 2005

_____. *The Lost Gospel of Judas Iscariot*, NY, Oxford, 2006

_____. *Peter, Paul and Mary Magdalene, the Followers of Jesus in History and Legend*, NY, Oxford, 2006

_____. *God's Problem*, NY, HarperOne, 2008

_____. *Jesus, Interrupted*, NY, HarperOne, 2009

_____. *Lost Scriptures, Books that Did Not Make It into the New Testament*, NY, Oxford, 2003

_____. *Did Jesus Exist?*, NY, HarperOne, 2012

_____. *How Jesus Became God*, NY, HarperOne, 2014

Fetzer, James H. *Render Unto Darwin*, Il, Peru, Open Court Publishing Co., 2007

Cambridge University Press, 2010

Friedman, Richard Elliot. *Who Wrote The Bible?* NY, HarperOne, 1987

Freke, Timothy and Gandy, Peter. *The Jesus Mysteries — Was the "Original Jesus" a Pagan God?* NY, Three Rivers Press, 1999

Galambush, Julie. *The Reluctant Parting*, CA, San Francisco, 2005

Granados, Luis. *Damned Good Company*, Washington, DC, Humanist Press, 2012

Greenberg, Gary. *101 Myths of the Bible*, Naperville, IL, SourceBooks, 2000

Harding, Nick. *How to be a Good Atheist*, Oldcastle Books, 2007

Harrison, Guy P. *50 Reasons People Give for Believing in a God*, NY, Amherst, 2008

Harris, Sam. *The End of Faith, Religion, Terror and the Future of Reason*, NY, W. W. Norton & Company, 2004

_____. *Letter to a Christian Nation*, NY, Vintage Books, 2008

Henze, Matthias. Editor, *Biblical Interpretation at Qumran*, MI, Rapids William B. Erdmans Publishing Co. 2005

Hitchens, Christopher. *God is Not Great*, New York, Twelve, Hachette Brook Group, USA, 2007

_____. *The Missionary Position*, NY, Verso, 1995

_____. *The Portable Atheist, Essential Readings for the Nonbeliever*, Philadelphia, PA, Da Capo Press, 2007

Huberman, Jack. *The Quotable Atheist*, NY, Nation Books, 2007

Hudnut-Beumler, James. *In Pursuit Of The Almighty's Dollar, A History Of Money And American Protestantism*, Chapel Hill, NC, University Of North Carolina Press, 2007

Johnson, Marshall D. *The Evolution of Christianity — Twelve Crises That Shaped the Church*, NY, Continuum International Publishing, 2005

Jordan, Michael. *In The Name of God — Violence and Destruction in the World's Religions*, Sutton Publishing, 2006

Joshi, S. T. *The Original Atheists, First Thoughts on Nonbelief*, Amherst, NY, Prometheus Books, 2014

Kasser, Rodolphe, Meyer, Marvin and Wurst, Gregor. *The Gospel of Judas*, Washington, DC, National Geographic Society, 2006

Konner, Joan. Compiler, *The Atheist's Bible*, NY, HarperCollins, 2007

Largo, Michael. *God's Lunatic's*, NY, Harper, 2010

_____. *The Unbelievers*, Amherst, Prometheus Books, 2011

Lewis, C. S. *Mere Christianity*, NY, Harper Collins Paperback, 2001

Lewis, James R. *Violence and New Religious Movements*, Oxford University Press, 2011

Loftus, John W. *Why I Became an Atheist*, Amherst, NJ, Prometheus, 2008

Maisel, Eric. *The Atheist's Way, Living Well Without Gods*, Novato, CA, 2009

Marshall, David. *The Truth Behind The New Atheism*, Oregon, Eugene, Harvest House Publishers, 2007

Meyer, Marvin. *The Gnostic Discoveries*, NY, HarperSanFrancisco, 2005

_____. *Judas*, HarperOne, 2007

Miles, Jack. *God: A Biography*, NY, Alfred A. Knopf, 1995

Mikul, Chris. *The Cult Files*, Pier 9, ?

Mills, David. *Atheist Universe, The Thinking Person's Answer to Christian Fundamentalism*, Berkley, CA 2006

Moorey, P. R. S. *A Century of Biblical Archaeology*, KY, Louisville, Westminster/John Knox Press, 1991

Moss, Candida. *The Myth of Persecution*, NY, HarperOne, 2013

Myers, PZ. *The Happy Atheist*, NY, Vintage Books, 2014

Nabarz, Payam. *The Mysteries of Mithras*, VT, Rochester, Inner Traditions, 2005

Navabi, Armin. *Why There Is No God*, Atheist Republic

Needleman, Jacob. *What Is God?*, NY, Penguin Books, 2009

O'Reilly, Bill and Dugard, Martin. *Killing Jesus*, NY, Henry Holt and Company 2013

Pagels, Elaine. *Revelations*, NY, Penguin Books, 2012

_____. *Beyond Belief*, NY, Vintage Books, 2004

_____. *The Origin of Satan*, NY, Vintage Books, 1996

_____. *Adam, Eve and the Serpent*, NY, Vintage Books, 1988

Paine, Thomas. *Common Sense*, NY, Fall River Press, 1995

Park, Robert L. *Superstition: Belief in the Age of Science*, Princeton, NJ, 2008

Phillips, Kevin. *American Theocracy*, NY, Viking Press, 2006

Picknett, Lynn. *Mary Magdalene*, NY, Carroll & Graf Publishers, 2004

Randi, James. *The Faith Healers*, Buffalo, NY, Prometheus, 1989

Rosenberg, Alex. *The Atheist's Guide to Reality, Enjoying Life without Illusions*, NY, W. W. Norton & Company, 2011

Rodwan, John G. Jr. *Holidays & Other Disasters*, Washington, DC, Humanist Press, 2013

Rowland, Wade. *Galileo's Mistake*, NY, Arcade Publishing, 2001

Russell, D. S. *The Old Testament Pseudepigrapha*, Philadelphia, PA, Fortress Press, 1987

S, Acharya. *The Christ Conspiracy*, Kempton, IL Adventures Unlimited, 1999

Sachar, Abram Leon. *A History of the Jews*, 5th Edition, NY, Alfred A. Knopf, 1964

Sagan, Carl. *The Demon-Haunted World*, NY, Ballantine Books, 1996

Schroeder, Robert. *Cults, Secret Sects and Radical Religions*, Carlton Books, 2007

Schweizer, Bernard. *Hating God, The Untold Story of Misotheism*, Oxford University Press, 2011

Shermer, Michael. *Why People Believe Weird Things*, NY, MJF Books, 1997

_____. *Why Darwin Matters*, NY, Henry Holt and Company, 2006

Smith, George H. *Atheism, The Case Against God*, Amherst, NY, Prometheus, 1989

Stenger, Victor J. *God, The Failed Hypothesis*, Amherst, NJ, Prometheus Books, 2007

Stewart-Williams, Steve. *Darwin, God and The Meaning of Life, How Evolutionary Theory Undermines Everything You Thought You Knew*, NY, Cambridge University 2010

Twain, Mark. *The War Prayer*, NY, Harper and Row, St. Crispin Press Book, 1951

Vermes, Geza. *The Resurrection*, NY, Doubleday, 2001

Wade, Nicholas. *The Faith Instinct*, NY, The Penguin Press, 2009

Walter, Philippe. *Christianity: The Origins of a Pagan Religion*, VT, Rochester, Inner Traditions, 2003

White, Mel. *Religion Gone Bad*, NY, Penguin, 2006

White, L. Michael. *Scripting Jesus*, NY, HarperOne, 2010

Wicker, Christine. *The Fall of the Evangelical Church, The Surprising Crisis Inside the Church*, NY, HarperOne, 2008

Zichterman, Jocelyn. *I Fired God*, NY, St. Martin's Press, 2013

Zondervan. *Zondervan's Compact Bible Dictionary*, MI, Grand Rapids, 1993

Printed in the United States
By Bookmasters